Structure and Change
in Economic History

Structure and Change in Economic History

Douglass C. North

W · W · Norton & Company

New York · London

Library of Congress Cataloging in Publication Data
North, Douglass Cecil.
    Structure and change in economic history.
    Includes index.
    1. Economic history. I. Title.
HC21.N66 1981   330.9   81–38368
ISBN 0-393-95241-x   AACR2

W. W. Norton & Company, Inc.
500 Fifth Avenue, New York, N.Y. 10110
W. W. Norton & Company Ltd.
25 New Street Square, London EC4A 3NT

4 5 6 7 8 9 0

For
Elisabeth Case
with My Love

Contents

Preface

The objective of this book is to provide a new framework for analyzing the economic past. A new framework is needed because the analytical tools used by economic historians have failed to come to grips with the central issues in economic history: explaining the institutional structure which underlies and accounts for performance of an economic system, and explaining changes in that structure. The development of a theory of institutional change is a major challenge to the social scientist. This book offers some—but certainly not all—of the elements of such a theory.

Since Adam Smith, economists have constructed their models on the firm bedrock of the gains from trade. Specialization and division of labor are the key to *The Wealth of Nations*. In constructing their models, however, economists have ignored the costs arising from such specialization and division of labor. These transaction costs underlie the institutions determining the structure of political-economic systems. The theoretical framework of this book therefore overlaps the other social sciences and explores both political organizations and ideology as essential ingredients in an explanation of institutional change. Accordingly, the book is aimed at a wider audience than economic historians; and with this in mind I have tried to keep the technical economic language at a minimum. Although in chapter 1 I present the issues in formal economic terms, I have taken pains there and throughout the rest of the book to make the argument clear to the non-economist.

The theory advanced in Part I suggests a recasting of much of the economic past into new molds; Part II does just that in chapters covering ten millennia of Western economic history, from the origins of agriculture to the twentieth century. The justification for exploring economic history on such a cosmic scale is that advances in explaining the economic past require a conceptual base. Our understanding of the past is no better than the theory that we use and that theory has been woefully deficient. The theory and the subsequent historical essays in this book offer a basis for systematic examination and testing of new hypotheses out of which will come a search for new evidence, followed by modification or refutation of the hypotheses.

In order to make a contribution to knowledge, the theory must be potentially refutable: testable either directly from hypotheses contained in the study or indirectly from logical derivative hypotheses that follow from the argument. To the degree that definitive tests of explanations of the economic past are not possible we can expect competing explanations to persist and to be used in the service of diverse and conflicting current-day policy prescriptions. I offer, however, a counsel of reality, not despair: we are simply deluding ourselves if we believe that a single scientific explanation of the past is possible, but we are selling the discipline of economic history short by not trying to work toward that goal. The persistent search for testable hypotheses and the constant accretion of evidence can gradually reduce the number of competing explanations. We shall never reach a consensus on all the issues, but we will on some, and on others we will narrow the range of alternative explanations.

This book is a continuation of the study of institutional change begun with Lance Davis in *Institutional Change and American Economic Growth* (1971) and with Robert Thomas in *The Rise of the Western World: A New Economic History* (1973). I am indebted to both co-authors of the earlier studies and in addition to a host of economists, economic historians, historians, and social scientists from other disciplines who have contributed to the present study. I owe a special debt to four readers of diverse backgrounds who provided me with detailed comments on the entire manuscript from a variety of perspectives. They are George Bentson, Stanley Engerman, Margaret Levi, and Mancur Olson.

In addition my understanding of transaction costs and economic organization owes a great deal to my colleague Steven Cheung.

Other colleagues at the University of Washington who have provided valuable comments on parts of the study are Yoram Barzel, Arthur Ferrill, Michael Hechter, Paul Heyne, Robert Higgs, Levis Kochin, Carol Thomas, and Dean Worcester.

I have tried out various parts of this manuscript at a score of universities and several conferences and I have sent chapters to individuals at still other universities for comments. Moses Abramowitz, Armen Alchian, Ray Battalio, Richard Bean, Carl Dahlman, Victor Goldberg, Jonathan Hughes, Charles Plott, Gaston Rimlinger, Tom Saving, Theodore Schultz, Vernon Smith, Gordon Tullock, Burton Weisbrod, and Oliver Williamson all provided me with particularly helpful comments; but my debt extends to many others at those colloquia and conferences which helped improve this study.

Elisabeth Case edited the entire manuscript. In the process she forced me to clarify my own thinking on almost every page.

BENZONIA, MICHIGAN
AUGUST 1980

Part I

Theory

Chapter 1

The Issues

I take it as the task of economic history to explain the structure and performance of economies through time. By 'performance' I have in mind the typical concerns of economists—for example, how much is produced, the distribution of costs and benefits, or the stability of production. The primary emphasis in explaining performance is on total output, output per capita, and the distribution of income of the society. By 'structure' I mean those characteristics of a society which we believe to be the basic determinants of performance. Here I include the political and economic institutions, technology, demography, and ideology of a society. 'Through time' means that economic history should explain temporal changes in structure and performance. Finally, 'explanation' means explicit theorizing and the potential of refutability.

This study focuses on two central but neglected tasks of economic history: to theorize about the structure of economies, and to account for either stability or change in those structures. I shall use a simple neoclassical model to focus on the total output and output per capita aspects of performance. To explain both the income distribution and the structure of an economy, however, we must extend the theory beyond the traditional neoclassical bounds.

Let me begin by delineating the essential characteristics of the neoclassical approach to analyzing the performance of an economy. This approach assumes that in the face of pervasive scarcity, individuals make choices reflecting a set of desires, wants, or preferences. These choices are made in the context of foregone opportunities. Thus the opportunity cost of working an additional hour (and receiving additional income) is the leisure foregone. This utility or wealth maximizing postulate assumes that individuals have a stable set of preferences for income, leisure, and so forth, and that the choice made at the margin (that is when an individual decides to work an additional hour) represents a tradeoff between what one gets (more income) and what one must forego (leisure).[1] This behavioral postulate operates in any kind of economic system: capitalist, socialist, whatever.

Since the maximizing postulate asserts that individuals prefer more goods (and services) to less and since more goods can be produced by increasing the productive potential (at the expense of producing for current consumption), therefore individuals in a society will devote part of their efforts to increasing the capital stock—since the size of that stock determines the flow of goods and services that constitute the output of the system. The size of the stock of capital is determined by the amount of human capital (labor), of physical capital (machines, factories, agricultural improvements, and so forth), and of natural resources. These in turn are dependent upon the available technology (that is, human command over nature), which determines the skills embodied in labor (human capital), the quality of physical capital, and what constitutes a natural resource. Technological change is considered endogenous and is viewed as the result of an investment by members of the society in inventions and innovations. However, the "invention potential" is in turn determined by the stock of knowledge (the understanding of the natural environment).

Thus the stock of capital which determines the output is a function of the stocks of physical capital, human capital, natural resources, technology, and knowledge. The maximizing postulate will result in investment in whatever part of the capital stock has the highest rate of return; that stock will increase in quantity relative to the other stocks thereby assuring that the rates of

[1] For an orthodox discussion of the neoclassical assumptions see Becker (1976) Introduction. I have benefited from an excellent elaboration of the neoclassical approach applied to economic growth by Floyd (1969).

return will become equalized. New types of physical and human capital, then, will be invented and new types of natural resources discovered when the rate of return to be earned by investing foregone consumption (that is, savings) in invention or in discovering particular techniques and natural resources exceeds the rate of return to an expansion of the existing types of machines and skills. If the size of the labor force increases relative to the capital stock, it will be profitable to adjust the forms which human and physical capital take to accommodate changes in the capital-labor ratio. Similarly, accommodations can be made concerning the stock of natural resources.

Under these conditions the growth of total output and the growth of output per capita will be determined by the fraction of income saved (and invested) and the rate of growth of population. If the fraction of income saved produces a growth of output just equal to the growth of the population then per capita income growth will be zero. On the other hand, a higher rate of saving than of population growth will produce a positive rate of per capita income growth.

From the viewpoint of the economic historian this neoclassical formulation appears to beg all of the interesting questions. The world with which it is concerned is a frictionless one in which institutions do not exist and all change occurs through perfectly operating markets. In short, the costs of acquiring information, uncertainty, and transactions costs do not exist. But precisely because of this nonexistence, the neoclassical formula does lay bare the underlying assumptions that must be explored in order to develop a useful body of theory of structure and change.

First of all, the model assumes an incentive structure that will allow individuals to capture the returns to society of investment at all these margins, that is, private and social returns are equated. Second, it assumes no diminishing returns to the acquisition and application of new knowledge because of the ability at constant costs to increase the stock of natural resources. Third, it assumes that there is a positive return to savings; fourth, that the private and social costs of having children are equated; and finally, coincidence between people's choices and the desired results. Let us examine each in turn.

Perfectly specified and costlessly enforced property rights (that is, zero transaction costs) are necessary for the first assumption to hold. Such conditions have never obtained; and today, as throughout history, many resources are closer to common property than exclusively owned. As a result, the necessary conditions for achieving the equi-marginal efficient solution have never existed—neither in the Roman Republic nor in the twentieth century United States or Soviet Union. The best that societies have ever accomplished is to raise the private return close enough to the social return to provide sufficient incentives to achieve economic growth. But the fact that growth has been more exceptional than stagnation or decline suggests that "efficient" property rights are unusual in history. In particular, individual capturability of the benefits to society from additions to the stocks of knowledge and technology has been either absent or very imperfect. As a result, not only has technological progress been slow throughout most of history, but diminishing returns to the stock of natural resources has been the most critical economic dilemma of mankind.

That dilemma brings us to the second assumption of the model. It is only in the modern era that science and technology have been wedded so that the overcoming of diminishing returns has been a reality. While Western nations have not experienced diminishing returns to natural resources in the past century, they certainly had in the more distant past.

The existence of a positive return to savings is also dependent on the structure of property rights. Throughout history the percentage of income saved and the rate of capital formation (physical and human) have usually been extremely low and sometimes have been zero or negative. The security of property rights has been a critical determinant of the rate of saving and capital formation.

Coincidence of the private and social costs of having children has implied not only that fertility was subject to human control but also that the structure of incentives and disincentives existed to adjust individual fertility decisions instantaneously to changes in the costs to society of additional population. The recurrence of Malthusian crises throughout history provides abundant evidence that this condition has not obtained.

And finally we come to the last assumption—the coincidence of choices with results. A powerful insight of neoclassical theory, with fundamental implications for economic history, is that under conditions of uncertainty it is impossible for individual profit, or wealth, maximization to exist (since no one knows with certainty the outcome of a decision), but that the wealth-maximizing result nevertheless occurs. It occurs simply because competition in the face of ubiquitous scarcity dictates that the more efficient institution, policy, or individual action will survive and the inefficient ones perish.[2] This insight is basic to an understanding of the evolution of institutional forms of economic organization, but in a world of non-market decision making inefficient forms of political structure do persist for long periods of time. Otherwise it would not be important that individuals, groups, and classes have different perceptions of reality, different theories to account for the world around them, and different and conflicting policies that they pursue. "False" theories that lead to inefficient consequences would lead to the demise of those groups relative to those with theories that produced more efficient results. But the persistence of inefficient political and economic structures in turn makes the existence of competing ideologies a critical issue in understanding economic history. The sociobiologist's insights into the survival characteristics of human society are an important contribution, but they must be melded with the evident fact that at least for long enough periods of time to be crucial to the historian, human culture produces diverse, conflicting, and inefficient solutions.

Laying bare the assumptions of the neoclassical model points the direction that I shall take in this book. Explaining economic performance in history requires a theory of demographic change, a theory of the growth in the stock of knowledge, and a theory of institutions in order to fill out the gaps in the neoclassical model briefly delineated above. In the case of the first requisite, I have simply drawn down from the existing literature on demographic change. Changes in the stock of knowledge are explored in the context of the changing structure of incentives incorporated in institutions. The primary focus of the study is upon a theory of institutions. The building blocks of this theory are:

1. a theory of property rights that describes the individual and group incentives in the system;

2. a theory of the state, since it is the state that specifies and enforces property rights;

3. a theory of ideology that explains how different perceptions

---

[2] See Alchian (1950) for the classic statement of this argument. The terms "efficient" and "inefficient" as used throughout this study are designed to compare implications of two sets of constraints—in one, maximizing behavior on the part of the participants will produce increases in output; in the other, it will not produce increases in output.

of reality affect the reaction of individuals to the changing "objective" situation.

In the next four chapters I shall develop the elements of a theory of the structure of economic systems, but first I must delineate the other basic problem the economic historian must resolve: the problem of change in history (or its obverse—the stability of an economic system).

Let me return to the neoclassical model outlined above. In that model there are no organizations or institutions except for the market, and change occurs in this framework via a change in relative prices in an impersonal market. Such a framework provides a powerful set of tools not only to explain the self-regulating market, but to show how with any parametric shift, the market will adjust. It is worth elaborating this point since it comprises one of the most powerful insights of neoclassical economics applied to history.

For simplicity purposes let us trace out the change that will occur in a political-economic unit with a fixed area of land and no external trade (or migration of productive factors) which experiences a growth of population. The immediate result is that the price of food (and raw materials) rises because the short-run supply curve is less than perfectly elastic. That is, a seller of foodstuffs finds that at the old price more people will want his food and thus he will run out of food so he raises the price. The real income of a worker declines because his wage buys less food; that of the landholder rises because the same amount of produce he sells brings in more income. Since the potential profitability of owning land rises, the price of land is bid up. Investors will increase the ratio of capital to land because it becomes more profitable to get more output from a given amount of land by using more capital (better drainage, more irrigation, and so forth). The exact amount of substitution depends on production functions (that is, the state of technology). By this process even over a fairly short period the supply curve of foodstuffs becomes more elastic. The adjustment process however is far from over. The cost of children to the worker has risen and in order not to have its standard of living fall, the working family will decide to have fewer children. Altering the production function by devising new technologies of food production (developing new fertilizer or seeds, or breeding more productive plants and animals) will raise profitability. In the long run, then, the rate of population growth declines and the supply of food expands (that is, the long-run supply curve may be perfectly elastic). The real wage of the worker rises and the price of land falls back to the original equilibrium.

It should be readily apparent to the reader that this neoclassical model assumes coincidence of private and social costs and benefits (that is, perfectly specified and costlessly enforced property rights). It is an integral part of the model that the adjustment process occurs by changes at the margin as a result of the "signals" provided by changing relative prices. The changes in the relative prices redirect factors of production into their most profitable uses without friction, and all of the changes are instantaneous responses to alterations in benefits and costs by maximizing individuals.

Now let us go over the same scenario but this time in a real world context of institutions and positive transaction costs. The initial shift in demand together with the inelastic supply curve of agricultural production does result in a rise in the market price, but the adjustment process depends upon the costs of information. The "thinner" the market and the more primitive the technology of information dissemination, the longer the period required for the adjustment process to take place. In addition, the worker (particularly the urban worker) who has enjoyed a customary living standard for a period of time may riot to protest the rising food costs or appeal to government to put a ceiling on prices to prevent the rise. The potential value of land will rise, but if there have been customary land agreements (or a prohibition on the alienation of land) the nature of the adjustment is uncertain. In the absence of exclusive ownership rights over land a farmer may not be able to capture the increased benefits of more capital-intensive use of the land. Farmers may petition the state to alter property rights so that they will be able to obtain the exclusive benefits of land ownership, but if individuals previously having use of the land would now be excluded, they will oppose such changes in property rights. While the social cost of having children will rise, the perceived private cost will not be as great (since in addition to the cost to the family there is the cost to society of one more member of the labor force, thereby depressing the wage rate, and of one more individual contributing to greater crowding and to the potential of disease spreading). The consequence may be a delayed response as compared to the social optimum. The profitability of investing in new knowledge and developing new techniques requires some degree of property rights over ideas and innovation. In their absence the new technology may not be forthcoming.

This scenario in no way exhausts the possible consequences of an increase in population but it does focus on the two fundamental issues of this book.

1. It is essential to specify the structure of an economic system in order to explore in meaningful fashion the dynamics of an economy's performance.

2. While some of the changes will occur at the margin in precisely the way neoclassical economics implies (that is, with changes in individual costs and benefits resulting in automatic changes in behavior), others will not. Specifically, it would not be in the interests of an individual urban worker to riot and incur the potential danger to life and limb by such action. The neoclassical individual would sit back and let someone else do it. Nor would it be worthwhile for the farmer to incur the costs of organizing to appeal to government to change property rights— nor for the losers to organize to fight such a change. In every case the free rider dilemma would suggest a different result.

Let me confront the free rider issue squarely. Mancur Olson (1965) extended the neoclassical paradigm to deal with the forms of group behavior which would exist in a neoclassical world. He found that small groups would exist where the individual benefits of their actions would exceed the costs or where individuals could be coerced into action and that large groups (for example, the American Medical Association and trade unions) would exist where the members could receive exclusive individual benefits not available to outsiders. He also demonstrated that when large groups were organized to create change but did not possess some exclusive benefits to members they tended to be unstable and disappear. In essence, rational individuals will not incur the costs of participating in large group action when the individual benefits can still be received by being a free rider.

Olson's work poses a fundamental issue to the economic historian. Casual everyday observation confirms the ubiquitous existence of the free rider behavior. But casual observation also confirms the immense number of cases where large group action does occur and is a fundamental force for change—action which, however, is simply inexplicable in neoclassical terms. The economic historian who has constructed his model in neoclassical terms has built into it a fundamental contradiction since there is no way for the neoclassical model to account for a good deal of the change we observe in history.

The Marxist finesses the entire issue by arguing that it is classes that are the initiators of structural change. That argument is no explanation at all, since the Marxist simply ignores the free rider problem and makes the immense leap of faith that people will set aside their own individual self-interest to act in the interest of a class, even at considerable personal sacrifice. The best evidence that this is not standard behavior comes from Marxist activists themselves who devote enormous energies to attempting to convince the proletariat to behave like a class.

The dilemma of explaining change can be put succinctly. Neoclassical economic theory can explain how people acting in their own self-interest behave; it can explain why people do not bother to vote; it can explain why, as a result of the free rider problem, people will not participate in group actions where the individual gains are negligible. It cannot, however, explain effectively the reverse side of the coin, that is, behavior in which calculated self-interest is not the motivating factor. How do we account for altruistic behavior (the anonymous free donation of blood, for example); for the willingness of people to engage in immense sacrifice with no evident possible gain (the endless parade of individuals and groups in history who have incurred prison or death for abstract causes)? How do we explain the large numbers of people who do vote, or the enormous amount of effort individuals devote to participating in voluntary organizations where the individual returns are small or negligible?

Neoclassical theory is equally deficient in explaining stability. Why do people obey the rules of society when they could evade them to their benefit? Certainly an individualistic calculus of costs and benefits would suggest that cheating, shirking, stealing, assault, and murder should be everywhere evident. We do observe all these kinds of behavior, but side-by-side with them we also observe individuals obeying rules when they could be violated with impunity at considerable benefit. Indeed, a neoclassical world would be a jungle and no society would be viable.

The premium that an individual places above his opportunity cost before engaging in an illegal act is a measure of the value he places on legitimacy (an ideological consideration). Likewise the net cost an individual incurs in attempting to force change is a measure of the injustice and alienation an individual feels. Something more than an individualistic calculus of cost/benefit is needed in order to account for change and stability. Individuals may ignore such a calculus, in an attempt to change the structure, because of deep-seated ideological convictions that the system is unjust. Individuals may also obey customs, rules, and laws because of an equally deep-seated conviction that they are legitimate. Change and stability in history require a theory of ideology to account for these deviations from the individualistic rational calculus of neoclassical theory.

Chapter 2

An Introduction to the Structure of Economies

In the ten millennia since humans first domesticated plants and animals and thereby accelerated the long climb from savagery to civilization, there has been a bewildering array of forms of economic organization interacting with other, non-economic, institutions. Can we distill from such a mass the basic structural aspects that determine economic performance? It is difficult to determine how non-economic institutions interact with those directly involved in production and exchange. Moreover, the construction and destruction of these institutions—economic and non-economic—do not occur in a vacuum, but are the result of people's perceptions stemming from historically derived opportunities and values. What is "reality" is relative to people's historically derived rationalizations of the world around them and is fundamentally colored by their views of the rightness or wrongness of the existing customs, rules, and institutions.

We can begin to develop the structure from surviving evidence by focusing on the basic tension that has been and remains the center of economic history—that between population and resources. Ever since Thomas Malthus wrote his first essay on population, in 1798, scholars have debated his dismal prediction that population tends to outgrow the resource base. Indeed, the reaction to the social implications of Malthus led to a divorce between demography and economics, which have rewed only in recent decades.

In spite of modern research there is much about this relationship between population and resources that is still unknown or beclouded by controversy. We do know that despite intermittent and sometimes lengthy periods of absolute decline, population has grown throughout prehistory and history. If the speculative notion that population may have totalled around eight million at the end of the Pleistocene era is correct, then the rate of increase over the previous one to two million years was perhaps .0007 to .0015 percent per year. After the establishment of agriculture the rate of growth appears to have accelerated to about .036 percent, until population may have reached three hundred million by A.D. 1. From then until 1750 the rate of growth may have been .056 percent—resulting in a population of about eight hundred million at that date. Thereafter there is a sharp acceleration to .44 percent from 1750 to 1800; about .53 percent in the next century; .79 percent in the first half of the twentieth century; and then 1.7 percent since 1950—producing a current world population of more than four billion.[1]

Controversy enters when we attempt to impute causation to the relationship between population and resources. Has the pattern of population expansion been consistent with the Malthusian theory? Ester Boserup (1965) has turned the Malthusian argument on its head and argued that population growth stimulates technological change (and hence an expansion in the resource base). Still another view stems from modern studies of primitive tribes which appear to show a homeostatic population. In the case of the bushmen of the Kalihari desert it was demonstrated that they took only four or five hours a day to obtain their food supply and that surviving children were spaced far enough apart to prevent significant population growth—thereby forestalling the drawing down of the resource base.[2] Can we attribute the same behavior to prehistoric tribes? It is a subject that will be examined in chapter 7.

The economic historian is also concerned with the feedback response to a change in resources. A reduction in the resource base surely led to increased mortality through famine and reduced resistance to disease. How long did it take for fertility to

---

[1] Coale (1974, p. 42). See also Cipolla (1962).
[2] For a discussion of the evidence see Dumond (1975).

decline, and what was the social mechanism (as contrasted to an automatic physiological reduction): delayed marriages, improved contraception, infanticide? With an expansion in the resource base how did population respond? Recent research has suggested that the immense growth of population in the modern era is less a consequence of reduced mortality via medical discoveries and immunization than a consequence of reduced mortality via improved nutrition and environment. And finally, how do we account for the fall in fertility that has followed rapid economic growth?

Since many of these issues are unresolved, the approach in this book must be speculative. It does appear that there have been significant divergences between the private and the social costs of having children and even delayed responses to changes in the private costs of having children. A strictly neoclassical approach to fertility—that is, the new economics of the household —is surely a valuable tool of analysis; but the jury is still out on just how much it explains and how much cultural, that is, ideological, considerations modify strictly cost/benefit calculi in demography.[3] It also appears that Malthusian population pressures have been a reality in history; moreover, at times population pressure has induced technological, social, or other changes which have (at least temporarily) reduced population pressure on the resource base.[4] It also is evident that plagues have played a major part in altering mortality throughout history and that climatic changes have altered the resource base (and hence mortality) at various times.[5]

But while the approach must be speculative, the argument of this book is straightforward.

1. There have been two major discontinuities in the population/resource rates in history; I shall call them the First and Second Economic Revolutions.

2. Between these two revolutions there have been periods of

[3] For an excellent summary of the state of historical demography see Tilly, ed. (1978).
[4] For evidence on Malthusian population pressure see the numerous studies of the Annales School, or for a more precise modeling of the issues, see Ronald Lee, "Models of Preindustrial Dynamics with Applications to England," in Tilly, ed. (1978). Boserup (1981) explores the relationship between population pressure and technological change.
[5] See McNeill (1976) on the role of plagues in history and LeRoi Ladurie (1979, chapters 17 and 18) for a discussion of climatic changes.

Malthusian population pressure which have been overcome sometimes by physiological and social responses, and sometimes by alterations in the efficiency of economic institutions which have altered the resource base. Let us examine this last point in detail. The quantity of resources is relative to the state of technology. In the simple neoclassical model of the preceding chapter, we could make land and natural resources disappear by the legerdemain of assuming that they broadly can be conceived as a part of the capital stock. That may be a reasonable modern assumption, but it does fundamental violence to explanations of the historic past—since it is only in the past century, with the Second Economic Revolution, that diminishing returns to natural resources have not been an ever-present threat or a reality when population growth occurred. The model does, however, lay bare the basic point that expansion in the resource base depends upon improvements in technology and ultimately in the stock of knowledge.

The inventive capacity of human beings separated man from other primates several million years ago, and even a modest exploration of technological history over the last ten millennia leaves one awesomely impressed by human ingenuity.[6] Invention and innovation appear to be inherent tendencies within human beings. Inventive activity is not the issue here, but what has determined its rate and direction in history is an issue. In this preliminary excursion into an analysis of economic structure, three points need to be brought out.

1. Throughout history there has almost always been an immense gap between the private and the social returns to invention and innovation. The problem is one of specifying property rights over ideas and their application to economic activity; it has been more difficult to devise property rights over technological development than over products or resource inputs. The difficulty of measuring the dimensions of intellectual property and innovations and of enforcing any such property rights has been a basic reason for the divergence between private and social benefits.

2. As Nathan Rosenberg (1976) and Paul David (1976) have emphasized, technological developments are interrelated. The innovative ideas in Leonardo da Vinci's magnificent notebooks

---

[6] For example, in order to dispel any notion about how backward people were in the ancient world, one has only to peruse Hodges (1970) to be struck by the extraordinary technological developments in the ancient world.

could not be realized without complementary developments in engineering, physics, and chemistry. Pasteur's discoveries were made possible only by complementary developments in optics, which produced the microscope. Technological developments, then, are built upon the prior accumulation of knowledge, which shapes the subsequent direction of inventive activity.

3. Ultimately the development of new techniques runs into diminishing returns unless the stock of basic knowledge is expanded. Basic knowledge depends on the development of the disciplines of the physical and natural sciences; the determinants of the growth of these scientific disciplines have until relatively modern times been quite independent of the development of new technologies. In the modern world of the Second Economic Revolution, which wedded science and technology, however, one can view the expansion of basic knowledge as a derived demand for technological advance.

The stock of knowledge and the stock of technology set upper bounds to human well being, but do not themselves determine how successful human beings are within those bounds. It is the structure of political and economic organization which determines the performance of an economy as well as the incremental rate of growth in knowledge and technology. The forms of cooperation and competition that human beings develop and the systems of enforcement of these rules of organizing human activity are at the very heart of economic history. Not only do these rules spell out the system of incentives and disincentives that guide and shape economic activity, but they also determine the underlying distribution of wealth and income of a society. The two essential building blocks to understanding the structure are a theory of the state and a theory of property rights.

A theory of the state is essential because it is the state that specifies the property rights structure. Ultimately it is the state that is responsible for the efficiency of the property rights structure, which causes growth or stagnation or economic decline. A theory of the state, therefore, must provide an explanation both for the inherent tendencies of political-economic units to produce inefficient property rights and for the instability of the state in history. This fundamental building block is, unfortunately, missing in economic history in accounting for secular change.

A theory of property rights is necessary to account for the forms of economic organization that human beings devise to reduce transactions costs and organize exchange. If one could assume a "neutral" state, then the forms of property rights which would emerge in the world of scarcity and competition would be efficient in the sense of being a least-cost solution, given the existing constraints of technology, information costs, and uncertainty. In fact, the property rights which emerge are a result of an on-going tension between the desires of the rulers of the state, on the one hand, and efforts of the parties to exchange to reduce transactions costs, on the other. This simple dichotomy actually is anything but simple, since the parties to an exchange will devote resources to influencing the political decision makers to alter the rules. But at least as an initial starting point for theorizing, it is useful to separate a theory of the state from a transaction cost approach to property rights.

Political and economic organizations have a common set of basic characteristics that are at the heart of this study. Both are devised to maximize the wealth of the principals by exploiting the gains from trade as a result of specialization (including a comparative advantage in violence). Both entail

1. the establishment of a set of constraints on behavior in the form of rules and regulations;

2. a set of procedures designed to detect deviations from and enforce compliance with the rules and regulations; and

3. the articulation of a set of moral and ethical behavioral norms to reduce enforcement costs.

The rules and regulations define the terms of exchange whether between principals (that is, ruler and constituents in the political organization or producer and consumer in markets) or between principals and agents (in hierarchical political and economic organization, rulers and bureaucrats, owners and managers, managers and workers). Constitutions, the legal framework, the specification of property rights, the bylaws of organizations, trade-union contracts—these all embody constraints on behavior.

Compliance procedures are concerned with detecting deviations from the rules, regulations, or stipulated contract agreements and with instituting and enacting punishment (or rewards). If one could costlessly measure the characteristics of goods and services in exchange as well as the performance of agents, then the problem of detecting deviations from the rules would not be important. Measurement constitutes the formalized description of a good or service, and therefore without some form of measurement, property rights cannot be established nor exchange take place. Compliance costs in addition consist of the cost of enacting penalties for nonperformance. Because measurement is costly (and the costs of perfect accuracy prohibitive) and because there are also costs of enforcement it pays parties to an exchange to maximize with respect to deviations from the agreement. If either party to a contract can with impunity receive the benefits of the exchange without fulfilling his or her part of the bargain, then it is to his or her benefit to do so. Tax evasion, cheating, shirking, opportunism, problems of agency (and the resources devoted to monitoring and metering) are at base issues that arise because of the costliness of compliance procedures. Therefore both the constraints on behavior in the form of rules and the procedures designed to detect and enforce compliance with the rules are devised to maximize the revenue of principals subject to these transaction costs constraints.

There is a substantial literature dealing with the organizational implications of maximization subject to the constraint of technology,[7] but that constraint must be melded with the transaction constraints arising from compliance costs to develop a theory of political and economic institutions. In the next two chapters the elements of constrained maximization models of the state and of economic organization are developed.

The argument, however, is clearly incomplete. Compliance is so costly that the enforcement of any body of rules in the absence of some degree of individual restraint from maximizing behavior would render the political or economic institution nonviable—hence the enormous investment that is made to convince individuals of the legitimacy of these institutions. A theory of the structure of (and change in) political and economic institutions must incorporate a theory of ideology, which is the subject of chapter 5.

[7] See the literature on production functions, or for historical description see Chandler (1977).

Chapter 3

A Neoclassical Theory
of the State[*]

I

The existence of a state is essential for economic growth; the state, however, is the source of man-made economic decline. This paradox should make the study of the state central to economic history: models of the state should be an explicit part of any analysis of secular changes. But while the long path of historical research is strewn with the bones of theories of the state developed by historians and political scientists, economists traditionally have given little attention to the issue.

Recently, however, modern extensions of neoclassical economic theory, which have proven to be powerful tools of analysis, have been applied to a variety of political issues.[1] Neoclassical theory conceived of as a theory of choice has provided at the very least a disciplined and logically consistent approach to a study of the state. This theory offers the promise of developing refutable propositions about nonmarket decision making. In addition, research into economic organization has revealed its close kinship

[*] An earlier version of this essay appeared in *Explorations in Economic History* (July 1979) under the title "A Framework for Analyzing the State in Economic History."

[1] See Baumol (1962); Buchanan and Tullock (1962); Downs (1957); Niskanen (1971); Breton (1974).

with political organization. A satisfactory theory of the firm would contribute immensely to the development of a theory of the state.[2] We must, of course, be cautious about the limits of neoclassical theory. Public choice theory—economics applied to politics—has at best had only a modest success in explaining political decision making. Interest group politics cannot effectively explain voting behavior; ideological considerations appear to account for a great many political and judicial decisions.[3] Further, the questions that must be asked are at a different level than the day-to-day political decision-making process. For the economic historian, the key problems are to explain the kind of property rights that come to be specified and enforced by the state and to explain the effectiveness of enforcement; the most interesting challenge is to account for changes in the structure and enforcement of property rights over time.

II

At the outset one is posed with the problem of defining precisely what a state is. Where, for example, does the medieval manor belong on the continuum from the voluntary organization to the state? For the purposes of this work, a state is an organization with a comparative advantage in violence, extending over a geographic area whose boundaries are determined by its power to tax constituents. The essence of property rights is the right to exclude, and an organization which has a comparative advantage in violence is in the position to specify and enforce property rights. In contrast to the theories frequently advanced in the literature of political science, sociology, and anthropology, here the key to understanding the state involves the potential use of violence to gain control over resources. One cannot develop a useful analysis of the state divorced from property rights.[4]

Two general types of explanation for the state exist: a contract theory and a predatory or exploitation theory. Contract theories of the state have a long history. Recently they have

[2] See Coase (1937); Alchian and Demsetz (1972).
[3] See North (1978).
[4] In an otherwise interesting analysis of the origins of the state Carniero (1970) fails to link the state with the establishment of property rights.

been resurrected by neoclassical economists because they are a logical extension of the theorem of exchange, in which the state plays the role of wealth maximizer for society. Because a contract limiting each individual's activity relative to others is essential for there to be economic growth, the contract theory approach offers an explanation for the development of efficient property rights that would promote economic growth.[5]

The predatory or exploitation theory of the state is held by a remarkably varied collection of social scientists, including Marxists (at least in their analysis of the capitalist state) and some neoclassical economists. This view considers the state to be the agency of a group or class; its function, to extract income from the rest of the constituents in the interest of that group or class. The predatory state would specify a set of property rights that maximized the revenue of the group in power, regardless of its impact on the wealth of the society as a whole.

The contract approach may explain why the state potentially can provide a framework for economizing on the use of resources and therefore can promote wealth. As both the third party to every contract and the ultimate source of coercion, however, the state becomes the field on which the battle for control of its decision-making power is fought. All sides wish to be able to redistribute wealth and income in the interest of their own group. While the contract theory explains the gains of initial contracting but not the subsequent maximizing behavior of constituents with diverse interests, the predatory theory ignores the initial gains of contracting and focuses on the extraction of rents from constituents by those who gain control of the state. Nevertheless, the two theories are not inconsistent. It is the distribution of "violence potential" that reconciles them. The contract theory assumes an equal distribution of violence potential amongst the principals. The predatory theory assumes an unequal distribution.

Property rights that produce sustained economic growth have seldom held sway throughout history, but even the most casual survey of the human experience makes clear that there have been political-economic units that achieved substantial economic growth for long periods of time. By sustained economic growth I mean that output has grown at a more rapid rate than population. This phenomenon is not confined to the two hundred years since the Industrial Revolution. There was an immense ac-

---

[5] The most careful analysis is that of Umbeck (forthcoming).

cumulation of wealth between the development of agriculture in the eighth millennium B.C. and the *Pax Romana* of the first two centuries A.D. It is true that during those centuries whole civilizations declined and disappeared, but there were also civilizations that experienced economic growth for lengthy periods in Mesopotamia, Egypt, Greece, Rhodes, and, of course, the Roman Republic and Empire. There is nothing new about sustained economic growth, then, despite the myth perpetrated by economic historians that it is a creation of the Industrial Revolution. Nor is there anything more inevitable than the ultimate economic decline of political-economic units.

In this chapter I shall develop a simple model of the state in order to explain two aspects that are fundamental to economic history: the widespread tendency of states to produce inefficient property rights and hence fail to achieve sustained growth; and the inherent instability of all states, which leads to economic change and ultimately to economic decline. Initially the model examines a state with a single ruler. However, I shall also explore the tension between ruler and constituents which leads to the dilution of the ruler's control and the emergence of political pluralism. The study of legitimacy and alienation will be deferred until chapter 5.[6]

This model of the state with a wealth- or utility-maximizing ruler has three essential characteristics. One specifies the exchange process between ruler and constituents; the other two specify the conditions that will determine the terms of exchange.

First, the state trades a group of services, which we shall call protection and justice, for revenue. Since there are economies of scale in providing these services, total income in the society is higher as a result of an organization specializing in these services than it would be if each individual in society protected his own property.

Second, the state attempts to act like a discriminating monopolist, separating each group of constituents and devising property rights for each so as to maximize state revenue.

Third, the state is constrained by the opportunity cost of its constituents since there always exist potential rivals to provide the same set of services. The rivals are other states, as well as individuals within the existing political-economic unit who are

---

[6] I also neglect in this chapter the impact of state policies on fertility and mortality.

potential rulers. The degree of monopoly power of the ruler, therefore, is a function of the closeness of substitutes for the various groups of constituents.

By exploring in more depth these three hypotheses, we may not only put flesh on the bare bones of the model but also draw out some useful implications for the economic historian.

III

The basic services that the state provides are the underlying rules of the game. Whether evolving as a body of unwritten customs (as in the feudal manor) or as a written constitution, they have two objectives: one, to specify the fundamental rules of competition and cooperation which will provide a structure of property rights (that is, specify the ownership structure in both factor and product markets) for maximizing the rents accruing to the ruler; two, within the framework of the first objective, to reduce transaction costs in order to foster maximum output of the society and, therefore, increase tax revenues accruing to the state. This second objective will result in the provision of a set of public (or semi-public) goods and services designed to lower the cost of specifying, negotiating, and enforcing contracts which underlie economic exchange. The economies of scale associated with devising a system of law, justice, and defense are the basic underlying source of civilization; and the creation of the state in the millennia following the first economic revolution was the necessary condition for all subsequent economic development. While the ten millennia since the creation of settled agriculture appear in historical retrospect as an endless saga of war and of butchery, exploitation (however defined), enslavement, and mass murder, most often done by the state ruler or his agents, it is still essential to stress the necessity of a state for economic progress. Throughout history, individuals given a choice between a state—however exploitative it might be—and anarchy, have decided for the former. Almost any set of rules is better than none, and it is not in the ruler's interest to make the rules so unpalatable that initiative is stifled.

There are three important implications of these objectives.

1. Put together, the two are not completely consistent. The second objective implies a completely efficient set of property rights to maximize societal output; the first attempts to specify

a set of fundamental rules that will enable the ruler to maximize his own income (or, if we wish to relax the assumption of a single ruler, to maximize the monopoly rents of the group or class of which the ruler is the agent). From the redistributive societies of ancient Egyptian dynasties through the slavery system of the Greek and Roman world to the medieval manor, there was persistent tension between the ownership structure which maximized the rents to the ruler (and his group) and an efficient system that reduced transaction costs and encouraged economic growth. This fundamental dichotomy is the root cause of the failure of societies to experience sustained economic growth and I shall explore it more precisely later in this chapter.

2. The creation of an infrastructure designed to specify and enforce a body of property rights entails the delegation of power to agents of the ruler. Since the utility function of the agents is not identical with that of the ruler, the ruler will specify a group of rules to attempt to enforce conduct by his agent that will be consistent with his own objectives.[7] There will be, however, a diffusion of the powers of the ruler to the degree that the agents are not perfectly constrained by the rules. The effect will also be a reduction in the monopoly rents of the ruler. We can predict the structure of this bureaucracy by exploring the transaction costs of the several parts of the economy.

3. The services provided by the ruler have differently shaped supply curves. While some services are pure public goods, others have typical U-shaped cost curves reflecting rising average costs beyond some range of output. The cost curve of protection would be relative to the state of military technology and would specify the size of the political-economic unit as "efficient" when the marginal cost of protection was equal to the incremental tax revenue. From the Greek city-state to the Roman Empire to the small decentralized political organization of the feudal era to the nation state, military technology and changes in military technology have played a major role in shaping the supply curve.[8]

---

[7] For a further discussion of agency theory see Jensen and Meckling (1975).

[8] One of the most neglected parts of economic history is the study of military technology in relationship to the size of states. While there is an immense literature on military technology itself, it has seldom been explored in terms of its implications for political structure. For an exception to this indictment see Bean (1973).

Two partial theories that have been advanced to account for the varying size of the state are consistent with the above stated marginal conditions. Wittfogel's hydraulic society (1957) was in effect a natural monopoly, with economies of scale derived from the indivisibility of an integrated water system. Friedman's theory of the size and shape of nations (1977) explores the relationship between the type of revenue and the size and shape of nations, arguing that if trade is the major political revenue source the result should be a large nation; that rent should imply small nations; and that labor should imply that nations will have closed boundaries or be culturally homogeneous.

IV

The economy consists of a diverse group of activities with varying production functions reflecting the technology, resource base, and population of the political-economic unit. The ruler will specify a set of property rights designed to maximize his monopoly rents for each separable part of the economy by monitoring and metering the inputs and outputs of each. The costs of measuring the dimensions of the inputs and outputs will dictate the various property rights structure for the diverse sectors of the economy, which therefore will be dependent on the state of the technology of measurement. Common property resources have persisted where the costs of measuring the dimensions of the resources have outweighed the benefits. The development of standardized weights and measurements is almost as old as government and has typically been fostered by the state. Standardization performs the function of lowering transaction costs and of allowing the ruler to extract the maximum amount of rent. The higher the cost of measurement of the multiple dimension of a good or service, the greater the dissipation of rent.[9]

Some of the historical forms of organization employed by the ruler include a loosely organized federal structure of local governors with their own bureaucracy; a centralized bureaucracy directly employed by the ruler; a bailiff system; and tax farming. Despite elaborate efforts at monitoring, in each of these organizational structures the agents of the ruler were imperfectly

---

[9] See Barzel (1974); Cheung (1974).

constrained, and their interests never completely coincided with the ruler's. The result typically was more or less dissipation of the monopoly rents of the rulers to the agents; in some cases there was collusion between agents and constituents to divide up some of the monopoly rents.

V

The ruler always has rivals: competing states or potential rulers within his own state. The latter are analogous to the potential rivals to a monopolist.[10] Where there are no close substitutes, the existing ruler characteristically is a despot, a dictator, or an absolute monarch. The closer the substitutes, the fewer degrees of freedom the ruler possesses, and the greater the percentage of incremental income that will be retained by the constituents. The opportunity cost of each of the various constituents will be different and will dictate the bargaining power each group has in the specification of property rights, as well as the tax burden it will incur. Opportunity costs will also dictate allocation of services provided by the ruler to the degree that they are not pure public goods), since the ruler will provide greater services to those with close alternatives than to those with none.

Constituents may, at some cost, go over to a competing ruler (that is, another existing political-economic unit) or support a competitor for ruler within the existing state.[11] The former alternative depends upon the structure of competitive political units. The more geographically proximate ones of course have an advantage. The ruler's efforts to gain or keep constituents will be determined by the supply curve of protection and the marginal benefits to be derived from additional constituents.

The latter alternative depends upon the relative violence potential of competing constituents. The ruler's own agents may be able to organize opposition and attract supporters from among the constituents by offering a better division of the existing rents. However, other individuals with command over sufficient resources to acquire military capability (or in the feudal world, lords with existing military capability) are potential rivals.

[10] For an analysis of the monopoly case see Demsetz (1968).
[11] These two choices are roughly analogous to Hirschman's Exit and Voice. See Hirschman (1970).

VI

The simple static model just described will give rise to two constraints on the ruler: a competitive constraint and a transaction cost constraint. Both typically produce inefficient property rights. Under the first, the ruler will avoid offending powerful constituents. If the wealth or income of groups with close access to alternative rulers is adversely affected by property rights, the ruler will be threatened. Accordingly, he will agree to a property rights structure favorable to those groups, regardless of its effects upon efficiency.

Efficient property rights may lead to higher income in the state but lower tax revenues for the ruler because of the transaction costs (monitoring, metering, and collecting such taxes) as compared to those of a more inefficient set of property rights. A ruler therefore frequently found it in his interests to grant a monopoly rather than property rights which would lead to more competitive conditions.

These two constraints together account for the wide spread of inefficient property rights. In effect, the property rights structure that will maximize rents to the ruler (or ruling class) is in conflict with that that would produce economic growth.[12] One variant of this is the Marxian notion of the contradictions of the mode of production, in which the ownership structure is incompatible with realizing the potential gain from an evolving set of technological changes. Economic growth is assured when the state behaves as specified in the contract case cited earlier (given reasonable assumptions about individual preferences with respect to savings and the number of children desired). Given the strictures in the foregoing model, however, it is clear that the pure contract case occurs only under the unusual circumstance that the ownership structure specified by the ruler is consistent with the kind of efficiency standards implied by neoclassical growth models (capitalism as described in the *Communist Manifesto*, for example). In effect, an ownership structure that provided

---

[12] Under the condition of zero transaction costs, the ruler could always devise first an efficient set of rules and then bargain for his rents, but this postulate from welfare economics simply ignores positive transaction costs, which is what the game is all about. Even the most casual observations from history and the contemporary world make clear that "inefficient" property rights are the rule, not the exception.

incentives for efficient resource allocation (that is, a set of property rights that made the private rate of return on innovation, investment in human capital, and so forth approach the social rate) would be essential. But we should note immediately that the consequences must be destabilizing, since technological change, the spread of more efficient markets, and so forth would alter relative prices and the opportunity cost of constituents and would lead eventually to conflicts with the fundamental ownership structure of property rights.

In short, the process of growth is inherently destabilizing to a state. I shall explore in the next section the adjustment process of a state to such changes.

If, however, growth is destabilizing, so is no growth, when a political-economic unit exists in a world of competing political-economic units. Relatively inefficient property rights threaten the survival of a state in the context of more efficient neighbors, and the ruler faces the choice of extinction or of modifying the fundamental ownership structure to enable the society to reduce transaction costs and raise the rate of growth. Again, however, we must note carefully that the ability to adjust assumes a single ruler and none of the complicating issues posed when there are multiple sources of decision making.[13]

Stagnant states can survive as long as there is no change in the opportunity cost of the constituents at home or in the relative strength of competitor states. This last condition usually implies that the state approaches the status of a monopoly and is surrounded by weak states (and there are no net gains to a ruler in acquiring these states).

VII

The inherent instability of the state as outlined in the previous sections should be evident. Changes in information costs, technology, and population (or relative factor prices in general) are all obvious destabilizing influences. Also significant is the fact that the ruler is mortal.

A change in relative prices that improves the bargaining power of a group of constituents can lead to alteration of the rules

13 Gerschenkron's relative backwardness hypothesis makes sense only in this context.

to give that group more income, or, alternatively, the constituents can force the ruler to give up some of his rule-making powers. Sometimes the emergence of "representative" government has come in the face of an external threat to the ruler. The transformation of the Greek city-state from monarchy to oligarchy to democracy (in the case of Athens) occurred as a consequence of a change in military technology (the development of the phalanx) which could only be accomplished with a citizen army; the price the ruler paid was the dilution of his rule-making powers. Similarly in early modern Europe, alterations in military technology (the pike, the longbow, and gunpowder) led in some instances to the delegation of rule-making powers to parliament or Estates General in return for the increased revenue needed for survival.

While changes in military technology were a major (though certainly not the sole) source of the growth of pluralist or representative government in the ancient and medieval world, the modern alterations in control of the state have been associated with the radical change in relative prices stemming from the Second Economic Revolution. The overwhelming dominance of agriculture in production in the Western world prior to the nineteenth century resulted in struggles to control the state being associated with the distribution of landed wealth and income (including the income from trade and shipping of agricultural and resource goods). With the Second Economic Revolution, the decline in the relative importance of land rent (and the landlord), the growth of manufacturing and services, the growing share of income going to labor, and in particular the growing importance of human capital have transformed the structure of production and created new interest groups; further, they are the basis of the struggle to control the state that has been going on in the past century.[14]

[14] The property rights and allocation implications of the rise of pluralism are explored elsewhere. Here I want simply to emphasize that whether constituents bargain with a ruler over property rights or gain some control over rule making power, the result may be the same as far as the efficiency or inefficiency of property rights is concerned and the argument advanced in section VI above still holds. I can make this point more forcefully by the following illustration. In the contemporary world there are immense differences in the control of the state as between the Soviet Union and the United States. The former is certainly close to my model of a single-ruler state; the latter is certainly a pluralist state. In the former, the bargaining over property rights takes place *within* the control structure; in the latter there is a ubiquitous struggle by interest groups to control the state. But I know of no a priori reason on the basis of *this difference alone* to predict the relative efficiency of property rights in one country or the other.

VIII

Instability is one thing; the process by which change and adjustment take place is something else. Here the separation between the application of economic principles and the application of other social science and Marxist principles is important. The former principles are inspired by the adjustment process in markets. In this process, changes at the margin lead to instantaneous adjustment. In politics as well as in economics, adjustments will occur only as long as the private returns exceed private costs; otherwise, the free rider problem will prevent adjustment. This condition severely restricts the willingness of constituents to adjust; and while it helps to explain the persistence of inefficient property rights, it obviously cannot explain the action of large groups to alter the property rights structure when private returns are negligible or negative.

Theories originating in the other social sciences and Marxism, on the other hand, account for large group action to alter property rights but have not provided any convincing theoretical underpinning to account for the way by which the free rider problem is overcome.

This theoretical gap is a crucial problem in any explanation of secular change. Casual empiricism provides ample evidence that large groups have sometimes acted to alter the structure of the state; but without some model we are unable to predict when the free rider problem will preclude action and when it will not. The study of ideology and the development of some positive model on the free rider problem are essential preliminaries to formulating a dynamic theory of change in the state.

We should note also the implications of adhering strictly to a neoclassical approach where the free rider problem will prevent large group activity. These implications point up the explanatory power of this neoclassical model at the same time that they delineate its limitations, and in concluding this discussion I wish to dwell briefly on a number of them.

First, the free rider accounts for the stability of states throughout history. The costs to the individual of opposing the coercive forces of the state have traditionally resulted in apathy and acceptance of the state's rules, no matter how oppressive. An historical counterpart of the low voter turnout in many current democracies is the failure of individuals to act as classes and of large groups to overthrow societies in the past. While the significance of this simple observation has not appeared to be properly appreciated in much of the literature on the state, it is amply (though inadvertently) attested to by the immense literature of Marxists on class consciousness, class solidarity, and ideology. Lenin and subsequent Marxist activists have been well aware of the very real problem that the free rider posed for Marxist theory and revolutionary practice.

Second, institutional innovation will come from rulers rather than constituents since the latter would always face the free rider problem. The ruler will, on his side, continue to innovate institutional change to adjust to changing relative prices since he has no free rider problem. Thus a change in the relative scarcity of land and labor which made labor scarcer would lead the ruler to innovate institutional changes to appropriate increased rents from labor. These innovations will be carried out as long as the opportunity costs of labor do not change (that is, there is no change in potential competition from other rulers).

Third, revolutions will be palace revolutions undertaken by the ruler's agents or by a competing ruler or small elite Leninist-type groups.

Fourth, where the ruler is the agent of a group or class, some rules for succession will be devised to minimize the opportunities for disruptive change or revolution upon the death of the ruler. As noted above, disruptive change or revolution will come most likely from the ruler's agents.

The foregoing four points help to explain a great deal about the stability of and the sources of changes in the structure of the state throughout history. Limiting one's analysis to instances where one could identify net private gains (in narrowly construed economic terms) to the actors, however, would put a fatal handicap on the study of structural change of the state. It is necessary to construct a theory of ideology to resolve the free rider dilemma.

Chapter 4

A Framework for Analyzing Economic Organization in History

I

Throughout history economic activity has occurred by means of an immense variety of organizational forms. From the so-called redistributive societies of the Egyptian dynasties, to the patron-client relationship in Republican Rome, to the feudal manor, these organizational forms have been the subject of historical investigation; but most of the research has been devoid of analytical content.[1] Much the same criticism can be made of economists' work dealing with modern-day economic organization. In fact, as recently as 1968, the *International Encyclopedia of the Social Sciences* included no essay on the market, the most fundamental institution of modern Western economies and central to the performance of economies of the past, as well.

To account analytically for economic organization we must use a theory of transaction costs together with a theory of the state. A theory of transaction costs is necessary because under the ubiquitous condition of scarcity and therefore competition, more efficient forms of economic organization will replace less efficient forms under *ceteris paribus* conditions. The state, however—as I

---

[1] An exception is the work of Karl Polanyi. For a review of his contribution see North (1977).

have argued in the previous chapter—will encourage and specify efficient property rights only to the extent that they are consistent with the wealth-maximizing objectives of those who run the state. Hence the need for a model that incorporates both. I shall begin here by developing a transaction-cost approach to economic organization and then I shall combine it with the analysis of the state developed in the previous chapter.

I pick up where we left off in chapter 2. Any form of economic organization must have provisions for the specifying and enforcing of the terms of exchange. Abstracting from the role of the state, the choice of organizational form will be dictated by the relative amount of resources required for a given amount of output. A market-price system is costly because it is costly first to measure the dimensions of the good or service transacted and then to enforce the terms of exchange. And there is really a third cost involved as well: that associated with the external effects that arise because measurement was imperfect. In contrast, hierarchical forms of organization substitute the directives of a central authority: a contractual arrangement restricts the options of the parties to exchange wherein one party gives up control of decisions to the other party.[2] The costs of this organizational form are the costs of measuring the performance of agents; the inefficiencies associated with imperfect measurement; and the costs of enforcement. Because the resource costs of compliance are different from those involved in the market-price system, they lead to different results. Let me illustrate market exchange, then explore the reasons for the existence of the firm (or other hierarchical organization), and then attempt to explain economic organization in history.

II

I begin by simply describing a transaction I make every week in my local public market. It is the purchase of a quantity of oranges (fourteen oranges for one dollar in 1980). I purchase oranges

----

[2] In this context, authority is simply a contract in which this delegation of decision making is implied and a structure of decision making specified. In the absence of coercion by the state, which can impose nonvoluntaristic forms of organization, the neoclassical definition will serve. However, I examine the issue further in examining the literature on the firm and in considering ideology.

for orange juice and therefore I want the oranges to contain a great deal of juice (rather than pulp) and to have a tart flavor. What I really would like to specify in the exchange is a certain quantity of orange juice with a combination of organic ingredients that produces the flavor I want. Why aren't oranges sold in a way that I can get precisely what I want? In part, they are. Valencia oranges are juice oranges and are sold separately from Navel or other eating oranges. But the amount of juice and the flavor that I will get from the oranges cannot be specified at low cost. If the measurement of these ingredients were possible at no or little cost, then I could obtain the precise combination I want. Instead, purchases are made by number, weight, volume, length; and resources are devoted to seeing that these objective measurement characteristics are met.

The seller of the oranges bought them from a wholesaler; within the crates he received were some oranges not in good condition. He stands to lose money on those oranges, since if he tries to give them to me for my dollar I will go to another stall at the public market to buy my oranges. In short, the competition of a large number of sellers constrains his behavior. Does he slip a few of the rotten oranges in the bottom of the sack where I won't notice them until I get home? He might if he never expects to see me again since it is the only way he can get rid of the oranges that otherwise would be a loss to him. But that is why I go to the same dealer, Morris, each week. He knows I will not return if he slips such oranges into my sack. I am valuable as a repeat customer; opportunism, then, is constrained by repetitive dealings. Morris, on his part, accepts my check for one dollar without inquiring whether I have sufficient funds in the bank to cover the check, or whether the dollar he gets when he cashes my check will be accepted unquestionably by his wholesaler or by anyone else from whom he wishes to purchase goods or services.

It should be readily apparent not only that this simple exercise was really complex in terms of its fundamental characteristics, but also that we have examined only its superficial manifestations. Underlying the transaction—making it possible—was a complex structure of law and its enforcement. Both Morris and I accept that we each have property rights over the oranges and the dollar—and that these rights are enforceable in a court of law. Morris accepts a piece of paper as a legitimate surrogate for a command over a certain amount of other resources and knows that he can use it for that purpose. In brief, uncertainty is reduced or completely eliminated by an accepted structure of property rights and their enforcement.

Let me summarize the implications of the foregoing illustration. One must be able to measure the quantity of a good in order for it to be exclusive property and to have value in exchange. Where measurement costs are very high, the good will be a common property resource. The technology of measurement and the history of weights and measures is a crucial part of economic history since as measurement costs were reduced the cost of transacting was reduced. The fourteen oranges in the illustration above are an imperfect surrogate for the quantity desired, which is a given quantity of juice with a certain flavor. The separation of oranges by type or the grading of oranges is a step in the right direction; but so long as *some* characteristic of a good that has economic value is not measured, then there is divergence between private and social cost.[3]

Information costs are reduced by the existence of large numbers of buyers and sellers. Under these conditions, prices embody the same information that would require large search costs by individual buyers and sellers in the absence of an organized market.[4]

Opportunism is constrained by the competition of large numbers (and by personalized exchange). We can think loosely of opportunism, at this point, as the ability of one party to an exchange to benefit at the expense of the other party by violating the agreement in his or her post-contractual behavior.

The transfer of property rights amongst individual owners through contracting in the market place requires that the rights be exclusive.[5] Not only must the rights be measurable; they must also be enforceable. Note that there are two stages to the transfer process. The first stage involves the costs of defining and policing exclusivity in the absence of exchange; the second, the costs associated with negotiating and enforcing the contracts for the exchange and transfer of rights.

[3] See Barzel (1974) and Cheung (1974).

[4] The original contributions were those of Hayek (1937 and 1945). See also Stigler (1961).

[5] The rights that are transferred must be exclusive, but we should note that the sale of a good or service does not imply unrestricted rights. When I sell my house the new owner is as constrained by zoning laws in his use of the house as I was. What I am transferring is a specific bundle of rights.

A third party, the state, can lower the costs of transacting through the development of an impersonal body of law and enforcement. Since the development of law is a public good there are important scale economies associated with it. If a body of law exists, negotiation and enforcement costs are substantially reduced since the basic rules of exchange are already spelled out. Finally before leaving this illustration, let me note one additional point. Even if Morris had known he would never see me again, he probably would not have slipped some rotten oranges in the bottom of the sack; and I know, on my part, that while Morris's back was turned, filling up the sack, I would not have slipped a couple of oranges into my pocket even though there was no chance of being detected. The reason is that both of us viewed the exchange as fair or legitimate, and we were constrained in our behavior by that conviction. This issue will be examined in chapter 5.

III

Why does the firm replace the market? That was the question Ronald Coase asked in his essay "The Nature of the Firm" (1937). He characterized the firm as that range of exchanges over which the market system was suppressed and resource allocation was accomplished instead by authority and direction. Alchian and Demsetz, confronting the same question (1972), emphasized the importance of monitoring the inputs where the gains of joint team production (resulting from specialization and division of labor) make it difficult to measure inputs; Jensen and Meckling (1976) extended the monitoring argument to the effort of principals (owners of a set of property rights) to control the behavior of agents (persons engaged by the principals to perform services in their behalf) so that they will act in the principal's interests. The difference between Coase and Alchian and Demsetz requires some elaboration.

According to Coase, the advantage of the firm over transacting in the market is a gain as a result of a reduction in transaction costs. (In effect, a firm has reduced one set of transactions—those in the product market—and increased another set —those in the factor market. Therefore, the efficient size of the firm is determined as that at which the gains and costs at the margin are equal.) Alchian and Demsetz stress the productivity gains from team production, which Coase ignores; but they then emphasize that a byproduct of team production will be shirking or cheating and that therefore a monitor is needed to reduce these transaction costs.[6] Both Williamson (1975) and Klein, Crawford, and Alchian (1979) stress the role of opportunism in inducing the vertical integration of economic activity. Where there are appropriable quasi rents (defined as the excess of an asset's value over its next best use) as assets become more specific, the costs of contracting will increase more than the costs of vertical integration; we will observe vertical integration to prevent a firm's being held up by another contracting party in the position of being able to cause the firm large losses by altering the terms of the agreement at a strategic moment.

Alchian and Demsetz (and Jensen and Meckling) emphasize that the firm is simply a legal fiction and a nexus of contracting relationships, whereas Coase emphasizes that the firm is governed by authority. Coase's position is in some respects close to that of New Left critics such as Marglin, who has argued (1974) that the productivity gains from the celebrated Smithian specialization and division of labor do not require the hierarchical organization of the firm, and that the reason for the existence of the firm is that it is an exploitative vehicle by which bosses exploit workers. The difference is that Coase emphasizes the real transaction cost gains from the firm (presumably at least partly in consequence of the authority), whereas Marglin and other New Left critics argue that there are no savings in real cost as a consequence of the hierarchy imposed by the firm. Marglin's argument, however, will not survive critical scrutiny. If there were no real costs savings from the disciplined hierarchical firm structure, then we surely would observe non-authoritative organizational forms effectively competing with firms. Since there have been literally thousands of utopian, cooperative, and other experimental organizational forms in American economic history, we would expect that many should survive in competition with the traditional firm. They haven't; and even a casual examination of the sources of their failure suggests that there were fundamental transaction cost problems impeding the sur-

---

[6] However, as McManus (1975) points out, Alchian and Demsetz are incorrect in asserting that team production per se is the cause of the problem. It is the costliness of measuring inputs and outputs that generates monitoring costs.

vival of such non-authoritarian forms of organization. If that evidence were not sufficient, we could equally turn to look at the many experiments in socialist countries. Clearly there are both production-cost (from economies of scale) and transaction cost advantages to hierarchical organization.[7]

IV

Let us see if we can fit the pieces from the two previous sections into a general transaction cost framework of economic organization, before adding the state to the analysis.[8]

The resource costs devoted to compliance differ with alternative forms of organized economic activity. These compliance costs consist of the costs of measurement in alternative organizational forms and the costs of enforcing an agreement. Clearly, measurement costs in markets contrast to those of hierarchical organizations.

Markets dominate the sale of goods to consumers, and there will be both a subjective measurement element (such as the freshness of produce or the flavor of the orange juice) and the less costly but less accurate objective measurement costs (such as the weight, number, color, or grade of the good—the observable surrogates used by consumers). When we shift from orange juice to more complex goods or services such as a television set, the quality of repair work on an automobile or the quality of a physician's service, the costs of measurement are increased immensely and we tend to rely on various surrogates such as brand names, trade marks, warranties, reputation; but the key element is the degree of competition which constrains the principals.

When we turn to intermediate goods and services, such as a machine tool which is used in making an automobile, the exchange may be a market exchange or one internalized inside a firm, but the measurement costs will be different. When the exchange consists of purchases in the market, competition constrains the seller to meet the measurement specifications of the contract or lose out to a competitor. The pecuniary income of

---

[7] For psychological experiments demonstrating and measuring shirking in groups as compared to individual performance, see Latane, Silliams, and Harkinds (1979).

[8] For an elaboration of the argument presented here see McManus (1975) and Barzel (unpublished 1980).

the seller therefore is directly tied to performance. When machine tool making is consolidated inside a firm, measurement is still necessary to see that the machine tool meets quality specifications and that the firm uses a variety of monitoring devices, such as quality-control inspectors and accounting methods, to measure performance. However, the income of the worker, now a part of team production in making the machine tool (and an agent rather than a principal), is no longer directly tied to his or her productive activity. The market no longer serves as a direct constraint on performance. If it were costless to measure the output (quantity and quality) of the individual worker, then the market would indeed be an equally effective constraint, the worker's income would be tied directly to performance, and the worker would be paid by his or her output (piece rate) rather than by input (hourly rate). But because it is costly to measure individual performance (and perfect measurement is frequently impossible), shirking, cheating, and so forth are common, workers are paid by input, and various costly but imperfect monitoring devices are employed to reduce shirking.

There are also costs in enforcing a contract: those of measuring the damages or injury to a party to the contract, of enacting penalties, and of compensating the injured party.

In order to measure damages one must first be able to measure performance; contracts therefore include detailed specifications, designed to spell out the characteristics of the exchange that indicate performance.

The enactment of penalties and compensation for damages not only entails a body of law, judicial process, and enforcement, but is heavily influenced by moral and ethical codes of behavior (that is, by the perceived legitimacy of the law and the contractual relationship). Personalized exchange in simple, unspecialized societies depends for enforcement upon such behavioral codes, and the perceived legitimacy of the contractual relationship significantly influences judges and juries. If measurement were perfect and the judicial process precisely awarded the "correct" amount of damages to injured parties in a contract violation, then opportunism would not play the part that it does in influencing economic organization. But the judicial process is implemented by rulers' agents who cannot themselves be perfectly constrained and who are guided by their own interests as well as their subjective evaluation of the justice of the contract.

Therefore enforcement is imperfect, particularly concerning such agreements as long lived contracts where future prices and risks cannot be specified.[9] It is equally imperfect where specialized physical or human capital, which can make hold-up or opportunism profitable, is employed.

With home production there are no transaction costs: therefore no proxy for subjective measurement is required, since individuals tailor their home production to their own utility function. There is complete vertical integration, but at the cost of specialization.

The greater the specialization and division of labor, the more steps in the production process from initial producer to final consumer and the greater the total costs of measurement (since measurement must occur at each step). The choice of organizational form will be influenced by the characteristics of the good or service and by the technology of measurement of the attributes.

Hierarchical organization replaces the market first of all because economies of scale arise from team production; but the scale economies come at the price of higher measurement costs of the performance of individual members of the team (agents). "A firm internalizes external effects [that is, realizes scale economies] by making an individual's productive activity external or independent of his pecuniary income from production" (McManus, 1975: 346). Hence the firm hires monitors to constrain the behavior of agents and reduce shirking and cheating.

Hierarchical organization will also replace market transactions where specialized human or physical capital investment makes the principals vulnerable to post-contractual opportunism because of imperfect enforcement. Vertical integration can reduce the likelihood of hold-up where substantial quasi-rents are appropriable; there will, however, be the same monitoring costs as above.

All of the modern neoclassical literature discusses the firm as a substitute for the market. For the economic historian this perspective is useful; its usefulness is limited, however, because it ignores a crucial fact of history: hierarchical organization forms and contractual arrangements in exchange predate the price-making market (like that for oranges). The first known price-

[9] Goldberg (1976) has termed such contractual relations "relational exchange."

making market was in the Athenian agora in the sixth century B.C., but exchange had been going on for millennia before that. We now possess the clue to account for such early forms of organization. In order to do so we must clarify a confusion that has been propagated by Karl Polanyi and many subsequent writers.[10] Polanyi made a *market* synonymous with a *price-making market*. It should be readily apparent, however, that any form of voluntary contractual exchange involves a market and that its form will be dictated by the considerations advanced above. Polanyi made a basic error in thinking that any deviation from the Agora-type market implied non-economizing behavior: even the era which, in *The Great Transformation* (1957), he regarded as the epitome of the market mentality was characterized by an enormous variety of contractual arrangements that were not price-making markets.[11] Two considerations militated against the existence of price-making markets before the 6th century B.C. One was the transaction costs considerations that have been the subject of this chapter; the second was the wealth-maximizing objectives of the rulers of the state.

Price-making markets require well-defined and enforced property rights. It must be possible to measure the dimensions of a good or service; moreover, the consequent rights must be exclusive and there must be an enforcement mechanism to police the exchange of goods. Small numbers involved in exchange, the possibility of opportunism, and uncertainty as a result of a lack of well-defined property rights or an inability to forecast changes in conditions over the life of an exchange agreement all result in alternative contractual arrangements designed to reduce the attendant transactions or production costs.

V

The foregoing analysis has assumed that under the ubiquitous conditions of scarcity and competition, more efficient organizational forms will replace less efficient and that it would be possible to predict the forms that would exist. Even in the presence

---

[10] While Polanyi has had little influence on economists, he has had a much larger impact on the other social sciences and amongst historians.
[11] See North (1977).

of a state that operated in the way that a contract theory would imply, modifications of the organizational forms would result since any form of taxation would alter the relevant measurement costs and the consequent organization; but the theory of the state elaborated in the preceding chapter implies much greater modification.

The state will specify rules to maximize the income of the ruler and his group and then, subject to that constraint, will devise rules that would lower transaction costs. Nonvoluntary forms of organization will exist if profitable to the ruler (nonvoluntary slavery, for example); relatively inefficient forms of organization will survive if more efficient forms threaten the survival of the ruler from within or without (the collective farm in the Soviet Union today, or the organization of the Athenian grain trade in the classical world, for example); [12] and forms of organization that have low measurement costs to the rulers for tax collecting will persist even though they are relatively inefficient (monopoly grants as in Colbert's France, for example).

Given this initial constraint, however, the ruler will provide the public good of a set of rules and their enforcement designed to lower transaction costs. Included will be the specification of uniform weights and measures,[13] a set of property rights to encourage production and trade, a judicial system to settle differences, and enforcement procedures to enforce contracts.

VI

The foregoing neoclassical approach to economic organization is deficient in at least two respects.

First, the more diffuse the distribution of political control as a result of the ability of groups of constituents to capture an interest in the state, the more difficult it becomes to predict or explain the ensuing forms of property rights which will develop. It is not too difficult to account for economic organization of the redistributive societies of the ancient dynasties in Egypt; it is much more difficult to explain the complex economic organization in

[12] See the account of the Athenian grain trade in Polanyi (1977).

[13] However, it should be noted that the way weights and measures will be devised will be with the objective of maximizing the ruler's income. The history of weights and measures makes sense only if we recognize the priority of the ruler's interest.

modern democratic societies where many interests compete with each other in controlling the state and modifying property rights and, hence, economic organizations.[14] A more serious problem is that the theory is incomplete, as even a casual inspection of the literature on industrial organization will attest. This literature is full of references to simple self-interest versus self-interest with guile (in opportunistic behavior); sometimes individuals will take advantage of each other and sometimes they won't; sometimes individuals are hard working and sometimes not. Honesty, integrity, and gentlemen's agreements are important in contractual arrangements; equally important are the ubiquitous loafing on the job, cheating, white collar crime, and sabotage.

To put it succinctly, the measurement costs of constraining behavior are so high that in the absence of ideological convictions to constrain individual maximizing, the viability of economic organization is threatened. Investment in legitimacy is as much a cost of economic organization as are the measurement and enforcement costs detailed in the preceding sections of this chapter. Indeed, as briefly discussed above, a major issue in enforcement is the perceived legitimacy of the contractual relations.

[14] The burgeoning literature in such specialized journals as the *Bell Journal* and the *Journal of Law and Economics* provides ample evidence of this difficulty.

Chapter 5

Ideology and the Free Rider Problem

I

In the two previous chapters I have specified a number of neo-classical assumptions concerning the state and economic organization. I turn now to an issue which such assumptions have illuminated but not solved.

The neoclassical model has an asymmetrical dilemma built into its behaviorial function because it assumes both wealth maximization and the Hobbesian model of the state, which will constrain behavior to produce a viable political system. If individuals are acting rationally with respect to the first assumption then they are acting irrationally with respect to the second. It is certainly in the interests of a neoclassical actor to agree to constrain behavior by setting up a group of rules to govern individual actions: hence the view that the Hobbesian state is a logical extension of the neoclassical model applied to a theory of the state. But it is also in the interests of the neoclassical actor to disobey those rules whenever an individualistic calculus of benefits and costs dictates such action. That action would, however, result in the non-viability of any state, since enforcement costs of the rules would be, if not infinite, at least so large as to make the system unworkable. Yet everyday observations provide abundant evidence that individuals obey rules when an individualistic calculus should have them act otherwise. Casual observation also provides evidence that an enormous amount of change occurs because of large group action which should not occur in the face of the logic of the free rider problem. Let me specifically examine this dilemma in neoclassical terms.

An immense amount of individual behavior can be accounted for in the context of the neoclassical behavioral assumption—hence the power of the neoclassical model. The free rider issue does account for the instability of large groups where no specific side benefits exist, for the disinclination of people to vote, for the fact that the anonymous free donation of blood does not provide sufficient blood for hospitals. But so far the neoclassical model does not adequately account for the obverse. Large groups do act when no evident benefits counter the substantial costs to individual participation; people do vote, and they do donate blood anonymously. I am not arguing that these actions are irrational—only that the calculation of benefits and costs that we employ is too limited to catch other elements in people's decision-making processes. Individual utility functions are simply more complicated than the simple assumptions so far incorporated in neoclassical theory.[1] The task of the social scientist is to broaden the theory to be able to predict when people will act like free riders and when they won't. Without a broadened theory we cannot account for a great deal of secular change initiated and carried through by large group actions.

While we observe people disobeying the rules of a society when the benefits exceed the costs, we also observe them obeying the rules when an individualistic calculus would have them do otherwise. Why do people not litter the countryside? Why don't they cheat or steal when the likelihood of punishment is negligible compared to the benefits? I am not talking about the actions of individuals that stem from reciprocity—for example, behavior such as courtesy and good manners, which pays off in reciprocal behavior by others with whom we come in contact. I am discussing the values inculcated by the family and by schooling that lead individuals to restrain their behavior so that they do not

[1] Sociologists such as Parsons and Shils have attempted to incorporate broader psychological elements into the concept of ideological behavior—in particular the societal stress elements from Durkheim. For a discursive but inconclusive exploration which stresses the importance of symbols and imagery on the formulation of ideologies, see Geertz (1973, chapter 8).

behave like free riders. For example, I will receive the aesthetic benefits of a beautiful countryside regardless of whether I litter; it is costly not to litter, and my behavior will have a negligible effect on the quality of the countryside. The question for the social scientists becomes, How much additional cost will I bear before I become a free rider and throw the beer cans out the car window?

I have posed the issue in the context of political organization, but it is equally basic to the viability of economic organization. The quality and quantity of individual labor can only imperfectly be controlled by rules, because of measurement problems. Piece-rate wages are a solution only where individual contributions can be measured at low cost and quality is constant. Other monitoring devices designed to measure labor output are equally imperfect. The difference between workers who are "diligent," "hard working," "conscientious," and those who are "lazy," "soldiers on the job," or "shiftless" is the difference in output as a consequence of the degree of success of ideological conviction that reduces shirking.

What applies to shirking is equally applicable to the quantity of stealing, cheating, white collar crime, padding expense accounts—of opportunistic behavior in general. Their myopic vision has prevented neoclassical economists from seeing that even with a constant set of rules, detection procedures, and penalties there is immense variation in the degree to which individual behavior is constrained. Strong moral and ethical codes of a society is the cement of social stability which makes an economic system viable.

Without an explicit theory of ideology or, more generally, of the sociology of knowledge there are immense gaps in our ability to account for either current allocation of resources or historical change. In addition to being unable to resolve the fundamental dilemma of the free rider problem we cannot explain the enormous investment that every society makes in legitimacy. This includes much of the educational system that can in no way be accounted for as either human capital investment or a consumption good. We cannot predict the voting behavior of legislators where a large residual remains after incorporating interest group explanations. Nor can we account for the decisions of the independent judiciary, where lifetime tenure and salary eliminate most of the standard interest group pressures, which frequently run counter to the major interest group pressures. What explains major judicial reversals of long standing and the radical changes in interpretation of the Constitution in the past century? And equally, we can neither explain the proclivity (and indeed the boast) of historians to rewrite history each generation, nor account for the charged emotional content of many historical debates.

In the rest of this chapter I explore these issues. I must warn at the outset that nothing as grand as a theory of the sociology of knowledge emerges. We are a long way from such a theory, and the more modest objective of this chapter is to point up some of the issues and suggest some tentative hypotheses that may be useful for the economist, the historian, or the economic historian attempting to break out of the theoretical strait jacket in which we find ourselves. Moreover, I give particular emphasis to the free rider problem because that problem plays a critical role in explaining structure and change in political and economic organization in history.

The next three sections explore successively the nature of ideology, changes in ideology, and the characteristics of successful ideologies. Section V examines the implications of ideology for economics and economic history and advances some hypotheses for a positive theory.

II

The sociology of knowledge is concerned with how knowledge is acquired.[2] At its most elementary level it is pretheoretical in the sense that the everyday behavior of individuals is guided by a set of habits, maxims, codes of behavior, which are acquired initially from family (primary socialization) and then through the educational process and other institutions such as the church (secondary socialization). But while we think of our everyday lives as guided by "common sense" knowledge, such knowledge is at base theoretical; and ideologies are intellectual efforts to rationalize the behavioral pattern of individuals and groups. Facts do not explain the world around us; explanation requires theory—not necessarily conscious, explicit theory but nevertheless theory. Theories cannot be proven "true"; they can

---

[2] A good discussion of the subject is contained in Berger and Luckman (1966).

only be refuted by evidence. But competing theories are employed to explain much of the world around us, and no definitive tests exist to eliminate all but one explanation.

The choice-theoretic approach to economics assumes that in making choices values exist but are fixed, and people are acting rationally in the sense of making efficient use of information. This second assumption is a neoclassical entering wedge since at least part of the explanation for the persistence of conflicting theories is information costs. Given any cost/benefit calculus of voting, it is simply not worthwhile for voters to acquire the information necessary to test competing explanations so that they can link the choice with the desired results. Moreover, even with the information available to professional social scientists there still exist competing theories. There simply is not the evidence available to perform the definitive tests that would eliminate competing explanations. Clearly ideology is ubiquitous, not confined to any class; and "false consciousness" is beside the point since it implies some "true consciousness," which no one possesses. It is important to stress three aspects of ideology.

1. Ideology is an economizing device by which individuals come to terms with their environment and are provided with a "world view" so that the decision-making process is simplified.

2. Ideology is inextricably interwoven with moral and ethical judgments about the fairness of the world the individual perceives. This situation clearly implies a notion of possible alternatives—competing rationalizations or ideologies. A normative judgment of the "proper" distribution of income is an important part of an ideology.

3. Individuals alter their ideological perspectives when their experiences are inconsistent with their ideology. In effect, they attempt to develop a new set of rationalizations that are a better "fit" with their experiences. However, it is important to stress here an analogy with the findings of Thomas Kuhn. In his *Structure of Scientific Revolutions* (1962), Kuhn emphasizes that there always exist anomalies between "normal science" and scientific evidence, and that it requires an accumulation of such anomalies to force the scientist into a new paradigm. Similarly with ideology: inconsistencies between experience and ideologies must accumulate before individuals alter their ideology. The implications for neoclassical theory are important. A single change in a relative set of prices by itself may not alter an individual's per-

spective and therefore decisions, but persistent changes that run counter to an individual's set of rationalizations or a change of fundamental consequences for his well-being will induce him to alter his ideology.

III

In terms of the foregoing section, we should be able to predict a good deal of change in ideology in strictly economic terms. Becker and Stigler (1977) do just that by considering the consequences of the value of time, human capital, and so forth on decision making. For example, in strictly opportunity cost terms one can predict that the ideology of a young adult will be different from that of a middle-aged adult. But Becker and Stigler's approach is far too confining to explain most of ideology, for two fundamental reasons. First, for most of the rationalizations or theories that individuals possess there are no conclusive tests by which to determine the consequences of alternative choices; individual experience does not provide for the unambiguous choices implied by the Becker-Stigler approach. People differently positioned in terms of experience have differing rationalizations or views of the world around them and have no way to confirm or reject definitively these different views.

Second, Becker and Stigler ignore the ethical and moral judgments that are an integral part of an individual's ideological makeup. An inherent part of everyone's ideology is a judgment about the fairness or justice of "the system." While this judgment extends beyond the particular terms of exchange that each individual confronts, nevertheless these terms are crucial in evaluating the fairness of the system. For example, let me suggest four alterations in relative prices that will alter an individual's perceptions about the fairness of the system and lead to an alteration in his or her ideological perspective:

1. an alteration in property rights which denies individuals access to resources which they had heretofore come to accept as customary or just (the enclosure of common land, for example);

2. a decline in the terms of exchange in a factor or product market away from what had come to be regarded as a just exchange ratio;

3. a decline in the relative income position of a particular group in the labor force; and

4. a reduction in information costs that results in individuals

perceiving that different and more favorable terms of exchange may prevail elsewhere.

I am well aware of the difficulties of introducing the notion of equity into the literature on property rights. How do individuals arrive at the notion of a just exchange ratio and at what point does a just ratio become unjust? If the concept is not crucial to the way in which choices are made, then we are left with the puzzle of accounting for the immense amount of resources invested throughout history in attempting to convince individuals about the justice or injustice of their position. Competing rationalizations of the world around us have been the basic ingredient of history since long before Pericles' rhetoric was decisive in his struggle with Cimon for the support of Athenian citizens. This ingredient has dominated historical conflict ever since. Becker and Stigler, however, would ignore Christ, Mohammed, Marx, and—in 1980—Khomeini, not to mention the thousands of other sources of ideology in history.

Ideologies can develop without the guidance of intellectuals (the IWW, for example), but they do so only exceptionally. I do not propose to analyze the reward system that produces what I call the intellectual entrepreneurs of ideology; however, entrepreneurs spring up whenever there develop contrasting views of the world around us as a result of differential experiences.

The origins of differential ideologies are geographic location and occupational specialization. Originally, it was geographic location that confronted bands with the experiences that coalesced into languages, customs, taboos, myths, religions, and, eventually, ideologies differing from those of other bands. These survive today in the ethnic diversity that produces conflicting ideologies.

Occupational specialization and division of labor also leads to diverse experiences and differing and conflicting perspectives about reality. Marx made "consciousness" dependent upon one's position in the production process and this insight was an important contribution in explaining the development of "class consciousness."

IV

Whether ideology is justifying an existing structure of property rights and terms of exchange or attacking the injustice of the current structure, it must have the characteristics discussed below to be successful.

Because ideology consists of an interconnected comprehensive view of the world, it must explain how the existing structure of property rights and terms of exchange are a part of a larger system. It is also crucial to account for the past in terms consistent with this set of rationalizations. If, as historians state, history is rewritten every generation, it is not typically because subsequent evidence has developed clearly refutable tests of previous hypotheses but because different weights are assigned to the existing evidential material to provide different explanations consistent with current ideology. I do not mean to imply that historians do not ever find new evidence; obviously they do, and to the degree that such evidence provides tests of previous hypotheses, there is an advance in the state of historical knowledge. But even in the present world, replete with immense quantities of information, the ability of scholars to develop unambiguous tests of the complex, large-scale hypotheses that are involved in explaining secular change is very limited. Therefore, competing explanations tend to have a heavy ideological cast. Marxists write economic history as a story of class struggle; free market ideologists write it as the development of efficient markets. Bitter controversies over historical debates such as those over the standard of living during the Industrial Revolution or over the condition of the American slave are simply not explicable as pure scholarly debates. They do make sense as part and parcel of larger views in which history is a battleground of contending ideologies. I am not arguing—as I shall make clear below—that all history or social science theorizing is nothing more than ideology. I am arguing that to the degree that definitive tests of competing explanations are not possible, there will be a number of scholarly explanations of the past—and theories to explain the present.

Successful ideologies must be flexible so that they can capture the loyalty of new groups or retain the loyalty of older groups as external conditions change. Two examples can illustrate this point.

As real wages have risen over the past century and a half and the blue collar proletariat has become a declining percentage of the labor force, Marxist ideology has adjusted to this seeming contradiction to Karl Marx's analysis. The ideology of Marxism, as contrasted with Marx's formal theory of surplus value and the reserve army of the unemployed, has attempted to account for these changes (and the lack of class consciousness in America) and at the same time to recruit from new groups that were candidates for Marxism as they perceived the injustice of their position. A flexible theory was required to attract racial minorities, women, and recently the residents of the Third World. The result has been, predictably, a spate of new theories to attempt to incorporate these groups into Marxist ideology and, equally predictably, conflict amongst Marxists over the "correct" theory.

The ideology of the free market has faced a similar crisis in recent years with the recognition of the widespread existence of externalities and the growth of non-market forms of resource allocation. Here, too, there has been the development of new theories to account for these observations; but in contrast to Marxism, free market ideology has not developed within a comprehensive framework of social, political, and philosophical (not to mention metaphysical) theory.[3] In consequence it has faced serious difficulties in holding and capturing the loyalties of groups in the face of these changing conditions.

Most crucially, any successful ideology must overcome the free rider problem. Its fundamental aim is to energize groups to behave contrary to a simple, hedonistic, individual calculus of costs and benefits. This is the central thrust of major ideologies, since neither maintenance of the existing order nor its overthrow is possible without such behavior.

The costs of maintenance of an existing order are inversely related to the perceived legitimacy of the existing system. To the extent that the participants believe the system fair, the costs of enforcing the rules and property rights are enormously reduced by the simple fact that the individuals will not disobey the rules or violate property rights even when a private cost/benefit calculus would make such action worthwhile. If everyone believes in the "sanctity" of a person's home, houses will remain unlocked while vacant without fear of vandalism or burglary. If a beautiful countryside is considered a public "good," individuals will not litter. If individuals believe in the values of political democracy they will vote as a matter of civic obligation. Labor will be hard working, and management, diligent in caring for the interest of the owners; contracts will be honored in the spirit as well as the

---

[3] The Austrian school of Von Mises and Hayek is a partial exception to this statement.

letter of the law. To put the issue precisely, the premium necessary to induce people to become free riders is positively correlated with the perceived legitimacy of the existing institution. The educational system in a society is simply not explicable in narrow neoclassical terms, since much of it is obviously directed at inculcating a set of values rather than investing in human capital. While recent Marxist literature stresses this value-inculcation aspect of the American educational system, some Marxist writers appear to neglect the point that it is not unique to "capitalism"; investment in legitimacy is an even more prominent feature of the Soviet and Chinese societies. Indeed, in Chinese communism such investment dominates both the formal and the informal educational structure. Either neoclassical economists have ignored (or missed) an essential ingredient of every society; or if they are correct, the enormous investment that every society makes in legitimacy is an unnecessary expenditure.

If the dominant ideology is designed to get people to conceive of justice as coextensive with the existing rules and, accordingly, to obey them out of a sense of morality, the objective of a successful counter ideology is to convince people not only that the observed injustices are an inherent part of the existing system but also that a just system can come about only by active participation of individuals to alter the system. Successful counter ideologies must not only provide a convincing image of the link between the specific injustices perceived by various groups and the larger system which the intellectual entrepreneurs desire altered, but also offer a Utopia free of these injustices and provide a guide to action—a path by which the individual can, through appropriate action, realize that Utopia. The immense literature of Marxists on class consciousness, class solidarity, ideology, and the role of the intellectual makes abundantly clear that Marxist revolutionaries are aware of the very real problem that the free rider issue poses for Marxist theory and revolutionary practice.

Again, casual observation suggests the widespread existence of behavioral patterns by individuals armed with nothing more than moral indignation as a benefit in a cost/benefit calculus. Protest movements, individual actions that incur the likelihood of imprisonment or death, are so common throughout history that they need no citation; they are no less evident in the modern world containing such varied groups as the clamshell alliance, Soviet intellectuals, and the Moslem rioters in the Iran of 1978–79.

V

From this discussion of ideology I want to draw out some implications for economics and economic history and to advance some hypotheses. Briefly stated, they are, first, that the introduction of the concept of ideology does not detract from the ability of economic theory to be scientific in the sense of deriving refutable tests of competing hypotheses. Second, that while the development of a positive theory of ideology is necessary to resolve the free rider dilemma (and such resolution is essential to further development in much of social science theorizing), it is equally necessary for further development of theory to account for non-market–resource allocation; and it is essential in explaining a great deal of secular change. Let me now expand on these ideas.

Since ideology is ubiquitous, the scholar is no more immune to it than is anyone else. As Schumpeter made clear in his presidential address before the American Economic Association in 1948, the economist approaches problems with a set of ideological convictions which influence the choice of problems selected and the initial approach to the issues, but to the degree that economists develop theories capable of providing refutable tests, it is possible to have scientific advancement of the discipline.[4] Because economists have been less than completely successful in developing unambiguous refutations so that there can be a complete consensus, a variety of theories and hypotheses persist alongside neoclassical economies; but the detractors of the neoclassical approach have lost sight of the extent to which it has provided such convincing explanations about resource allocation in markets as to make them no longer be issues in scholarly debate. Put simply, neoclassical economics predicts a lot of aspects of market relationships so well that we have simply forgotten how much of a scientific contribution such developments were.

Economic theory concerned with contractual relations between principals and between principals and agents must make investment in legitimizing the appropriate institutions an essential cost of constraining the contracting parties. Without in any way minimizing the difficulties, a positive theory of ideology is essential for the further development of transaction cost analysis. Constrained maximization models limited to constraints of rules

---

[4] "Science and Ideology" (1949).

and their enforcement leave an immense residual which can be narrowed only by measuring, additionally, the strength of moral and ethical codes that determine the premium necessary for individuals to act as free riders. The greater the specialization and division of labor in a society, the greater the measurement costs associated with transacting *and also* the greater the cost of devising effective moral and ethical codes. This paradoxical dilemma is the root cause of many of the problems of modern society stemming from the Second Economic Revolution (to be explored in chapter 13) and hence is crucial to further development of economic theory.

The allocating of resources through the political and judicial process provides ample opportunity for ideological conviction to dominate the decision-making process. Recent studies have shown that the best predictor of legislative voting behavior is not any evident interest group but ideological conviction as measured by the Americans for Democratic Action and other rating systems.[5] It is not that interest group pressures are not important sources of political decision making; they are, and public choice theory is a valuable vehicle to explore the decision-making process. It is rather that legislators, regulators, and the executive branch are faced with many choices which allow ideology to be the decisive factor where the costs of ideological conviction are small or negligible, interest groups are relatively evenly divided on an issue, or the diffusion of costs and benefits is so widespread and individually small that it is not worthwhile for any individual or group to devote substantial resources to interest group pressure. And finally, strong ideological conviction may, and frequently does, lead political decision makers to make decisions that run counter to organized interest group pressure.

But even more important, the composition and actions of interest groups themselves are not explicable in terms of interest group pressure that excludes ideological convictions. It is possible in some cases to identify interest group pressures that mirror positive net private benefits to the participants of sufficient magnitude to explain such behavior; but in many it is not possible The modern environmental movement is one such case.

The clearest instance of the dominant role of ideology is the case of the independent judiciary. Judges with lifetime tenure are relatively immune from interest group pressure. It is true that

[5] See Kau and Rubin (1979) for a summary of the literature and evidence.

their initial appointment may reflect such pressure (although frequently based on broad ideological attitudes); but their subsequent decisions over a wide range of policies reflect their own convictions of the "public good." Efforts to explain the independent judiciary in an interest group perspective (Landes and Posner 1975) are simply unconvincing, as J. Buchanan (1975) and North (1978) have pointed out. The Miranda decision, and indeed many of the Warren Court decisions, were not only reversals of legal developments over a long precedent but ran counter to the major interest groups. The Courts' support of school busing and the decision of Judge Boldt on Indian rights over the fishing in Washington State are still other instances; indeed such judicial decisions are so common that observations reflecting a judge's view of the public good are everyday occurrences. A positive theory of ideology is essential to an analysis of the role of the independent judiciary in affecting resource allocation.

The need for a positive theory of ideology to explain secular change is equally pressing. Neoclassical economics applied to economic development or economic history may account very well for the performance of an economy at a moment of time or, with comparative statistics, contrasts in the performance of an economy over time; but it does not and cannot explain the dynamics of change. The major source of changes in an economy over time is structural change in the parameters held constant by the economist—technology, population, property rights, and government control over resources. Change in political-economic organization and its consequent effect on incentives are basic to theorizing about all these sources of structural change; and alterations in institutions involve purposeful human activity. Present theory is not designed to explain such changes except in the relatively trivial cases where a change in relative prices produces an automatic and instantaneous response. But institutions involve vested interests in which there are gainers and losers, both of whom marshall resources for and against the prospective changes. The gainers very seldom compensate the losers, and the resources devoted by both sides to the conflict are seldom explicable in cost/benefit terms. I do not mean to gainsay Mancur Olson's (1965) explanation of group behavior around coercion and side benefits available to members only. This is valid for a great deal of group behavior such as that of the American Medical Association, trade unions, or the Farm Bureau. Olson himself, however, acknowledges that his theory does not account for a wide variety of groups (Olson, pp. 160–63), although in explicitly downplaying the importance of ideology in "stable, well-ordered, and apathetic societies that have seen the 'end of ideology'" he overstates his case.[6] He points up the instability of farm protest movements that did not have side benefits, but he neglects the point that they should not have existed at all under his model. Nor does he acknowledge that they significantly affected political and legal policy: indeed, most of their objectives were eventually incorporated in new legal interpretations, including *Munn* vs. *Illinois,* and in the platform of the Democratic party. We also are left wondering how he accounts for the anti-market mentality that dominates most Third World countries today, for the mass movements he assigns to unstable countries, or for periods of "revolution and upheaval" (p. 112).

The simple fact is that a dynamic theory of institutional change limited to the strictly neoclassical constraint of individualistic, rational purposive activity would never allow us to explain most secular change ranging from the stubborn struggle of the Jews in antiquity to the passage of the Social Security Act in 1935. Secular economic change has occurred not only because of the changing relative prices stressed in neoclassical models but also because of evolving ideological perspectives that have led individuals and groups to have contrasting views of the fairness of their situation and to act upon those views.

---

[6] Olson: 162. The quote within a quote is the title of Daniel Bell's 1960 book. But Bell's title makes sense only if we consider it as meaning the decline of large-scale integrated ideologies such as Marxism in the United States. All that such a statement implies, however, is that with the modern fall in information costs ideologies have become more fragmented and partial and no intellectual entrepreneur has been able to weld them into a single coherent ideology that has captured a large percentage of the populace (but see the Moslem movement in 1979 Iran).

Chapter 6

Structure and Change
in Economic History

I

The cumulation in the stock of knowledge has largely been irreversible throughout history, but human economic progress has not: the rise and the decline of political economic units, not to mention entire civilizations, are certainly indisputable. The contrast makes clear an important point—it is the successes and failures in human organization that account for the progress and retrogression of societies. Knowledge and technological advance are necessary conditions, but we must cast a wider net if we are effectively to explore the sources of the rise and fall of economies. In this chapter I shall pull together the threads from the previous chapters and use this loose framework to provide an overview of Western economic history that will set the scene for the historical chapters that follow in Part II. The only building blocks that the economic historian has to work with are classical, neoclassical, and Marxian theory, and I begin by sorting out the elements of those theoretical constructs that have been of use in this theoretical framework.

Picking up where we left off in chapter 1 in describing the effect of a change in relative prices—an increase in population—on an economy, we see that the neoclassical result was a series of adjustments that when completed resulted in a new equilibrium.

The fundamental forces affecting the long-run (secular) growth path would still be determined by the function of income saved; per capita growth rate would then be a result of population growth rate. Contrast this model to the classical model of Malthus and Ricardo. The dismal results of the classical model obtain because there exists a fixed factor—land and resources—which when taken in conjunction with the ubiquitous tendency of population to expand lead to a secular tendency for a subsistence wage. Both the optimistic model of neoclassical economics and the pessimistic model of classical economics provide powerful insights into economic history. The former with its elastic supply curve of new knowledge and substitutability at all margins approximates the unparalleled growth experience of western economics since the Second Economic Revolution. The latter sets economic history in a persistent tension between population and the resource base and is a far more useful starting point to explore the human experience in the millennia prior to the middle of the nineteenth century.

Both are incomplete. The original neoclassical model, which had as test conditions a neutral state, zero transaction costs, and constant tastes, could serve as a useful framework for analysis only when those test conditions were approximated, although a modified version incorporating positive transaction costs and a theory of the state provides us with parts of the theory. The classical model provided no escape from its dismal implications, although as Ester Boserup has persuasively argued (1965) population sometimes acted as a spur to induce new techniques (but she provides no theoretical bridge to account for the overcoming of diminishing returns to a fixed factor).

It is difficult to pin down the Marxian model since there appear to be almost as many interpretations of Marx as there are Marxian theorists. Marx regarded technological change and not population growth as the primary engine of change. He was critical of Malthus's view that people tend to breed to subsistence and regarded fertility as culturally determined.[1] In the Marxian model, technological change leads to production techniques whose potential cannot be realized within the existing economic

---

[1] See Meek (1953) for Marx and Engels view of Malthus. However, Samuelson points out that when you add the limitations of land and natural resources to Marx's model you end up with the same classical model as did Smith, Ricardo, and Malthus. Paul Samuelson (1978).

organization. The result is to energize a new class to overthrow the existing system and develop a new set of property rights which will allow that class to realize the potential of the new techniques.

The Marxian framework is the most powerful of the existing statements of secular change precisely because it includes all of the elements left out of the neoclassical framework: institutions, property rights, the state, and ideology. Marx's emphasis on the crucial role of property rights in efficient economic organization and on the tension that develops between an existing body of property rights and the productive potential of a new technology is a fundamental contribution. It is technological change that produces the tension in the Marxian system; but it is through class conflict that change is realized.

The limitations of the Marxian model include the absence of a theory to account for the *rate* of technological change and an emphasis on technology at the expense of other sources of change.[2] Marx slights, for example, the crucial role of population change in history. It is understandable that Marx did not want population change to play a crucial role in his model; but incorporating population growth into a Marxian model substantially increases its explanatory power. Technology alone simply cannot account for a great deal of secular change where the technology does not appear to have altered significantly, or where technological change does not appear to have required fundamental organizational changes in order to realize its potential.

Moreover, classes are far too large and varied a group to serve as a primary unit of action. Marx's informal analysis at many points recognizes this fact and discusses divisions amongst the bourgeoisie or proletariat, but that discussion amounts to ad hoc reasoning. The individualistic calculus of neoclassical economics is a better starting point. Aggregation determined by commonality of interest allows for more flexibility in the model without sacrificing consistency. Aggregation indeed may be as large as a class—as when the members view themselves as having common interests. This emphasis on commonality of interest also allows one to explore the conflicts within a class which in fact account

---

[2] See, however, Rosenberg (1974) for an elucidation of Marx's sophisticated views on technology which explores the demand for and supply of technological knowledge.

for an enormous amount of secular change. Neither the Marxist nor the neoclassical approach, however, resolves the free rider problem, which is central to explaining group action.

Neoclassical economics, with the tool of opportunity costs and its emphasis on relative prices, is a far more sophisticated tool of analysis than the cumbersome Marxian model built upon a labor theory of value. As the analysis in chapter 4 attempted to make clear, extending neoclassical analysis to incorporate transaction costs provides the crucial theoretical bridge by which to analyze economic organization and to explore the tension between an existing structure of property rights and the production potential of an economy.

But the approach to transaction costs and property rights developed in the foregoing chapters has very different implications from much of the standard neoclassical literature. Not only is there no implication that economic organization is necessarily "efficient," but it is stressed that all organization involves dissipation of income because of imperfect measurement and positive enforcement costs. Given both the interests of the rulers of the state and the aforementioned positive transaction costs in economic organization, it is not surprising that economic organization that induces economic growth may very well do so by internalizing the benefits and externalizing the costs and hence raising the private rate of return to "productive" economic activity at the expense of costs imposed on other groups in society. An idealized national income accounting would of course take into account all social benefits and costs. The divergence between the ideal and what we currently employ in economic history is so wide, however, that we are a long way from really determining the social rate of return on much of the investment and economic activity which we have traditionally associated with economic development.

Still another contrast between neoclassical and Marxian reasoning is important. Change in a neoclassical model is change at the margin induced by a change in relative prices. The relationship between stocks and flows in the neoclassical model is important for the economic historian. The stocks reflect the historically derived constraints of knowledge, technology, and physical and human capital, which can only be incrementally changed at a moment of time. The essential continuity of historical experience and the incremental character of economic change are effectively captured by this approach. Moreover, the importance of changing relative prices as a force in secular change is hard to over emphasize. While the stocks that affect economic performance can be increased only slowly (although they are subject to drastic decreases), revolutions that alter control of the state are not readily amenable to a neoclassical approach; nor has ideology played a role in the neoclassical framework. As noted above, the Marxian framework has incorporated a more complex analysis of secular change into its framework than has the neoclassical approach.[3]

II

Where does all that leave us? As the foregoing pages make clear, these models are disparate (disparate although having a common origin in classical economic theory including the behavioral assumption of wealth maximization); but in the five earlier chapters I have melded and shaped ideas from all of them into my own framework. Let us apply this framework in the form of an explanation sketch of human economic history so that we can see where we are going in Part II, and I can then point up what is still missing.

We first introduce population expansion, which appears to be a ubiquitous secular tendency of the past million years. With a constant technology, the result is eventually a Malthusian crisis. Moreover, as long as all resources are common property, improved techniques (such as the invention of the bow in a hunting/gathering environment) will simply lead to a more rapid drawing down of the resource base. Diminishing returns and declining living standards may have led to efforts to curtail population growth although with competition amongst tribal bands such efforts would be irrational in the sense that large bands could exclude smaller bands from resources. They surely led to the development of exclusive property rights over a territory by a band and in consequence a rise in the rate of return to acquir-

[3] Recent Marxist research exploring secular change such as Perry Anderson's *Passages from Antiquity to Feudalism* (1974) have demonstrated the valuable insights that can be derived from this framework. Moreover some recent Marxist research has begun to confront the free rider problem. See A. Buchanan (1979).

ing knowledge about the resources. The result was the First Economic Revolution, which is the subject of the first chapter of Part II.

The development of exclusive *communal* property rights resulted in increased specialization and division of labor and the emergence of a specialized form of organization—the state—to specify, adjudicate, and enforce the property rights. Whether the state originated as a predatory group attacking and exploiting a peasant village (a predatory origin of the state) or developed out of the communal needs for organization of the peasant village (a contract origin of the state) cannot be resolved. What is more interesting is the long-run consequence of a group with a comparative advantage in coercion producing a state which on the one hand devised a set of property rights to maximize the returns to the rulers and on the other hand, within that framework, developed a body of law and its enforcement aimed at promoting economic efficiency and hence, tax revenue.

The physiography and resources of the regions together with the state of military technology played decisive roles in determining the size and characteristics of the state and in shaping the forms of economic organization (given the technology of measurement which determined the costs of monitoring agents and the forms of property rights that evolved). The eight millennia between the origins of agriculture and the decline of the Roman Empire were characterized by population expansion, the creation of increasingly sophisticated and efficient forms of economic organization, and a growth in the size of states. The working out of the organizational implications of the First Economic Revolution are explored in chapter 8.

Growing specialization and division of labor in history produced diverse experiences and consequent diverse constructions of "reality," in contrast to the common experiences and ideology of a tribal society. Conflict arises over the division of output (that is, income distribution) associated with division of labor. Successful political-economic units have been associated with the development of ideologies that convincingly legitimized the existing structure of property rights and consequent income distribution. Such constructs have been most successful when built around a common religious movement; identifying the ruler with a god (as in Pharaonic Egypt) has been the most convincing form of legitimation.

Cost of maintaining an ideological consensus is inversely related to the costs of information and directly related to the stability of relative prices. While a ruler may be able effectively to control the first, he has had far less control over the second for reasons outlined in earlier chapters. Reductions in the relative well-being of groups of constituents from what has come to be accepted as just will lead to a reassessment of the legitimacy of an existing economic order. Opportunities will be offered the ideological entrepreneur to build on the alienation of those groups to construct a counter ideology. This ideology must overcome the free rider problem if it is to activate groups to change the existing economic order. Just as the rise of a political-economic unit is associated historically with a consensus on values, the decline is associated with a disintegration of a common value system.

During the eight millennia there were recurrent periods of population pressure and reactions in the form of efforts to reduce fertility, to colonize, and to create more efficient institutions and technologies. Some were successful for periods of time: for example, Athens in the fifth century B.C. or Rhodes in the fourth century; or the Roman Empire in the first two centuries A.D. These were extraordinarily prosperous periods characterized by substantial economic growth. But Athens eventually was defeated by Sparta and ultimately absorbed in the Roman Empire. Rhodes too lost out to Roman jealousy, and its period of hegemony over the trade of the Eastern Mediterranean was ended by Rome's establishing Delos as a free port. And Rome itself finally fell to barbarians. Whether decline came from without or, by internal decay, from within, the source was conflict among states and/or the internal instability inherent in the structure of political-economic units. Some of the changes during the classical era can be accounted for in relative price terms, but others require the introduction of ideological considerations. In particular the great religious movements, from the resistance of the Jews to the great schisms of the Christian church, wrought changes that require a theory of ideology. In chapter 9 I attempt to sort out the changes that can be explained in relative price terms from those that require ideological considerations without in any way denying that elements of both were continuously involved in economic change.

In the perspective of ten millennia of economic history the

decline of Rome is only an incident in an apparently endless succession of civilizations rising and falling. But from the perspective of Western history it was a dramatic break in economic expansion, growing sophistication of economic organization, technical progress, and growth in size of political-economic units. Only gradually do islands of order reappear in the sea of chaos in western Europe.

Again it was military technology and changes in that technology that dictated change in the size and structure of political units. The ability of a warrior class to build a viable economic organization was conditioned by the relative prices of land and labor and transaction costs. The feudal and manorial systems that emerged led to a revival of trade and population expansion and the crises of the fourteenth century. Changes in military technology led to the obsolescence of the feudal lord, an increase in the optimal size of the political unit, and (together with changes in relative prices) radical alterations in property rights. The rise and decline of feudalism and manorialism are explored in chapter 10.

The period from the end of feudalism to the Industrial Revolution has been characterized as the age of exploration and commercial expansion which (in the seventeenth century) included an era of crisis over control of the state. The consequence of exploration and expansion was, ultimately, to integrate the rest of the world into the expanding economies of western Europe and to impose the diverse property rights structure of the mother countries on their colonies with long-run consequences for the viability of these colonies. The conflict over control of the state led to the diverse results of creating both states that produced relatively efficient forms of economic organization and states that in relative or absolute terms declined. The relative bargaining power of rulers and constituents was decisive in these results. Both the expansion of western Europe and the crises of the states of western Europe are explored in chapter 11.

The Industrial Revolution customarily has been regarded by economic historians as the watershed of economic history. Was it a revolution? The argument of chapter 12 is that growth in the size of the market induced increased specialization and division of labor that resulted in an increase in transaction costs. The increase induced alteration in economic organization which in turn lowered the cost of technological change and accelerated economic growth; these changes paved the way for a much more fundamental transformation, the Second Economic Revolution.

The wedding of science and technology in the late nineteenth century was a revolution in the same sense as the development of agriculture. The First Economic Revolution was a fundamental change because it made possible the increase in the effective resource base and raised the private rate of return to improving that resource base through the incentives provided by property rights. Over the next ten millennia humans worked out the implications of that change. Admittedly these years were punctuated by numerous Malthusian crises, but these crises could be and were overcome by devising more efficient economic organization and technical change. Ultimately, however, there was a relatively fixed factor. The progress of technology finally depended on the systematic development of science, which required raising the rate of return on "pure" knowledge. Without the development of science, the growth of population would ultimately have led to an inability to expand the resource base further at constant costs.

The Second Economic Revolution resulted in an elastic supply curve of new knowledge, a capital intensive technology, and the necessity for a drastic change in economic organization to realize the potential of that technology. It involved far greater specialization than heretofore and hence an increase in the costs of measurement and enforcement of rules in the lengthening chain of the production and distribution process and, therefore, the need for new organizational forms to constrain principals and agents. But specialization also produces ideological diversity: a further consequence of the Second Economic Revolution has been alienation and political instability on the one hand and persistent problems in devising effective economic organization on the other. The Second Economic Revolution and its organizational implications are explored in chapter 13.

In the final chapter of Part II, I explore in more detail how structural change—and specifically the growth of government—occurred in the United States as a consequence of the Second Economic Revolution.

In Part III I pull together the theory from Part I and its application to economic history in Part II and suggest the elements of a theory of institutional change.

III

Before we move on to the historical essays it is important to stress what is missing from the theoretical part of my presentation. It does not form a theory of economic history. Such a theory could come only from the melding of theories of demography, the stock of knowledge, and institutions together with neoclassical production theory (chapter 1). What I have attempted to do is first to reframe the questions that economic historians ask so that at least they squarely face the task of explanation in economic history and second to provide an interconnected set of hypotheses that allow me to suggest the promise of this approach. The major lacunae should be explicitly brought out.

1. There is no theory of demographic change. The emphasis of this book is upon political and economic institutions, and I have simply made some assertions about demographic change which are consistent with the historical evidence.

2. There is no theory of the development of military technology and as both the chapter on the state and the foregoing explanation sketch make clear, military technology and changes in military technology were crucial to the structure and size of the state in history.

3. The model of the state is deficient in other ways too, but it is particularly deficient when we move from a single ruler to the modern pluralist state. A theory of the resolution of the conflicts in such a state has baffled modern political scientists.

4. While most of the elements of a theory of institutional change are developed (chapter 15), there is no neat supply function of new institutional arrangements specified in the framework. What determines the menu of organizational forms that a society devises in response to changing relative prices? Institutional innovation is a public good with all the characteristics of such goods, including the free rider problem.

5. Finally I again remind the reader that we have a way to go before we develop a positive theory of the sociology of knowledge.

But enough caveats. Let us see what we can do with the tools at hand.

Part II

History

Introduction

The eight historical chapters in Part II focus upon secular structural change in western economies; their function is to suggest the promise of this approach to economic history. I must emphasize that the theoretical framework in Part I has been used as the organizing focus of Part II but that I have not carried out the detailed specification of the historical forms of political and economic organization necessary to provide a solid basis for testing the model.

The use of secondary sources in these historical sketches imposes significant qualifications on their explanatory value. I have no apology to make for using secondary sources. That is what they are for: they are in effect intermediate products between raw materials and explanatory syntheses. The qualifications come from the selective use of such sources and the limits of available evidence.

While I have sought the advice of specialists in chronological periods in which I am, at best, an amateur, the results nevertheless reflect my lack of specialized knowledge of these periods. For chronological periods concerning which I possess some familiarity with the materials, I was frustrated by the lack of organized evidence that directly confronted the theoretical issues that I raised. Historians seldom have focused their scholarship on the questions that I am examining. I hope these exploratory historical essays will induce them to undertake that task.

Chapter 7

The First Economic Revolution*

I

For more than a million years after men and women had become distinguishable from other animals, they roamed the earth hunting and gathering plants. The evidence available, while scanty, makes clear that Paleolithic man had a lifestyle that distinguished him from lower animals, although like theirs, his ability to survive was affected by the vagaries of nature. Man lived in small groups or bands; caves, or sometimes simply the open, were his dwelling places. The groups had to be ready to move whenever they had exhausted the animal or plant supply in an area.

During this long era of hunting and gathering there developed many variations of man's lifestyle and culture. Examples of Paleolithic man's artistry are to be found in the Dordogne Valley in France, where depictions of animals and hunting scenes still survive on the walls of caves. While this Magdalenian culture has been viewed by archeologists as the most brilliant achievement of the Pleistocene period, there is evidence of a developed culture in other parts of Europe as well. Archeologists have found tools and weapons engraved or carved with animal or floral designs;

* This chapter is based on an essay by Douglass C. North and Robert Paul Thomas entitled "The First Economic Revolution," *Economic History Review*, May 1977.

small figurines (Venuses) have been found that accentuate the pregnant features of women; and burial sites suggest that prehistoric humans were concerned with life after death. Despite these artistic and aesthetic achievements, however, man lived very much as other animals, taking from nature what he could kill or gather. The limits of livelihood were fixed by a resource base which he could not yet improve; he could exist only within the earth's biological constraints.

Approximately ten thousand years ago, humans began to develop a settled agriculture: to herd and breed animals and to cultivate plants for food. The results of a developed ability to increase the resource base amounted to a fundamental economic revolution. The transition from hunting and gathering to settled agriculture, which the archeologist V. Gordon Childe termed the Neolithic Revolution, fundamentally altered the rate of progress of human beings. It led to an enormous acceleration in the process of learning, which accounts for the extraordinary developments in, say, the past ten minutes of man's chronological history in contrast to the previous twenty-three hours and fifty minutes.

Making sense of this change is extremely difficult and to some degree must be conjectural. There is, of course, no written word to provide evidence and only a few artifacts survive. Nevertheless, the brilliant detective work of archeologists has helped us a great deal, and the combined efforts of botanists, biologists, geologists, physicists, and geographers have given us a number of clues to help us reconstruct, however tentatively, what must have taken place.

Before examining this first economic revolution it is well to outline that generally accepted significant evidence about man's prehistoric past with which a theory of the revolution should be consistent.

1. The development of settled agriculture occurred approximately ten thousand years ago, but man is distinguishable from other animals more than one million years ago. The rate of material progress of man has accelerated dramatically since the development of agriculture.

2. This development appears to have occurred independently in such areas as the "Fertile Crescent," Meso-America, and probably Peru, North China, and others, and at different times.[1]

----

[1] For essays providing evidence on the timing and location of agricultural development see Struever (1971).

3. The spread of agriculture took thousands of years. The rate of spread across Europe appears to have averaged only about one kilometer per year. (L. L. Cavalli-Sforza, 1974)

4. The extinction of a variety of large animal species occurs in the later Pleistocene period. Some two hundred species have been listed as disappearing. (Paul Martin and N. E. Wright, 1967)

5. Before the development of agriculture man had begun to exploit a wider source of food. Larger animals played a lesser role in man's diet, and small animals, fowl, shellfish, snails, nuts, and seeds played a larger role. This exploitation is called the Broad Spectrum Revolution. (Flannery, 1968)

6. Human population increased and man migrated into new regions; the most dramatic was his movement into the New World and into Australia. (Davis, 1974)

II

Let me begin by examining, within the context of a comparative static economic model, the conditions that would account for the First Economic Revolution. The purpose of this model is to derive the conditions under which the scarce labor resource of the band would shift from its traditional occupation of hunting/gathering to agriculture.[2] The major resource of the band, it is assumed, is the labor of its members. The band may choose how to employ its labor to produce the goods and services desired. It will attempt to allocate resources in the manner that will maximize the value of the scarce labor resource and, therefore, the economic welfare of the group. In the absence of a market to determine the relative prices of the two kinds of output (hunting/gathering or agriculture) the band's preferences will establish these relative valuations. I assume for purposes of analysis that they remain unchanged. Hence, the marginal product of labor or the opportunity schedule in each activity becomes the crucial variable in the band's determining how it will allocate its labor between the two sectors.[3]

[2] The term "band" is adopted from Colin Renfrew (1972: 363). See his discussion of the anthropologist's distinction between band, tribe, and state: 363–65.

[3] Throughout this section I am assuming that man actually possessed sufficient knowledge of plants and/or animals to have engaged in cultivation

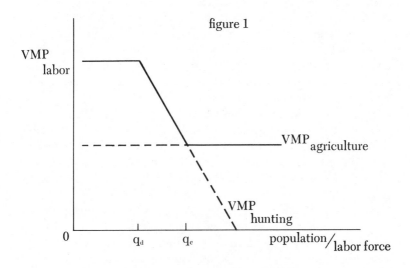

figure 1

Initially assume that the work force is fixed. The opportunity for labor in the hunting sector is the value of the marginal-product schedule for labor in hunting.[4] Assume also that the stock of resources is biologically determined and, therefore, subject to diminishing returns as hunting effort is increased.[5] Thus, the value of the marginal-product schedule in hunting when graphed will after a period of constant returns (oq_d in figure 1) eventually slope downward. The relevant downward-sloping portion of the demand for labor in the hunting sector is $q_d \cdot q_c$ in figure 1. The agricultural sector, reflecting the abundance of land at this time suited to this purpose, exhibits constant returns to

and/or herding prior to the actual transition. I shall derive from the model what these conditions were. In the final section I shall relax this assumption in order to demonstrate that the results will be the same once exclusive property rights are created. What I am asserting is that the invention of agriculture is not the most important issue. Rather, it is the incentive change resulting from exclusive property rights that will inevitably create agriculture.

[4] Hereafter "hunting" should be understood to mean hunting/gathering.

[5] A more precise assumption is a model that specifies a biological growth law for animals. See Smith (1975), who suggests a model consistent with the analysis in this chapter. The distinction is that Smith provides a formal and elegant comparative static model. This is an essay in economic history which attempts to describe the time-path of the transition from hunting/gathering to agricultural society and identify the institutional changes that were required to make the transition. More specifically, it attempts to explain the characteristics of development that archaeologists have discovered.

scale for additional units of labor. Thus, the relevant portion of the demand for labor in agriculture is the horizontal section beyond q_c. The total effective demand for the band's labor can be viewed as the solid line in figuire 1. This schedule, when combined with the quantity of labor available, determines the marginal-value product of labor and how the available labor will be allocated between the two sectors.

Man would devote his efforts exclusively to hunting if the value of the marginal product of labor in hunting after fully employing all the available labor is still above the value of the marginal product of the first unit of labor employed in agriculture. This would occur if the size of the labor force was, in figure 1, q_c or less.

Assuming that for a time the size of the work force remains below q_c, then there are only two parametric shifts that can result in the reallocation of labor from hunting to agriculture. One would be a shift to the left of the value of the marginal product of labor in hunting reflecting a general decline in productivity in this sector. If such a shift took place, then the band would reallocate to agriculture that portion of the work force previously devoted to hunting whose output was now below what it would be if employed in agriculture. This result also implies a decline in the band's standard of living.

A second parameter shift that would reallocate labor from hunting to agriculture would be an upward shift in the value of the marginal-product schedule for labor in agriculture reflecting an increase in the productivity of labor in this sector. A shift of this nature would have some of the same results as described above: the productivity of a portion of the work force previously employed in hunting would now be higher if reallocated to agriculture, and so a transfer of labor would occur. The standard of living of the band in this event, however, would rise. If either or both of these parameter shifts were pronounced enough, the effect would be to transfer all of the labor out of hunting into agriculture. If we allow the labor force to grow while holding the opportunity schedules for labor constant in each sector, then a transfer of labor to agriculture would eventually result. If the initial work force were less than q_d on the graph, then additions to it after reaching that point would result in declining marginal productivity of labor employed in hunting. This would continue until the labor force reached q_c on figure 1. Thereafter, additional increments to the labor force would be added to the agricultural sector under our assumptions with no further reductions in the marginal productivity of labor. Eventually, if population continued to expand with each addition being allocated to agriculture, that sector would come to dominate economic life. In sum, there are three changes that could account for the transition from hunting to agriculture. Individually or acting in concert, a decline in the productivity of labor in hunting, a rise in the productivity of labor in agriculture, or a sustained expansion of the size of the labor force could have resulted in the transition of man from being exclusively a hunter to increasingly a farmer.

III

Archaeologists have advanced a number of explanations to account for the shift from hunting to agriculture. Each of them offers some insight into this transition and can be accounted for in terms of the above model; but no one of them is completely satisfactory—either because it does not account for the evidence summarized above or because its theory is incomplete. V. Gordon Childe (1951) maintains that with the recession of the last ice age the climate was radically altered. The Near East and North Africa, which once had been adequately watered, verdant areas filled with wild animals and plants easily available to humans, became relatively desiccated. As a result, available food supplies, both animals and plants, were concentrated near the water holes and oases that survived. In these few oases man was in close contact with animals and plants. He could observe them carefully and was in a position to protect some of the animals from their predators. Grass-eating animals gradually became domesticated as humans found it to their advantage to protect and herd them and to provide them with grass and grain.

Childe's theory, considered within the context of the historical evidence presented above, rests on a change in the environment which produced a decline in the natural resource base including the extinction of animals. A decreased natural-resource base suggests a decline in the productivity of labor employed in hunting, which in turn necessitated man's acquiring greater control over the remaining resources in order to survive. In the process man learned how to increase the productivity of this labor in agriculture, forced to do so by the decline in his hunting opportunities. Childe's explanation consists of a shift to the left of the VMP_H (value of the marginal product in hunting) so that some part of the population would gain by shifting into agriculture. The Childe theory has been criticized on two grounds. First, why did this development not occur after prior glacial recessions? Second, and perhaps more substantive, historical meteorologists have not found that the climatic changes coincide with the timing and location of shifts into agriculture. Furthermore, climatic change did not always accompany the disappearing of a species. Nor does Childe's hypothesis explain the rate of adoption of agriculture or the expansion of human population in the Neolithic period. Nevertheless, it is likely that climatic change did reduce the resource base and lead to increasing relative scarcity of plants and animals in some areas.

A second theory, the so-called nuclear-zone theory, has been advocated by Robert J. Braidwood (1963). The nuclear-zone theory of Braidwood rests on a view of cultural development in which man becomes gradually better acquainted with the plants and animals around him. Braidwood defines a nuclear zone as "a natural environment which includes a variety of wild plants and animals both possible and ready for domestication." Braidwood (1960) summarized this theory as follows:

> The food producing revolution seems to have occurred as the culmination of the ever-increasing cultural differentiation and specialization of human communities. Around 8,000 B.C. the inhabitants of the hills around the Fertile Crescent had come to know their habitat so well that they were beginning to domesticate the plants and animals that they had been collecting and hunting. . . . From these nuclear zones, cultural diffusion spread the new way of life to the rest of the world.

Braidwood's explanation consists of a shift upward of the VMP_A (value of the marginal product in agriculture). An appealing aspect of Braidwood's nuclear-zone theory is that in some areas the plants and animals were probably better suited initially for domestication than in others. Moreover, Braidwood stressed that man did not suddenly acquire an intimate knowledge of plants and animals, but learned it gradually and inevitably. What is missing from Braidwood's explanation is any causal nexus for change. Braidwood's description is not a complete explanation of the cause, the timing, the independent development, or the slow spread of settled agriculture; the rise in population; or the extinction of certain animal species. It is obvious that getting to know plants and animals well is not a sufficient condition for the agricultural revolution even though it appears a necessary one.

These two theories do not consider population growth as an integral part of the explanation of man's transition to agriculture. A third theory, by Lewis R. Binford, elaborated by Kent Flannery, does. In this theory, population expansion via immigration puts pressure upon the resource base and creates competition among rival groups for survival. Binford (1968) speculates that in particular areas, different socio-cultural groups produce a disequilibrium:

> From the standpoint of the population already in the recipient zone, the intrusion of immigrant groups would disturb the existing density equilibrium system and might raise the population density to a level at which we might expect diminishing food resources. This situation would serve to increase markedly for the recipient groups the pressure favoring means for increased productivity. The intrusive groups, on the other hand, would be forced to make adaptive adjustments to their new environment. There would be strong selective pressures favoring the development of more efficient subsistence techniques by both groups.

Flannery (1969) elaborates on Binford's explanation in a study detailing the process which may have occurred. He ascribes to population pressure changes in hunting and gathering patterns: man turned from larger mammals to smaller ones and eventually from gathering to the development of agriculture.

The Binford and Flannery explanation consists of an expansion of population beyond q_c and, as a result, a part of the population shifting to agriculture. It suffers, however, from having no demographic theory on which to base the explanation, nor does it provide any explanation of why population expansion led to the development of agriculture.

IV

The model presented here assumes that when prehistoric man was presented with the choice between two alternatives, he would tend to choose the one that made him better off. I do not suggest that this assumption accurately described the behavior of any one individual or band of prehistoric men. In a world of uncertainty it is impossible to know a priori which choice is the "correct" one. Instead, as many bands faced a similar decision, a few of the groping responses to a new situation would turn out to be the "correct" ones in terms of the struggle for survival; that is, these decisions made the band materially better off, hence increasing its chances for survival vis-à-vis other bands. The bands that select the "correct" alternative, whether consciously or by chance, will be favored by a process of natural selection. Other groups initially selecting other actions and as a result doing less well will over time either change over to the techniques of their more successful rivals or perish.[6]

Prehistoric man, as postulated by the simple comparative static-equilibrium model presented above, had two basic alternative employments for his secure labor. Those bands which chose the alternative that maximized the value of production would over time be favored over those that did not. The simple comparative-equilibrium model with which I began this chapter is therefore acceptable as far as it goes. That model, however, is incomplete for our purposes in that it does not explicitly consider the nature of the existing property rights within which prehistoric man existed; nor does it include any demographic hypothesis. Since the existing structure of property rights channels man's economic behavior, the individual will find it in his interest to behave differently under one set of rights than under another. Prehistoric man employed his labor in conjunction with natural resources to produce his living. The natural resources, whether animals to be hunted or vegetation to be gathered, were initially held as common property. This type of property right implies free access by all to the resource. Economists are familiar with the proposition that unconstrained access to a resource base will lead to its inefficient utilization. This inefficiency as the demand for the resource increases eventually leads to the depletion of the resource. The depletion can take the form, in the case of a reproducible resource, of a reduction in the biological stock below the level required for sustained yield harvesting.

This instance is an example of incentive failure caused by cultural or institutional (property rights) inadequacies. The individual or band has an incentive to ignore certain costs which results in the resource being overutilized and perhaps even its continued existence endangered.

---

[6] The scarcity of resources guarantees competition which in turn ensures that observable behavior consistent with the wealth-maximization hypothesis will emerge via the selection process, if not as a result of conscious design.

Let us examine the situation where several bands compete for the same commonly held migratory animals. The animals are valuable to the bands only after they are captured. The band then has the incentive to exploit the resource to the point where the value of the last animal killed is equal to the private costs of killing it. The collection will continue until all of the income the scarce resource would have earned under private property rights is dissipated.[7] That is, in a competitive situation no band has any incentive to conserve the resource, since the animals left to reproduce probably would be taken by its rivals. The stock of animals thus could be placed in danger of extinction. The crucial element causing this inefficiency is the lack of any barrier to the exploitation of the commonly owned resource base. Individuals or bands enter the hunt when they perceive their private returns to be greater than the benefits of doing the next best thing. The result is too many hunters. After some level of exploitation, the size of the stock would begin to decline, thus raising costs (reducing productivity) to all hunters. The opportunity for labor in hunting schedule (VMP_H) shifts back; this fact, however, will not dissuade new hunters from joining the hunt as long as their productivity in hunting remains above what it would be in their next best alternative, agriculture.

It has been shown that if some of the potential entrants are excluded from utilizing the resources not all of the income will be dissipated (Cheung 1970). Thus, primitive agriculture, which must have been organized as exclusive communal property, had the advantage over hunting in terms of the efficiency of the property rights. It is inconceivable that, from the very beginning, the first farmers did not exclude outsiders from sharing the fruits of their labors. Furthermore, the band was probably a small enough group to monitor easily the activities of its members to ensure that collective behavior did not overutilize the scarce protected land resource held in common by the group. Thus, the band in principle at least could have exploited its opportunities in agriculture by constraining its members with rules, taboos, and prohibitions, almost as effectively as if private property rights had been established.[8] We shall see that this difference

---

[7] The classic article developing the common-property resource model is by Gordon (1954). See also Smith (1975) and Cheung (1970).

[8] Economists' solutions to the common-property dilemma are a user charge, a change to private property, or enforcing rules of behavior. See Smith (1975).

between common property rights in hunting and exclusive communal rights in agriculture is crucial to an explanation of the First Economic Revolution. The hunting sector must be considered within the framework of a common-property resource and the agricultural sector as exclusive-communal property regulated so as to border upon private property in its influence upon man's behavior.[9]

The difference in the nature of the two types of property rights governing hunting and agriculture respectively has important implications for the effect technological change would have upon the band's welfare in the long run. There is no doubt that prehistoric man was inventive. The progress made in the development of tools is ample testimony to this fact. Learning by doing and by experimentation characterized this era. Under incentive provided by conditions of scarcity, man concentrated his efforts on one task, became more proficient at doing it, and discovered ways to do it better.

The long-run influence of these changes upon the economic well-being of prehistoric man would be very different if these improvements were applied to activities where common property rights prevailed than they would be if improvements were applied to activities where exclusive communal rights ruled. The short-run effects are similar. Technological change which improved man's productivity in hunting would make hunting initially more rewarding relative to the alternative of agriculture (the opportunity for labor schedule in hunting, the VMP curve in figure 1, would shift out). The same would be true of a technological change in agriculture which shifted the VMP_A curve upwards, hence making agriculture a relatively more rewarding pursuit. Over the long run, however, the increased rewards to pursuing agriculture would remain while those in hunting would be dissipated by the effects upon the resource base of increased effort in that area. The opportunity for labor schedule in hunting would initially shift out, attracting more resources into hunting and hastening the depletion of the stock of animals held as common property, eventually causing the schedule to shift to the left of its original position. The different types of property

[9] While there is no evidence that property rights existed over megafauna in Palaeolithic times, there have been widespread attempts to establish such rights amongst hunters in subsequent eras—Smith loc. cit. The costs of measuring and enforcing such rights have their contemporary counterpart in the case of whaling.

rights in hunting as against agriculture ensure that technological change would eventually cause a shift of labor into agriculture.[10]

V

Another crucial element in the analysis is a hypothesis about man's prehistoric demographic performance. It is clear that the number of people upon this earth has increased through time but not either continuously or at a constant rate. The secular trend is upward but the trend has been uneven and at times even interrupted. A complete explanation for the fluctuations in the human population is beyond my task here. However, detailing some of the elements that such an explanation would contain is necessary for our purposes.

The simple arithmetic of population change over the first million years suggests a very slow rate of growth. But it does appear that population did grow. Thus, despite probable setbacks during climatic changes, fertility tended to exceed mortality.[11] So long as the standard of life was above a certain level, there was a tendency for man to increase in numbers. The trend would have been upward despite the effects of factors that periodically would tend to increase mortality. This line of argument runs directly counter to the observations of anthropologists who have discovered that contemporary Stone Age tribes tend to have stable populations. In addition, the level of population maintained by such tribes seems well below that which would damage the resource base. This modern observation has suggested to anthropologists and archaeologists that the view of population dynamics developed above is inappropriate and should be rejected in favor of an assumption that prehistoric humans tended toward a homeostatic population.

There are several difficulties in making this extension from modern Stone Age tribes to their historical antecedents. Let us examine the conditions under which a homeostatic population could be established and maintained. First, fixed resources must be present to create diminishing returns to additions to the population. Second, exclusive communal property rights to the

---

[10] Another way of viewing this process is that technological change in hunting would reduce the private costs of hunting, increasing the rate of exploitation of the common property resource, hence hastening the overexploitation of the resource.

[11] See Coale, "The Human Population" (1974).

resource must exist to eliminate competition between rival groups. And, third, some form of communal regulation of access to the resource must exist to regulate the economic behavior of members of the group.

The first must exist or additions to populations would impose no cost upon the group—hence no reason for the group to attempt to limit population. The second and third are necessary if the common property result is to be avoided. Suppose for the moment that one band was engaged in exploiting a common resource and had succeeded in limiting its population to the level that did not threaten the resource. Then suppose another band appeared which desired to share the resource. The ability of the first band to exclude the second is surely a function of the size of its population. The larger the population, the better its changes of successfully excluding others. Thus the bands that do not attempt to limit their population will tend to dominate those that do when they come into contact with one another. A homeostatic population can exist only among isolated bands. Indeed, that is where they are found today—in areas remote from the rivalries of other peoples.[12]

In the world of prehistoric man those bands that attempted to adjust their population to the size of the local resource base would eventually lose out to those bands that encouraged large and increasing populations, even if it meant migration and the subdivision of the band. Thus, the human population of the prehistoric era had built into its behavior, whenever the standard of living permitted, a collective tendency for population to grow.

VI

Now let us look at this model in the context of the evidence developed by the archaeologist and anthropologist. Humans lived in small bands that had to be ready to move whenever the local food supply dwindled. Small children and old people were a burden. Humans lived in whatever natural shelters they could find as the band moved after the animals being hunted. There is little evidence of permanent villages, although a few half-buried huts have been found. As population grew over the million or so years of man's history as a hunter, bands divided and subdivided

---

[12] Modern-day survivals are discussed in Binford (1968).

and migrated in search of food. At first man hunted the larger animals. A number of kill sites with great quantities of bones have been found, indicating that the hunting tactic of driving large animals over a cliff was employed. It is possible that man's increasingly efficient ability to hunt the great cold-weather animals—the mammoth and the woolly rhinoceros as they retreated northward—contributed to their extinction in the period between 25,000 and 12,000 years ago.[13] About 30,000 years ago, population expansion pushed humans across the Bering Strait from Asia into America. Thereafter, they moved throughout that land mass. Coincident with the appearance of humans was the disappearance of several species of large animals.

Let us put this very general description into our economic framework. Initially, this was a world in which the supply of animals and plants upon which man could feed appeared endless. As human population expanded and threatened the supply of foodstuffs in a given area, bands would subdivide and move to new areas, thus gradually spinning off new groups. This process is described by anthropologists as an open-donor system. In terms of the model this was a world of constant returns to an increasing labor force, so that growth in population resulted in a proportionate increase in output. This world of constant returns persisted as long as there was empty land of equal productivity for a growing population to exploit. So long as this condition existed, there was no incentive to attempt to delineate exclusive ownership over plants or animals. We should expect, however, that groups that found themselves inside the population frontier would initially try to develop stable relationships between the population of the band and the resource base since they were bounded by other bands and as yet had no way to expand the resource base. Such population groups would attempt to reach precisely the kind of homeostatic relationships that the anthropologists have described as existing among contemporary primitive societies. These bands would limit fertility by taboos, infanticide, and various other means in an attempt to keep the relationship between the population and the resource base constant. Moreover, we should expect that these bands attempted to develop a set of customs and rules to regulate hunting, and in a way that would maintain stability. This

---

[13] For an economic analysis of this phenomenon, see Smith (1975).

attempt is due to fail for the reasons discussed above: a homeostatic population can exist only among isolated bands.[14]

Once population had expanded to the point where the resource base was fully utilized, then any further increase in population led to a decline in the marginal produce of labor in hunting/gathering. Nevertheless, given the characteristics of competing tribes and a common property resource, population would continue to grow. I can illustrate the consequences in figure 1 above. Population expansion to q_d could occur without a diminution in the stock of the resource base, but further increases produced diminishing returns. Big animals increasingly became scarcer and gradually man was forced to search for new sources of food among the lower orders of animals. We do know that beginning about 20,000 B.C. man began to adapt himself to different kinds of animals and plants to eat (Flannery 1969). This era can itself only have been a transitional phase because as population pressure continued to grow and compete for these common property resources even they would become increasingly scrace and relatively more "costly" in labor time to gather.

The solution to the common-property dilemma in which prehistoric man found himself was the development of exclusive communal property rights. While animals and plants remained abundant relative to the demands of the human population, there was no incentive to incur the costs of establishing property rights over them. It is only during this transitional phase of increasing scarcity that it became worthwhile to incur the costs necessary to develop and enforce property rights that could limit the rate at which the resources were exploited.

The evolution of property rights has historically consisted of first excluding outsiders from harvesting the resource and then devising rules that limit the intensity of exploitation of the resource by insiders. As Flannery points out (1968: 68), "We know of no human group on earth so primitive that they are ignorant of the connection between plants and the seeds from which they grow." In terms of figure 1, when population reached q_c additional labor could be more productively used in cultivation and herding. Prior to reaching this point, as the marginal return to hunting diminished, more effort would be spent in gathering. At some point, it is a logical step for the band to attempt to find

[14] In Meso-America the Broad Spectrum Revolution appears to have occurred after about 5,000 B.C.

a naturally fertile area, settle, and repel new arrivals. Bands living inside the frontier thus became increasingly sedentary. As the population of these bands grew, the natural resources of the area were exploited more intensively.

It is interesting that the viewpoint of Flannery described in the above quotation has led some anthropologists and archaeologists to suspect that the first domestication of plants and animals did not occur where they were naturally in abundance. Instead, they reason, domestication would first have occurred where the natural harvests were less rich because if man could obtain sufficient wild wheat by gathering, he would not have bothered to cultivate. Harlan and Zohary comment (1966), "Why should anyone cultivate a cereal where natural stands are dense as a cultivated field? . . . farming itself may have originated in areas adjacent to rather than in the regions of greatest abundance of wild cereals." [15] This argument ignores the fundamental dilemma of growing population pressure and the common property resource problem. It is more likely that man found rich areas where there was an abundance of wild grain that could be harvested with a sickle and then began to defend these areas against intruders. Thus, we would speculate that the intensive wild cereal cultivation, which in Jean Perrot's view (1966) was practiced by the semi-sedentary Natufian culture in Palestine, is a more likely step toward the development of domestication than the alternative of growing the seeds on marginal land.[16]

The evidence concerning the Natufian culture suggests that it is likely that agriculture was an already existing alternative to hunting. The independent developments of agriculture in different parts of the world and the slow rate of its spread northwest across Europe seems to be consistent with this assumption. But it is important to note that even if new knowledge were necessary to engage in cultivation and herding the basic argument that exclusive property rights will raise the incentive to acquire new knowledge is not damaged. The explanation sketch in this section can be read either as a story of the shift to an already known alternative or as one in which bands developed property rights over rich stands of wild grain and then had the incentive to acquire the knowledge necessary for cultivation

[15] Harlan and Zohary (1966: 1074–80).
[16] Perrot (1966).

and domestication. Probably the first step was the establishment of exclusive territory such as has been observed among primitive bands and tribes in modern times. Demsetz (1967), citing the anthropologist Eleanor Leacock, describes the creation by the Montagnais Indians of exclusive hunting territory for beaver in response to the growing demand by the Hudson Bay Company.[17] An exclusive territory could be established at relatively low cost for plants and nonmigratory animals, but only at much higher cost for migratory animals. Once exclusivity was established, weeding, primitive irrigation, and seed selection would gradually develop in a trial-and-error process of learning by doing. The productivity of cultivation thereby increased and the marginal-value product of labor employed in agriculture shifted upward.

The difference between cultivation and domestication is a subtle one. The latter implies a genetic alteration in the plant or animal to improve its value to humans.[18] Two famous examples from prehistory were the evolution of emmer and einkorn wheat from the shattering to non-shattering form and the modification of wild sheep to a quieter, more tractable animal. Both instances of domestication may have come about as accidental results of the selection process. But under exclusive property rights the rewards from domestication would encourage the trial-and-error process of seed and animal selection.

There is no implication that the transformation from hunting to agriculture occurred rapidly. The evidence accumulated by archaeologists suggests that it required a substantial period of time. The transition occurred as a result of persistent population pressure which produced changes in the relative scarcities of the resources exploited by prehistoric man. In response to these developments, individual bands began to attempt to exclude outsiders from access to the resource base. In the process such bands became sedentary. The establishment of exclusive communal property raised the bands' return to attempts to increase the productivity of the resource base. Many groups probably failed to make this transition, but some by luck or chance man-

---

[17] See, however, the caveat by McManus (1972) which indicates that a group survival criteria overcame the individual internal allocation. Smith (1975) describes a number of anthropological studies of primitive property rights.

[18] For a discussion of cultivation and domestication, see Isaac (1970).

aged to make the transformation; it is from these beginnings that we see the development of civilization and economic growth that has occurred in the ten thousand years since.

The First Economic Revolution was not a revolution because it shifted man's major economic activity from hunting and gathering to settled agriculture. It was a revolution because the transition created for mankind an incentive change of fundamental proportions. The incentive change stems from the different property rights under the two systems. When common property rights over resources exist, there is little incentive for the acquisition of superior technology and learning. In contrast, exclusive property rights which reward the owners provide a direct incentive to improve efficiency and productivity, or, in more fundamental terms, to acquire more knowledge and new techniques. It is this change in incentive that explains the rapid progress made by mankind in the last 10,000 years in contrast to his slow development during the long era of primitive hunting/gathering.

Chapter 8

The Organizational Consequences of the First Economic Revolution

I

Between the beginning of settled agriculture and the peak of the Roman Empire was a span of approximately eight thousand years. As the length of time is not matched by quantity of evidence, we may tend to think of these years in terms of an endless parade of kingdoms, empires, and whole civilizations appearing and then disappearing in warfare, treachery, intrigue, and murder. Yet there were, as well, more mundane developments underlying these societies; and despite scanty evidence, it is possible to reconstruct certain of these developments. We would like especially to know the structure of the economies that supported the civilizations and permitted the existence of great empires—some of which endured for centuries. We would like also to know more about their demise than the story of a great battle or the sack of a capital city and the death, or enslavement, of its inhabitants.

Let me frame the questions specifically. In Part I, I maintained that the performance of an economy is dependent upon its organizational structure. Over the eight-thousand-year period I want now to consider, there appeared a bewildering array of economic organizations, most of them very different from those with which we are familiar today. In the modern world, for example, markets are used to allocate goods and services as well as the factors of production. During much of the ancient era, organized markets did not exist. What types of organizations took the place of such markets? What kinds of property rights existed and how did exchange take place? What accounts for the size of political-economic units and the different forms that government organization took? And most important of all, what were the consequences of these institutions for economic performance? Did economic growth occur?

In the next section I survey broad trends in the structure and performance of economies during this period before specifically turning to examine the evolution of the state. It was the distribution of "violence potential" both *within* and *between* political-economic units that became the most important underlying influence upon the structure and hence performance of economies in the classical world. While geographic constraints produced diverse results with respect to the viable size and survival ability of states, these constraints must be melded with the characteristics of military technology to explain the internal control structure and the consequent structure of property rights that evolved. In section III, I briefly discuss the evolution of the state before examining, in sections IV through VII, in rough (sometimes overlapping) chronological order the centralized Egyptian State of the New Kingdom, the decentralized Persian Empire, the Greek Polis, and then the Roman Republic and Empire. The consequent economic structure is briefly described in each case. The final section assesses overall economic performance in the classical world.

II

Certain broad trends can be identified as occurring during the eight thousand years that span the ancient era.

1. It is clear that population grew and at a then unprecedented rate. The area of human settlement also increased. The land surrounding the Mediterranean, for instance, became fairly densely populated during this era.

2. There was a gradual transition from hunting/gathering to farming, and over time the dominant form of economic activity became settled agriculture.

3. The political organization of the state emerged for the first

time. The particular forms that the state took during this era were many and varied, ranging from the despotic to the democratic. But despite the variety of forms, each undertook the duties of government. The rise of the state was accompanied by war and political instability. The size of the state tended to grow until the entire Western world was united in the Roman Empire.

4. Significant progress was made in the development of technology, and over those eight thousand years the Bronze was succeeded by the Iron Age.

5. Trade developed and expanded. Especially interregional trade grew in importance during this era. Eventually impersonal markets were created and then increasingly used to allocate resources.

6. Urban places developed for the first time. Cities grew in size and complexity of function and spread across the Mediterranean World.

7. A variety of economic organizations emerged. The redistributive economies of Sumer, Egypt, and Mycenaean Greece represent one extreme; the extension of price-making markets in Hellenic Greece and Rome, the other.

8. A variety of property rights underlay the various types of economic organizations. Initially, exclusive communal rights were established by the first agricultural communities; in some places these gave way to exclusive state-owned property rights and in others to individual private property rights. Where individual private property rights were established, these rights were developed over goods, land, and labor in the form of slavery.

9. Significant economic growth occurred. Part of this gain was used to support a growing population, part to raise the general standard of living.

10. The distribution of income became decidedly more unequal, with wide disparities appearing very early.

I want to examine these trends in more detail. I begin by contrasting the organizational characteristics of a hunting/gathering community with those required for settled agriculture. A hunting/gathering community consisted of a band who foraged for food. The members of the band hunted together and were mostly composed of family units. Other than the coordination involved in hunting there was little organization required. There was relatively little differentiation among the members of the band—in our terminology income distribution was very equal.

In contrast, settled agriculture necessitates a much more complicated social and economic organization. Foremost, a set of exclusive property rights must be established to exclude nonmembers of the community from sharing in the output generated by community action. The development of such a set of property rights over animals and plants involves some form of community defense.

The successful practice of agriculture requires that decisions must be taken with respect to what to plant, when to plant, when to harvest, and how to handle the assorted activities necessary between planting and harvesting. Besides decisions about what and when, important decisions must be made as to who will perform these tasks, and some system must be implemented to insure that the assigned tasks are properly completed. A settled society also has the opportunity to store goods against periods of famine and drought. The inventorying of goods necessitates coordination and the creation of storage facilities. An organization for making and implementing communal decisions is an absolute prerequisite for a viable agricultural community.

If early agriculture involved irrigation, as some of the archaeological remains in Palestine, Egypt, and the Tigris-Euphrates suggest, the organization problem was even more complicated. The capital involved in an irrigation system must be acquired; canals, for example, dug and maintained; drainage systematically organized; and sluices and floodgates arranged so water is distributed over the area to be irrigated.

Settled agriculture involved a division of tasks. In a hunting/gathering society specialization is limited to a simple role assignment: hunting is usually done by men and gathering by women. In contrast, settled agriculture saw a more complex assignment. Among early farmers, some individuals specialized in providing protection; others served as priests to handle "the rationalizing" of man with his environment. Within the agricultural community, new occupations emerged. By the second millennium B.C., craft specialization was well developed. Potters, metal workers, weavers, masons, carpenters, shipbuilders, bronzesmiths, and goldsmiths are some of the specialized occupations listed in Linear B tablets of the Mycenaean civilization (Renfrew 1972:341). Such specialization and division of labor marks an enormous change from the relatively undifferentiated society that hunting and gathering produced. A society made up of specialized individuals requires the establishment of a mechanism for distributing the community output among the population. This is a relatively simple task in a hunting and gathering society but involves far more coordination and decision making in a society in which specialization and division of labor exist.

The problems that an agricultural community faced in deciding what to produce, how to produce, and for whom to produce were therefore much more complex than those faced by bands of hunters/gatherers. Some means of organizing a common defense; insuring against famine; making decisions over what, when, and how to produce; managing and coordinating the increasingly specialized tasks necessary for a settled existence; and making decisions over the distribution of increasingly varied numbers of goods among the population had to be established.

The institutions which developed probably were not created *de novo* but evolved out of the communal decision-making mechanism of the simpler nomadic bands. Such a mechanism would have posed no serious problems for the emerging agricultural communities. Since they were small in size each member would recognize his or her stake in the community. The cost of making such community decisions would be minimal. When shirking did occur it would be easily detected.

The very success of an agricultural community, however, would tend to put the communal decision-making apparatus under stress. Agricultural productivity would tend to increase over time and the ability to store food would decrease the damage a crop failure could do. Both of these changes would tend to favor population growth. In turn, a growing population would increase both the costs of making community decisions and the incentive for any individual to shirk his community assignments (since the measurement of shirking would be more costly). A growing community would also increase the costs of coordinating production decisions and distributing the community product.

III

The emergence of the state with its concomitant body of rules to order internal structure and its coercive power both to enforce those rules and to compete with other states was the most fundamental achievement of the ancient world. This chapter focuses on the positive side of that achievement: the role its creation played in the development of complex civilizations and in the immense economic expansion of the ancient world. In the next chapter the emphasis will be on its inherent instability and the inevitable decline that eventually overtakes each state. While archaeological evidence continues to turn up new evidence of very early urban sites such as Jericho, going back to 8000 B.C., and Catal Huyuk in Anatolia, dating from 6000 B.C., there are still four millennia between the beginnings of agriculture and the "city-states" that developed in the plain of Sumer and Akhad in Mesopotamia and the first dynasties in Egypt.[1] Whether the origins of the state were by contract or by force, it was a lengthy process to innovate the institutional organization to produce a viable political structure. Religion played a crucial role in legitimizing the coercive power of the ruler and these early states were characterized as temple societies; the Egyptian Pharaoh was both the ruler and a god. Their size increased and by 2350 B.C. Sargon had reduced the importance of the city-states in Mesopotamia and created a centralized government. Upper and lower Egypt had also been consolidated by 3100 B.C. In both cases geography played a crucial role in shaping development and in determining the changing size of the state. Both depended upon an irrigation system that required integration and coordination of decision making; the indivisibility of such a system encouraged the increasing size of the state, but the efficient size of the hydraulic system in each case was different. In Mesopotamia the economies of scale undoubtedly encouraged consolidation beyond a single city-state, but they were far more limited than in Egypt, where the entire Nile Valley below the first cataract was a natural unit. The other major geographical difference was that Egypt was isolated by desert and water from invaders and was not overrun until the invasion of the Hyksos at the end of the twelfth dynasty. In contrast Mesopotamia was repeatedly invaded and overrun by Indo-Europeans (Hittites) and Semites (Amorites); as a result there was a bewildering succession of rulers and empires of varying size. More important, the form of political-economic organization evolved away from the temple economy in contrast to Egypt, where the economy continued to be dominated by an all-powerful Pharaoh.

[1] In the Indus Valley, Mohenjo-Daro and other urban places had developed by 2500 B.C.

It is more than a millennium from Hammurabi's reign in Babylon (1792–1750 B.C.) to the Persian Empire (550–331 B.C.), but with the advent of this empire under Cyrus the Great the size of the political economic unit was enormously extended and reached from the Aegean Sea to beyond the Indus River. Under Darius (521–466 B.C.) the empire was divided into twenty provinces, or satrapies, each with a governor, court, and treasury of its own.

Hellenic civilization, which eventually came in conflict with Persia and under Alexander conquered the Persian Empire, exhibited a radically different structure. The center of Greek political-economic organization was the city-state, or polis. Its small size was viable in consequence of the rugged mountainous country indented by the sea with small plains interspersed throughout. While Athens included a territory of approximately 1000 square miles and Sparta 3300, most of the Greek poleis were less than 400 square miles. If Greek unity was fostered by a belief in a common ancestry, a common language and religion, use of the same oracles, and a common participation in the Greek games, Greek competition was fostered by the rivalry of city-states. Not even the Persian invasion in 481 B.C. fully united them. Ubiquitous competition produced endless coalitions and internal warfare, culminating in (but not concluding with) the Peloponnesian war between Athens and Sparta. It was not until 338 B.C. that Philip of Macedon enforced Greek unity; his son Alexander created the Hellenistic world and empires that followed upon his death. While Greek culture was being superimposed on the Persian Empire and the society of the Egyptian Pharaoh, the Romans in the West were in a death struggle with the competing empire of the Carthaginians. The success of the Romans was followed by, first, hegemony over the Eastern Mediterranean, and then unity under the Roman Empire of the first two centuries after Christ.

The trend over these millennia is clear: the state became larger. The explanation for the variations in size throughout this time is, however, far from clear. The hydraulic society may account for Egyptian unity and help explain the expansion of the city-states in Mesopotamia, but one must invoke considerations of military technology to account for the viability of larger political economic units. The horse, the composite bow, the war chariot, and the phalanx successively altered the technique of warfare.

While the size of military units undoubtedly increased, the superiority of the Greeks over the Persians suggests that discipline and organization were substitutes for size beyond some critical minimum level (the march of the ten thousand as recounted by Xenophon is a striking illustration).

IV

The long dynastic history of Egypt bore witness to varying degrees of dominance of the Pharaoh over the nobles; however, the New Kingdom beginning in 1580 B.C. presents a classic picture of centralized Egyptian political structure.[2] While the Pharaoh was still theoretically a god as in the Old and Middle Kingdoms, his power in the New Kingdom was grounded in absolute control of the machinery of government: legislature, judiciary, army, police, and "apparently also the priesthood" (CAH, 1970:2, 314). The administration of the country was a tightly organized chain of command with the country divided into two parts, the North and the South, each with its vizier and treasurer. The vizier was directly responsible for the administration of economic activity in each area. Directly answerable to the vizier were the officials who were mayors of towns and surrounding rural areas. The monitoring of output, income, and tax collection was in the hands of the treasurer, who, while under the general supervision of a vizier, had his own extensive organization. Closely associated with the treasury were the overseer of the granary and overseer of cattle under whom accountants were charged with an annual census of cereal grains and livestock.

Taxation itself was under an official called the "Scribe of the fields and the Lord of the Two Lands" (CAH 1970:2, 359). The annual taxes were collected, in the name of the Pharaoh, on the output of the worker; the word labor was also a general expression for taxes (CAH 1970:2, 381). The taxes were imposed on the tenants and managers of economic activity, who managed to retain some profits in excess of the revenues required by the Pharaoh. Taxes were collected in kind. For example, the harvest tax was collected in emmer and barley with the rate varying according to the productivity of each piece of

[2] The following description is drawn from the *Cambridge Ancient History* (hereafter, *CAH*), vol. II, part I (third edition), chapter 9.

land as evaluated by the "Scribe of the Fields," who resurveyed and reevaluated the land each year. Similar monitoring and taxation were undertaken in every sphere of production: there was even a tax on wild game. Tributes were levied on foreign land; tolls, on waterways; and custom duties further increased tax revenue. In addition, communities had to lodge and feed all government officials; the army, navy, and police force could requisition supplies from districts (the amount to be deducted from taxes). The Pharaoh also directly possessed vast estates.

The Egyptian army of the New Kingdom was a professional, standing army which had learned its lessons from the Hyksos. There were squadrons of war chariots; the composite bow; and heavy bronze axes, swords, and spearheads. Strategy and military tactics had become a part of the training program of the professional officers. Under Tuthmosis III, the New Kingdom consolidated and expanded its control over Nubia and northern Sudan and extended its conquests into southern Syria.

This account of the political-administrative structure of the Eighteenth Dynasty is a brief portrayal of the Egyptian structure during its most successful and efficient period. It was a society with a single absolute ruler, with all property rights vested ultimately in the Pharaoh, no close substitutes to offer alternatives to constituents (such as the contests between nobles and Pharaoh of the Middle Kingdom) and a highly centralized bureaucracy designed to monitor and meter output and maximize the rents accruing to the ruler. It proved to be so durable in its general outlines that when, following Alexander's death, the Persian Empire was divided, Ptolemaic Egypt (part of that empire) simply imposed Greek rule on top of the centralized administration structure it had inherited.[3] The Ptolemies did, however, introduce an additional monitoring device: specifically, the tax farmer was required to underwrite the amount collected by administration officials. He made good any deficiency and pocketed any surplus. The result was to provide an effective check on the administration officials (Rostovtzeff 1941:1, 328–29).

The economy of Egypt under the New Kingdom—and later— was one in which ultimate property rights were vested in the Pharaoh. There does appear to have been some private ownership of land, and the temples possessed (probably only for *use*)

---

[3] See Rostovtzeff (1941), vol. I:271–331.

vast amounts of wealth and exercised control over large land areas; but the entire economic structure had at its apex a single figure. International trade was virtually a monopoly of the state carried on primarily by the Pharaoh's agents; the internal economic organization was hierarchically structured, either directly as part of the Pharaoh's estates or indirectly via the bureaucratic organization of officialdom (briefly described in the foregoing section) which funneled revenues to the Pharaoh.

Since total agricultural output was dependent on controlling the annual flooding of the Nile, the construction, repair, and efficient functioning of the irrigation system not only occupied a substantial part of the total labor force during certain seasons of the year but also occupied a substantial part of the bureaucracy in overseeing its efficient functioning.

Surviving records make it impossible to determine the amount of slavery, the exact form of labor services, or the nature of the corvee which appears to have been required of all labor to harvest crops, repair the irrigation system, and construct the vast public monuments and buildings; the servile role of labor in the economy nevertheless is apparent. Peasants, while technically free and capable of possessing some ownership rights over property, provided labor dues to government or the temple. In general all workers were paid in kind. There do appear to have been some small retail markets and local trade. While there was no circulating medium there was a weight ratio of gold, silver, and copper, which served as units of account.

Whereas Weber (1976) describes a gradual relaxation of the rigid hierarchical structure, including a growth of free labor, increasing individual land ownership (though still associated with obligations), expansion of a money economy, and internal trade (Weber 1976:126–30), Rostovtzeff maintains that the basic hierarchical structure had not been fundamentally altered by Ptolemaic times and that the Greeks simply attempted to make it more efficient by reducing rent dissipation by agents of the hierarchy (by the tax farmer, for example: Rostovtzeff 1941: 271–322).

It should be noted in passing that Alexandria emerged in the Ptolemaic period as the greatest city in the Western world and the center of culture and learning; however, it was not an integral part of Egypt but rather a city-state "which acted as if it were a free and autonomous Greek City" (Rostovtzeff 1941:415).

V

While Egypt was a homogeneous unit, the Persian Empire was a vast conglomerate of disparate religions, economies, and political units welded into a highly decentralized empire.[4] At its center politically and militarily were the Persians. One of seven noble families furnished the "great king"; his advisers and administration were largely Persian nobles, and the standing army was predominantly a Persian army. The empire was divided into twenty satrapies, each of which possessed substantial though widely varying autonomy. They typically had their own courts, civil administration, and judicial authority, and they even received envoys from neighboring states. The satraps, or governors, were men of high birth. Sometimes the rulers of a previously existing independent kingdom became de facto heriditary satraps with the ruling house continuing for successive generations. It was the duty of the satrap to collect the taxes or tribute specified by the Persian ruler; according to Herodotus this varied from 4680 talents of gold dust from India, to 1000 talents from Assyria and Babylonia, to as little as 170 talents from the Seventh Satrapy (lying between India and Bactria). In addition there were taxes in kind including a land tax and tolls. These payments typically went to support the army and the households of the king, the satraps, and the sub-satraps.

The heterogeneity of the Persian Empire was accompanied by tolerance of widely diverse religions and economic organizations. The success as well as the inherent weakness of the Empire was a function of its decentralized structure. There was success because any attempt to impose a uniform centralized structure on each diverse unit would have been enormously—indeed prohibitively—costly. Religious tolerance and the active adoption of local religions was a crucial stabilizing influence. For example, Darius took names claiming relationship with the Egyptian god Re in an attempt to involve an element of legitimacy in the Persian domination of Egypt and thereby reduce enforcement costs.

Restructuring the separate economic organizations would have led to chaos and an enormous loss of tax revenues. Instead the

[4] The account is largely drawn from the *CAH,* vol. IV, chapter 7 and Rostovtzeff (1941:1, 77–90).

existing economies were favorably influenced by peace and a vast internal market, but at the cost of heavy taxation and tribute. The weakness was that the satrapic system created potential alternative and competing rulers and a continuing problem of the King of Kings was to devise monitoring practices which would anticipate and prevent independence. There were periodic inspections as well as the stationing of garrisons of Persian troops independent of the satrap's command. But the semi-autonomous satraps were a continuing base for rivalry and revolt and ultimately a source of the breakdown of the Empire.

Rostovtzeff describes the center of the Empire, Persia, as "feudal and tribal" (1941:77); Babylonia as carrying out the ancient tradition from the time of Hammurabi of an elaborate bureaucracy of officials and priests but continuing its flourishing economy based on private ownership of land, merchants, bankers and an extensive long-distance trade (1941:78–79). Then there were Phoenicia with its long seafaring and colonizing tradition and its thriving seaports of Byblos, Ugarit, and Al Mina; the Greek cities of Asia Minor with similar political-economic structure to those of Attica and the Peloponnesus; and the nomadic Bedouin tribes in the Syrian and Arabian deserts. There was in addition Lydia, where the first metallic coins made from stamped electrum (an amalgam of gold and silver) were circulated as early as 700 B.C. In addition there were the satraps of the Far East and Egypt. In Rostovtzeff's own words:

> Such was the great Persian monarchy—a medley of economic contrasts and yet an economic unit in the hands of the Persian kings, who never gave up the difficult task of holding together the disparate components of their empire. Their success resulted mainly from their sound policy of decentralization. They seldom interfered with the social and economic life of their satrapies. At the same time they gave them the military protection that they needed and new and welcome opportunities of developing their economic relations and their interchange of goods. Excellent "royal" roads connected the various parts of the Persian Empire; new sea routes (for example from the mouth of the Indus to the Red Sea and the Nile) were explored; and a "royal" gold and silver currency of perfect soundness and integrity facilitated the exchange of goods. The heavy taxation to which the satrapies were subjected was not excessive if compared with the advantages that they derived from being, not independent States, but constituent parts of a world empire.
>
> It is not surprising that Persia had the reputation of being a very rich country. We have no means of measuring its wealth. That of the Persian kings is, of course, well known. We know the

amount of their yearly revenue and the quantity of gold and silver stored in the Persian capitals. Royal riches do not neccessarily imply the well-being of subjects. But the ever-increasing prosperity, in Persian times, of the Phoenician cities, of the caravan cities of Syria and Mesopotamia, and of Babylon is evidence that the wealth of the rulers was based on the wealth of their subjects. It should be noticed that most of the satrapies of Persia, other than Egypt and Asia Minor, enjoyed a lasting peace for at least three centuries, a rare phenomenon in the history of the ancient world. (Rostovtzeff, 1941)

Weber (1976), while acknowledging the perpetuation of diverse economic organization, paints a very different picture of the consequences of Persian rule. According to him it was a period of economic stagnation: the Babylonian canal system was in decline and neither the Phoenician nor Greek cities flourished, "even though this meant peace and unity throughout a vast area" (Weber 1976:222). He concludes as follows: "The State Sector of the Persian Empire's economy was not dynamic and this must have had an effect on foreign trade. In fact economic development evidently came to a stop throughout the vast area which was unified for 150 years" (Weber 1976:223). Weber attributes this stagnation to the heavy taxes, the requisitioning system, and the lack of the necessary stimuli connected with political expansion (Weber 1976:222). Whether the Persian Empire promoted economic growth or throttled the thriving economies of Babylonia, Phoenicia, and the Ionian Greeks cannot be settled here. And the issue is not crucial, since the supremacy of Greek organization and the Greek defeat of the Persians and eventual conquest of the Persian Empire by Alexander are the main threads of the economic history of the ancient world. The Hellenistic empires that followed Alexander's death in 331 B.C. superimposed the Greek structure on the ancient world and eventually merged with and were integrated into the Roman Empire.

VI

The Greek polis was conditioned by a geography that made possible the viability of small political-economic units.[5] Aristotle maintained that a polis of more than one hundred thousand citizens (free adult males) would cease to be a polis. Side by side

[5] This section is drawn from Ehrenberg (1969); Weber (1976); Dickinson (1958); Forrest (1966); *CAH*, vols. IV, V; Starr (1977).

with its small size was a survival requirement that it could recruit a sufficient male population for military duty in the face of the ubiquitous competition and rivalry of a large number of contiguous independent units. Thus the traditional evolution, described by classical historians, from aristocratic polis to hoplite polis to citizen polis, mirrored the necessary expansion of the military base (from a few well-armed mounted knights to the hoplite phalanx and in the case of Athens and a few other states to the manning of its naval fleet) as well as the transformation of the political base from the few to the many and the creation of a democratic society.

The conflict in Athens between aristocrat and peasant produced reformers (Solon) and tyrants (Peisistratus); but by the time of Pericles, Athens was a direct democracy ruled by an assembly of all its citizens with most of the offices (excluding the military command) filled by lot from the whole citizen body.[6]

While democracy prevailed in Athens, in other Greek states there were oligarchies; there, the tension between rich and poor, creditor and debtor—in short over the distribution of wealth and income—was a phenomenon equally as pervasive as the tension between city-states.

In Athens and certain other democracies the citizen participated in running the state: sitting on the juries and, of course, serving in the military. Such participation entailed a good deal of the citizen's time and he was paid at the rate of two and then three obols a day for his political and juridical participation. While voluntary participation was an essential ingredient of the Greek polis, it was made possible by a structure of law and property rights which produced revenue from non-citizens (slaves and metics—resident aliens), voluntary contributions from the wealthy (liturgies), and, during the period of Athenian hegemony, tribute from Athenian allies. Themistocles' decision to divert the revenues of the slave-worked silver mines of Larium from distribution to the citizens to the building of a naval fleet in the face of the Persian threat in 483 B.C. illustrates not only the primitive state of the public finance of the Athenian polis but also its economic base.

The city-state, however, was not viable in isolation, and end-

---

[6] Sparta in contrast remained a monarchy with two kings, and a militaristic structure consisting of a relatively small number of citizens and a large servile population.

less coalitions, confederations, alliances, and periods of hegemony of one state with or over others was as ubiquitous a part of the classical Greek scene as was the internal strife over control of the polis and the distribution of wealth. The Peloponnesian War between Athens and Sparta was only the most famous of the innumerable conflicts that characterized the endless competition.

The Greek state was one in which the opportunity cost of constituents was conditioned by the military requirements necessary for survival. A widening of the electoral base was a necessary condition for survival and inevitably was accompanied by a continuous struggle over the distribution of wealth, just as the necessity for coalition with other city-states produced a parallel struggle for hegemony between city-states. Greek democracy was inseparable from Greek slavery (or helotry in Sparta) since the structure of political-economic organization which permitted direct democracy of citizens required a labor force of slaves or helots to perform the basic functions of the economy in order that citizens could be released for political, judicial, and military activity.

The Greek city-state economies which evolved in the centuries following the demise of Mycenaean Greece were based on individual land ownership which had replaced collective clan ownership. Whether the Kleros—the family plot—was alienable before the fifth century B.C. has been the subject of debate, but Starr maintains that the weight of evidence supports the alienability (Starr 1977:150–51). The clan divisions of Solon's new economic order (which replaced the old class divisions based on military capabilities: that is, knights who could afford to keep horses, zeugitai who could equip themselves to fight in the hoplite phalanx, and finally thetes—laborers) were based on land holding. The property qualifications were based on annual production of grain, wine, or olive oil (a unit being approximately 1½ bushels, equal to 8½ gallons) with thetes producing less than 200 units; zeugitai, 200 to 300 units; a knight, over 300 units; and "first class" knights, over 500 units. However, by Starr's estimates there must have been a substantial number of Athenian citizens in 600 B.C. who either owned no land or did not possess enough to be self-sufficient (Starr 1977:155).

Solon's celebrated reforms suggest that land consolidation as well as personal servitude for debt had been a growing phenomenon. The dramatic alteration in property rights in land by

Solon and then Peisistratus strengthened the economic (and political) position of the two lowest classes of citizens (and concomitantly guaranteed a broader base of military support). If debt slavery was eliminated for Athenian citizens, however, it was no accident that there was substantial subsequent expansion of slavery of aliens (mostly Thracians, Phyrygians, and Syrians). This growing slave population was mostly employed in domestic service, mining, and other non-agricultural economic activity. The extent of slavery in agriculture is a matter of dispute.

Between 800 and 500 B.C. there is clear evidence of growing specialization, division of labor, and in consequence both internal and international trade accompanied by the rise of a money economy.[7] Much of the growing artisan activity and trade was in the hands of metics, and both wages and interest appear to have been generally free of government restrictions (CAH, vol. V, chapter 1). The growing dependence of Athens on grain imports from the Black Sea was also largely in the hands of metics and foreigners who also made sea-loans as a part of the organization of international trade.

The fifth century B.C. between the defeat of Persia and the Peloponnesian War was the great age of Athens. Politically and militarily, Athens dominated the Greek world; economically it was an era of prosperity based on growing international trade and internal commerce. The imports of grain, timber, slaves, and luxury items were paid for with silver, olive oil, pottery, and other exoprts. Tribute from Athens's "allies" helped support the naval might of the Athenian Empire, which reduced piracy and therefore improved the safety of international trade and particularly guaranteed protection to the grain trade which was essential to Athenian survival. Underlying this economic prosperity was a structure of property rights in people (slavery) and other factors of production as well as in goods and services which gradually evolved as a body of law from Draco through Solon, Cleisthenes, and Pericles.

Classical scholars are certainly correct in emphasizing the fundamental underlying role of the polis in this evolution of Athe-

[7] In terms of the theoretical framework of this study, the development of money would depend on the technology of measurement and the interests of the ruler. Hicks (1969) provides an excellent outline of the emergence of money (pp. 63–68) consistent with this framework. His argument about the importance of the city-state for the rise of the market (chapters 3, 4) is also generally consistent with the argument advanced here.

nian political economy. Moreover one can agree with Polanyi that the evolution of price-taking internal markets as well as the growth of "administered trade" in international markets was also a consequence of the Athenian polis (Polanyi 1977); but the logical implication of this structure (as well as the subsequent economic organization of the Roman Republic and Empire) has led to one of the more sterile debates in history. As noted in chapter 4, Polanyi would separate out markets, economizing behavior, and capitalism on the one hand from reciprocity and redistributive and household economies on the other hand. The latter are motivated differently than the former and cannot usefully be analyzed by modern neoclassical (or Marxian) economics. For Polanyi, the supremacy of the polis suggests that the latter consideration dominated not only Greece but all economies until modern times. But this separation is spurious. The state specifies the property rights according to the interest of the dominant group in power (in this case Athenian citizens) and then, subject to those constraints, specifies the forms of economic organization that minimize transaction costs: in this case a free internal market for goods and services undergirded by a structure of property rights that on the one hand provided ownership rights and alienability in land, capital, and labor and, on the other, controlled international trade in grain in order to guarantee a food supply (frequently at subsidized prices). Polanyi is certainly correct in emphasizing that Athens could not afford a free international market in grain when its survival depended upon the uninterrupted flow of that import. The strategic importance of grain imports to Athens (and later Rome) is paralleled in the late twentieth century by the strategic importance of oil to the importing countries; the parallels in political economy are quite striking (but no one would argue that the motivation involved in securing oil imports was noneconomic).

Long after the relative decline of Athens, the political economy that evolved from the polis played a dominant role in the classical world. While the heritage of Philip of Macedonia was a monarchical state, the structure that his son Alexander imposed on the Hellenistic Empire he created was derived from the Greek polis. It is true that in the Seleucid Empire a Greek superstructure simply was imposed on the Persian Empire; and in Ptolemaic Egypt, a layer of Greek authority on the Egyptian hierarchical structure; but the dynamic centers of economic expansion in the

Eastern Mediterranean carried on the polis tradition. Rhodes, in particular, emerged as the economic center of the Eastern Mediterranean in the third century B.C. It not only became the entrepôt for grain, slave, and other trades of the eastern Mediterranean; it also provided banking services, a body of commercial law, and a navy to reduce piracy. Until Rome's jealousy cut short its hegemony by making Delos a free port (and attracting much of the grain trade away from Rhodes) the commercial expansion that characterized the Hellenistic world was centered in this island.

VII

The subsequent economic history of the western ancient world is a history of Rome; and the core of that history, as with Greece, was the developing political structure and consequent evolution of a body of property rights codified into Roman Law, the heritage of which has survived into modern times in continental Europe. Like the Etruscan before it, the Roman city-state had many parallels with the early Greek polis. It was aristocratic; but as in the case of the Greek polis, the military necessity of having a self-equipped hoplite army wrung concessions from the aristocracy. Weber maintains that military clientage (where the client was provided with military equipment and followed the patron into battle) was rendered obsolete and replaced by free clientage (where landless individuals and manumitted slaves provided service to patrons in return for protection and support) when the simple combat of knights was replaced with the hoplite phalanx of plebs (Weber 1976:280–89). The twelve tables (450 B.C.) gave the plebs representation in the government. The controversy over debt, land holding, and distribution of the *ager publicus* (public lands) paralleled Greek history in many respects. Yet the parallels differ in three important respects. First, while the plebs gained increasing political representation over the next three centuries and the ager publicus expanded as Roman conquests opened new land for its citizens, the evolving political structure never became democratic like that of Athens: rich plebs joined the patricians in running the state, and its political structure expanded from an aristocracy to an oligarchy. Second, the struggle over land distribution was the focus of repeated internal strife and even civil war for the next four centuries, but the end result, despite the reform and revolutionary leadership of the Gracchi brothers and others, was increasingly unequal land distribution, a growing portion of the citizenry who possessed no land and eventually became a part of the urban *proletarii,* and the development of the latifundia based on a slave labor force from Roman conquests. Third, and perhaps decisive, was the alteration from the polis to a bureaucratic empire. An important step was the extension of citizenship first to other Italian cities and then under Caesar and Caracalla beyond the boundaries of Italy so that the city-state of Rome gave way to a political structure that would eventually govern a Mediterranean empire. The evolving administrative structure of Rome from city-state to a vast administrative bureaucracy during the Empire was marked during the period of the Republic by senatorial control of foreign affairs (*CAH,* vol. VIII, chapter 12) and a gradual shift from alliances with friendly powers to dominance over dependent states—along with a continuing reluctance to undertake the administration of extra-Italian area (*CAH,* vol. IX, chapter 10).

Yet grow the Empire did. In 146 B.C. it possessed six provinces: Sicily, Sardinia, the two Spains, Africa, and Macedonia; in 133 B.C. Attalus, the king of Pergamum, left his kingdom to Rome. The administrative structure in all provinces was primitive. A governor was sent out from Rome and taxes were collected (unlike Italy), but in general local self-government was fostered since no civil service existed during the Republic (*CAH,* vol. IX, chapter 10:466).

One consequence was an expanding role for the *publicani,* private contractors, who both provisioned supplies and collected taxes.[8] Whether this system was as inefficient and led to such extensive rent dissipation via unscrupulous governors and enormous enrichment of publicans as many historians have maintained is a matter of some debate.[9] But it was inevitable that the Roman Empire under Augustus resulted in the development of more elaborate control systems which had more in common with the Persian Empire and the Hellenistic monarchies. Periodic censuses were undertaken, a civil service established,

---

[8] See Badian (1972).
[9] The traditional view is described in *CAH,* vol. X, chapter 7. For a contrary view of the publicani see Badian (1972).

experienced governors of senatorial rank appointed to run the provinces, and a professional paid standing army established. The tax structure was altered to be less dependent on the *publicani* and the burden of taxation extended to fall on Roman citizens resident in Italy (who heretofore had paid only a 5 percent tax on the manumission of slaves) as well as provincials. Accompanying this political transformation was the development and elaboration of Roman law with its base in exclusive individual property rights in both factor and product markets. While the Athenian structure of property rights was based on law, the contribution of Rome was the elaboration of a complete system of civil law undergirding the contractual relationships of the highly developed exchange economy which developed throughout the Mediterranean world in the first two centuries A.D. The codification of commercial law was a major economic achievement of Roman society. Equally important were the laws of property which dealt with the ownership of slaves, the major source of the labor force of the early Empire.

VIII

Population growth was the most fundamental underlying factor in ancient economic history; and it is with population growth that an assessment of the economic performance of the ancient world surely begins. The expansion of the food supply with settled agriculture led to an increase of the rate of population growth. It probably also produced greater periodic checks to population growth because the concentration of population in settled villages would have increased the spread of communicable diseases. But population grew, and the migrations that created and overturned the early Empires in the Tigris-Euphrates valleys were at least partly a response to population pressure, as indeed may have been the Dorian expansion in Greece. We are on more positive ground in relating the colonization of the Mediterranean and Black Sea by the Phoenicians, Greeks, and Romans as a reflection of growing population as much as a reflection of developing settled trading patterns between the home city-state and areas with complementary resources. If migration and colonization were one reflection of and response to population growth, the development of exclusive individual property rights and conflict over land distribution were others. As long as there was an available supply of good quality land we would expect that the costs incurred in migrating, colonizing, and creating individual property rights would not make such endeavors worthwhile; but in periods of diminishing returns there could be an acceleration in such activities.

Population pressure, then as now, is a two-edged sword. It is a major factor in internal and international conflict, political instability, and decline; but here I follow the cutting edge that induced societies to innovate forms of political-economic organization that promoted productivity increase leading to periods of sustained economic growth. There can be no doubt that substantial growth did occur. I am not referring to the extensive growth which led to the settlement of the entire Mediterranean basin and spread throughout northern Europe and North Africa in these millennia. Rather I refer to per capita growth in income that meant that for lengthy intervals output grew faster than population. It is evident in fifth century Athens before the internecine warfare with Sparta, in the era of Rhodian domination of the Eastern Mediterranean in the third century B.C., and in the first two centuries of the Roman Empire. The description of contemporaries provides abundant qualitative evidence of thriving economies and standards of living of significant segments of the population. True, there were large numbers who were barely above subsistence; but their living standards would have been universal in Neolithic times. In 500 B.C. only the rich drank wine; by 200 B.C. wine consumption extended to lower income groups. The use of olive oil was similarly extended and there is equally contemporary evidence for a broadening of the diet to include more meat, fish, fruit, and vegetables (Forkes 1955). The widespread extension of slavery itself is an indication that free laborers were themselves above a subsistence standard; otherwise, slavery would not have been a viable institution.

We do not have to search far to account for the economic sources of the productivity increase that underlay the thriving civilizations of the ancient world. The improving institutional organization of the state that we observe in the sequence from Egypt to Persia to Greece to Rome led to the reduction in transaction costs, growing regional specialization, and widening of the markets. The growing security of property rights in periods of peace such as the first two centuries A.D. led to a Mediterranean-wide market. In addition to the productivity gains associated with improving economic organization, there was immense technological change over these eight millennia. The rate was slow in comparison to that in the modern world; but the shift from bronze to iron, the development of writing (essential for the specification of contracts and the reduction in measurement costs which permitted the growth of impersonal exchange) from pictographs and hieroglyphics, the improvements in agricultural techniques, and the developments in engineering were but a few highlights of the immense technological transformation of these millennia.[10]

That substantial growth occurred in the ancient world cannot be doubted. That per capita income of the free population of the Roman Empire of the second century A.D. may have exceeded that of any society until the nineteenth century is possible. But these statements are incomplete without any accounting of the distribution of wealth and income that accompanied this growth, and our knowledge in this respect is as imprecise as it was in the discussion of growth. That incomes became more unequal is not in question. There was little differentiation in the Neolithic village, and the emerging specialization and division of labor surely produced greater inequality. But this pattern was not uniform. The inequality of the Egyptian dynasties may have been as great as the inequality in the Roman Empire, where the wealth of some senators was legendary (Pliny is quoted as saying that in Nero's time six senators owned half of North Africa). Yet the impression one gets from the literature of fifth century B.C. Athens is one of a rather modest dispersion of wealth amongst the free population. The trend thereafter, however, appears to have been toward greater inequality in wealth and income amongst the free population and toward an increasing percentage of the labor force being slave.

This chapter began with the primitive neolithic village and ends with the splendors of Rome at the height of its power in the second century A.D. The vestiges of primitive societies which anthropologists are examining today in New Guinea, Africa, and South America give us some inkling of what that primitive village must have been like. For the accomplishments of the Greek and Roman world we can still observe the Parthenon; see the

---

[10] For an informative summary account see Hodges (1970).

engineering accomplishments of the Romans in the viaduct at Nimes; read the histories of Thucydides, Polybius, or Livy; watch the plays of Aristophanes performed. The creation of such civilization was surely an accomplishment as impressive as that of modern times; but it has been obscured and ignored by economic historians because the intervening "dark ages" appear to render it a curiosity rather than an integral part of the evidential material which constitutes the economic historian's laboratory. Yet the achievements, whether measured in terms of cultural accomplishments or of the more prosaic economic ones, both are our heritage and comprise four-fifths of our economic history.

Chapter 9

Economic Change and Decline in the Ancient World

I

Eventually all societies experience economic decline, whether defined in absolute terms as a decline in per capita real income or simply in relative terms as compared to competing political-economic units. Usually economic decline leads to the state's disappearance as a sovereign nation; and given the inherent instability implied by the model developed in Part I this is not surprising. Some societies, however, have exhibited exceptional survival ability for long periods of time; others showed little ability to adjust. The survival of Rome for almost one thousand years is as remarkable as its demise, which more sharply delimited the end of an era than any other event in history.

Chapter 8 ended with a brief discussion of the distribution of wealth and income in the ancient world. That is the point at which to begin an exploration of economic change and decline since the struggle over this distribution, both within and between states, is the most fundamental source of such change and decline.

The focus of the preceding chapter was on the innovation and evolution of political forms of organization and the consequent property rights structures which they produced. The Egyptian dynasties were characterized by freedom from external competition, except for the Hyksos invasion; an internal structure under the New Kingdom with no close substitutes for the Pharaoh; and a stable economy—but one with probably little or no productivity increase. The question of growth under the Persian kings is unresolved, but the continued existence of potential competitors to the king among the satraps was a major influence on Persian internal policies. The evolution of the Greek city-state was basically conditioned by the tension between the requirements of military security and the internal struggle over the distribution of land ownership (the basic source of wealth). A similar tension existed throughout the development of the Roman Republic.

A distinguishing feature of the ancient world was that war often paid off for the victor. The Roman Triumphs were a dazzling display of the spoils of victory in the form of slaves and gold; the land acquired by these conquests also was distributed among the victors. In the latter period of the Roman Empire the barbarians could extract huge sums of gold from the Romans simply by threatening invasion. Successful military expeditions with subsequent division of the spoils to faithful underlings and soldiers were a major avenue of political success for ambitious Romans, just as enlargement of the subject area provided a larger tax base as well as a cheap supply of labor in the form of slaves.

II

Even in the absence of population growth the struggle over control of the state to redistribute wealth would have occurred; but it was population growth that was the deep underlying influence in shaping the pattern of conflict and adjustment in these millennia.

In chapter 7 population pressure was described as the initiating force in the replacement of hunting/gathering bands by settled agricultural communities. In the model used in that chapter the contrast was between diminishing returns to additional hunting/gathering efforts and constant returns to additional inputs into agriculture. The consequent growth of agriculture led to the gradual emergence of civilizations described in chapter 8. It also permitted immense expansion of population in these eight millennia as compared to the limits of a hunting/gathering world. Since the development of communal property rights raised the rate of return on acquiring new knowledge, there were two complementary sources of expansion allowing population expansion. One was the supply of land and resources that could be opened up and used for agriculture; the second was the productivity increases that came from improvements in the domestication of plants and animals and technological changes in agriculture. But there was a limit to the supply of land and resources available; and there is no logical basis for the conviction that productivity increase will automatically keep up with population growth. The adjustment process was sometimes successful: chapter 8 emphasized the growth of civilization. The other cutting edge of the population sword, however, was equally present in the ancient world.

We can briefly delineate the characteristics of decline as a consequence of population growth and diminishing returns as follows. Some political economic units could be experiencing continuing per capita growth because of still abundant good land, of increasing returns in the non-agricultural sector outweighing diminishing returns in agriculture, or of alterations in property rights in agriculture resulting in productivity growth to offset diminishing returns. At the same time other states would be experiencing falling real income and thereby have a growing inducement to invade and conquer rich neighbors. As a result, the prospering economy faces ever-growing costs of either bribing the invaders or making increased military expenditures. The increase in the tax burden falls on those groups with the least political influence; but as the costs continue to rise, the rulers of the state are forced to seek revenue wherever they can, even at the risk of alienating constituents or stifling productive activity. The result is either to have constituents switch their allegiance to a competitor offering better terms—including in some instances the potential invader—or to have stagnation and absolute decline in output in the goods and resources sector and, ultimately, reductions in tax revenues (and defeat at the hands of the invaders). In effect, taxes and confiscations alter the structure of property rights so that there is a reduced incentive to undertake productive activity.

Such a scenario might be labelled "the barbarians at the gate." There was a second scenario as well—decay from within. Population growth and diminishing returns in agriculture, which resulted in falling real wages in a political-economic unit, typically stimulated a variety of efforts to escape the dilemma. As noted earlier, colonization was a frequent method; conquest of a neighboring country with still abundant land was another. Failing these, the internal political structure faced growing tension. The agrarian small farmer at least initially has little influence on the ruler of the existing state. In comparison, large landholders not only have better access to the ruler but also wish to reorganize property rights to eliminate common property aspects and to capture the rising rents. Such a redefinition of property rights will deny the agrarian small landowners or landless peasants the access to land heretofore available to them and in effect redistribute wealth in favor of large landlords. The rulers of the state have an incentive to so redefine property rights because their action will increase output and tax revenue. The rulers of the state may become far more insecure, however, since such action invites potential competitors into the field to capture the allegiance and support of the disaffected groups. Without a great deal more specification, the outcome is indeterminate. Various compromises, such as "bread and circuses," partial land distribution schemes, and, of course, conquest and colonization, may delay a denouement. Population growth will slow and may even adjust to a low enough fertility rate to permit a reversal to per capita output growth—particularly if property rights have been redefined to provide an incentive for more productivity. Alternatively, a rival with the support of the landless may replace the existing rulers and redistribute land in such a way as to give land to the landless but also alter property rights so that growing productivity is not encouraged—for example, by making land inalienable or imposing price ceilings on the sale of agricultural goods.

III

Both stability in the ancient world and change as outlined in the foregoing stereotyped scenarios are in large part amenable to classical and neoclassical analysis as set out in Part I. In this section I undertake some specific application.

1. The active agents of change were overwhelmingly individu-

als with a direct interest in altering the system. The great bulk of the population was typically passive and inert. Societies that exhibited stability over long periods of time were characterized by a monolithic structure which did not permit the emergence of competitors to challenge the rulers. In the Egyptian dynasties, for instance, the competition was limited to that over succession; before the New Kingdom there had been struggles between nobles, priests, and Pharaoh, but thereafter the system persisted with little change. Marx (and others) at one time considered the Oriental mode of production a distinct and changeless system. What was distinctive was the monolithic political structure which did not permit the development of internal rivals, as well as a geographic isolation which raised the cost of invasion by external rivals. There were, however, two important additional characteristics. The genuine economies of scale in an integrated control of the Nile led to the structuring of a centralized bureaucracy and permitted such a monolithic structure.[1] And, the expansion of Egyptian population over the three millennia preceding the beginning of the Roman Empire must have been at a relatively low rate so that diminishing returns did not occur. While the distribution of income was extremely unequal, Egypt was looked upon as one of Rome's richest provinces and its major source of food supply. It is likely that the extremely unequal income distribution which kept the peasants at a very low level of well-being was a major influence in keeping population growth at a low level and therefore producing long-run stability rather than the dynamic secular pattern which characterized the rest of the western ancient world.[2]

2. Population growth elsewhere in the ancient world acted through the growing relative scarcity of land (that is, relative price changes) to induce change. From the Hittite and Amorite movements in Mesopotamia, to the Helvetii request that Rome permit a crossing of Gaul and thus an escape from the pressure of the advancing German hordes (which led to Julius Caesar's important victory in 58 B.C.), to the growing barbarian hordes pressing against the Roman lines on the Danube and the Rhine

---

[1] Egypt provides a better fit to Wittfogel's hydraulic society than most of the other cases he cites.

[2] William McNeill's suggestion in *Plagues and People* (1976) that population stability resulted from the debilitating effects of parasitic diseases upon the peasant population is consistent with this argument (p. 40).

in the late Roman Empire, population pressure resulted in migration, conquest, and war. Where still empty land existed colonization could occur—and the end result was the settlement of Europe and the Near East. Internally, the rising shadow price of land led to growing pressure to develop exclusive individual property rights and the ubiquitous struggle over land that characterized the ancient world.

3. Change in the form of conquest and revolution was instigated by rulers or their agents. From Sargon's creation of the first Empire in Mesopotamia to Alaric's sack of Rome in 410 A.D. (traditionally considered as the end of the Empire in the West), it was kings, Pharaohs, chiefs who initiated wars. Revolutions on the other hand were most commonly instigated by agents of the ruler—satraps, provincial governors, dependent monarchs, or military commanders. Internal strife over land brought forth competing aspirants for control of the state: Pericles versus Cimon in Athens, or the chief figures in the Roman Civil War—Tiberius and Gaius Gracchus, Marius, and Sulla.

4. Kings, usurpers, and reformers courted followers with selective incentives: a division of the spoils of victory amongst the victorious soldiers (including grants of land), military and free clientage, and the promise of land redistribution to the landless; they sometimes simply bribed and incited mobs.[3]

5. The growth and decline of slavery reflected its changing profitability. The supply of slaves was augmented during the Classical Greek period and to the Roman Empire by conquest, and during the first two centuries of the Empire by slave breeding when, because of peace, the price of slaves rose dramatically (Jones 1966:296). The demand for slaves reflected the relative profitability of slaves versus a free labor force: first in the mines and domestic service in Greece; and then, in addition, in the latifundia in the Roman Republic as growing markets made large-scale agriculture profitable. Even the widespread manumission of slaves in the Roman Empire is largely explicable in economic terms since the incentive system it provided to the slaves led to a sufficiently incremental marginal effort to compensate owners for the future loss of the manpower of the ex-slave. The decline of slavery reflected its declining profitability. When slave prices rose high enough it became profitable to substitute free labor as

---

[3] For a discussion see Brunt (1966).

evidenced in the first two centuries of the Empire (Jones 1966: 296). Conversely when the price of free labor fell or the demand for agricultural products declined with the disruption of trade in the late Empire, the transformation of slaves (and free labor) into *coloni* was a rational response.[4]

6. The changing locus of economic activity in the ancient world was sometimes a consequence of war, chaos, and the consequent lack of secure property rights; sometimes, as in the case of Rhodes, a change in tariff and trade barriers; but often it was the result of technological diffusion and changing relative prices. Athens was the technological leader in the production of wine, olive oil, and pottery and had preeminence in the trade of these commodities starting in the fifth century B.C. Once the new technologies became standardized and widely disseminated, however, production tended to get diffused and spread to other areas as production costs (of constant quality) became equalized and transport costs dictated location.[5] In the second century A.D. central Italy faced increasing competition from African grain, Gallic wine, and Spanish olive oil (Gunderson 1976:54). As cities grew in Gaul the size of the local market led to a shift of industry from Italy to Gaul, and the reduced transport costs via the river systems of that region made Gaul a center of commerce and industry (Rostovtzeff 1926:91, 150).

7. The bureaucracy of Empires—Egyptian, Persian, Hellenistic, and Roman—reflected the persistent tension between rulers attempting to maximize their revenues and control their constituents and agents whose interests seldom completely coincided with those of the ruler. While the evolving structure of the bureaucracy reflected the ruler's efforts to prevent the dissipation of rents by better monitoring of his agents, the efforts met at best partial success.[6]

8. The major crises of political stability came from the problem of succession. The throne of Augustus in the Roman Empire was never legally hereditary, but de facto hereditary succession

[4] The classic account is Marc Bloch's "Comment et pourquoi finit l'esclavage antique?" (1947).
[5] For a discussion of the diffusion effect of technological leadership in the ancient world in wine, olive oil, pottery, and glass blowing see Gerald Gunderson (unpublished).
[6] For example, the persistent efforts to stamp out *suffragia* (sale of offices) was never successful in the Roman Empire from Constantine to Justinian despite enormous efforts to root it out. See Jones (1966:148–50).

was the rule. Sometimes emperors, to assure succession, made their sons emperor during their own lifetime. Often, however, emperors died without having a successor, conflicts arose over the legitimate successor, or usurpers got acclaimed emperor by a part of the army; the result was a seemingly endless succession of civil wars. The Roman Empire became increasingly a military state, and the army was the decisive factor in this change. Frequently powerful generals governed through puppet emperors.[7]

IV

If the theme of the preceding section appears banal and self-evident it is important to recognize that historians and other social scientists examining the ancient world have maintained that the motive forces underlying classical and neoclassical economics are not amenable to analyzing the ancient world.[8] It is equally important to remember that the section opened by stressing that stability and change could *in large part* be explained in these terms. There remains an important residue that defies such analysis and that requires the introduction of ideological considerations.

1. The stability of early societies and Mesopotamia and throughout the millennia of the Egyptian dynasties was reinforced by the identification of the ruler with a god (and a consequence was to lower enforcement costs).

2. While population pressure and the ubiquitous struggle for control of the state to redistribute wealth and income were the major secular forces for change in the ancient world, they do not completely account for the stubborn struggle of the Jews to maintain their identity through centuries of persecution. Their persistence forced the Romans from Julius Caesar's time to grant them special dispensations. Jews could not be summoned or sued on the Sabbath, nor be conscripted into the army; while they could not build new synagogues they could repair those that were destroyed. The Christians before Constantine's conversion (312 A.D.) exhibited similar survival characteristics in the face

---

[7] For a discussion of succession under the Empire see Jones (1966: 125–28).

[8] See the discussion on Karl Polanyi in the preceding chapter and Finley (1971). However, much of Finley's study really fits economic analysis (even though he appears to be unaware that it does) and his explanation of the demise of the empire is essentially economic, as he himself admits (p. 176).

of the intermittent persecution of Roman emperors. Moreover, once Christianity was adopted the struggle over correct theological interpretation wracked the Roman empires (East and West) with dissension. The doctrine Constantine imposed on the Council of Nicaea (325 A.D.) did not bring lasting unity but was followed by endless schisms which were frequently accompanied by violence and warfare. One does not need to accept Gibbon's view of the role of Christianity in the fall of the Roman Empire to be impressed by the crucial role that Christianity and Christian doctrinal conflict played in the affairs of the late Roman empires. Gibbon's vivid portrayal of the conflict and bloodshed that ensued from the Arian controversy, the Donatist schisms, and the claim to the truth on the part of a myriad of other sects is, however, still a sober reminder of the religious zealotry that characterized the late Empire.[9]

3. The agents of change too were not all kings, emperors, or their agents; they included such persons as Rabbi Akiba ben Joseph and his pupil Rabbi Meier, who began to systemize the codes of the Jews; [10] Jesus of Nazareth; Saul of Tarsus, who was perhaps the decisive influence in the spread of Christianity; and in the seventh century A.D. Mohammed.

4. It was not simply selective material incentives that provided the basis for continuing Jewish struggle against Hellenism and led to their resistance against Vespasian at Jerusalem (70 A.D.) and Masada (72 A.D.). The spread of Christianity is equally replete with actions based on ideological conviction.

V

Few subjects have engrossed historical scholars as has the demise of the Roman Empire. Long before Gibbon's masterpiece it was a central theme of historians and it has continued to be so to this day. Moral decay, Christianity, a manpower shortage, poisoning from using lead pipes are only a few of the explanations for the decline. Most scholars have considered economic forces as critical; [11] but the ancient world has not been a province of scholars trained in economics, and much of the evidence al-

[9] See Gibbon (1946). See in particular volume I, chapter 21.
[10] See Roth (1954), chapter 12.
[11] An excellent survey is by Bernardi (1970:16–83).

leged to explain decline is either ambiguous with respect to its implications or is simply irrelevant.[12]

There are really two questions to answer about the demise of the Roman Empire: (1) why did it collapse and (2) why was it not replaced by another empire in the West. The second helps to set the scene for the first. From the period of Pompey and Julius Caesar in the Republic to the third century A.D. Roman military superiority was clear. Even in the fifth century small Roman contingents still could defeat larger barbarian armies (Jones 1966:228). But the margin of superiority was much less and the growing military sophistication of the barbarians simply reduced the Roman comparative advantage. When the relative decline in military superiority is taken together with the growing costs of bureaucratic control of the Empire, it seems clear that the result was a disequilibrium followed by increasing local autonomy and autarky.

The Roman line of defense along the Rhine and the Upper Danube imposed an increasingly heavy financial burden as time went on. Not only were larger and larger payments in gold made to barbarian groups to bribe them not to invade, but the expenses of the legions rose: the army under Diocletian may have numbered 350,000 men. At the same time, Rome was feeding 120,000 of its citizens free. While these increases in expense, and therefore demands on the tax structure, were continuing, the tax base was eroding. Those who enjoyed good political ties were freed from taxation, thereby increasing the burden on the groups who had little access to political favoritism. Increasingly, townsmen and peasants were apathetic as to which side they belonged in the struggle between Romans and barbarians (Jones 1966:368).

It is important to note that increased taxation per se does not cause economic decline if the increased spending results in more public goods. But in the case of Rome, continually increased taxation was required to provide the same amount of defense. Moreover, the shift in the burden of taxation ultimately provided such a disincentive to economic activity that it was self-defeating—eventually eroding the tax base. In effect, property rights had been so altered as no longer to result in a viable economic system.

In some respects we have been misled ever since the time of

[12] For an economist's review of this evidence see Gunderson (1968: 43–68).

Gibbon in talking about the decline of the Roman Empire. What really appears to have happened is that the events described above ultimately led to decline and what is frequently described as the Dark Ages; the process at the time does not, however, fit a neat pattern of decay. A more apt description is that the gains to individual constituents of being members of the world-wide empire called Rome had significantly declined as their taxes had grown and the protection of trade that they enjoyed had eroded. More and more individual parts of the empire found that local units provided them with more protection than they could get from the bickering, internally agonized Roman state. Thus they came to the conviction that their well-being depended upon local autonomy.[13] The short-run result was undoubtedly that they no longer bore the burdens of the Roman state; but the long-run consequences were the growth of local autarchy, a decline in trade as there was no longer protection for long-distance trade, and a fundamental shift and transformation in economic structure. Slavery was no longer profitable because there were no longer large-scale markets, and, increasingly, servile labor serfs were more suited to a world of local autonomy and very little trade.

As a corrective to the account of *decline*, we would say that the *reasons* for the Roman Empire's existence simply disappeared as its military advantages evaporated and the large-scale state no longer provided for the protection and enforcement of property rights.

The disintegration of the Roman Empire is perhaps the most striking watershed that exists in economic history. For the Western world, it presaged almost a millennium of small-scale political-economic units. Whatever advantages had existed in large-scale political-economic organization were absent or at least significantly weakened in the era that followed. It is true the Roman Empire persisted in the East until Constantinople was finally captured by the Turks in 1453 and that the Moslem world, building on the charismatic faith of the new religion, created an empire in North Africa which reached into Europe. These exceptions, and the short-lived Carolingian Empire, do not, however, gainsay the major point that the economies of scale that made possible a single empire governing the entire Mediterranean world had disappeared.

---

[13] For an elaboration of this argument see Gunderson (1968).

Chapter 10

The Rise and Decline
of Feudalism

I

The Roman Empire disappeared in the chaotic conditions of the fifth century A.D.; a more or less arbitrary historical chronology dates the end of feudalism about a millennium later, in 1500. In between these dates western Europe gradually emerged from the anarchy that followed the collapse of Roman order and developed a political-economic structure which produced sufficient order and stability to in turn induce changes leading to its breakdown and presaging the development of the nation-state—and then the economic development that has characterized the last four centuries.

It is important to point out at the outset that while the Germanic hordes that overran western Europe were relatively primitive tribal groups, the history (such as we know it) of the "dark ages" is not a recapitulation of the earlier emergence of Greek and Roman civilization. It is true that population change and the character of warfare play a decisive role in both instances. The emergence of western Europe, however, was basically conditioned by the heritage of Greco-Roman civilization, which persisted (particularly in southern Europe) and modified and ultimately shaped many of the institutional arrangements that emerged in the sixth to the tenth centuries. The manor appears to be a lineal descendant of the Roman villa and the dependent *coloni* a predecessor of the serf of the feudal world. Slavery, too, persisted into the Middle Ages. The heritage of Roman law continued and reemerged in full force in early modern Europe to shape the structure of property rights.

It was the Church that carried over the cultural heritage of the classical world to the Middle Ages; the Church was the repository of learning—a lonely center of literacy. Monasteries were frequently the most efficient farming centers in the Middle Ages.[1] The Church's role defies simple categorization. On the one hand it was the top-heavy bureaucracy of the late Roman Empire and the major center of material wealth, selling salvation in return for treasure and land. On the other hand it was the Church of asceticism, extreme austerity, hermit life, and devout missionaries such as St. Boniface, who converted inner Germany in the eighth century and suffered martyrdom in Frisia in 754 A.D.[2] In its former capacity it has the characteristics of a state, with the pope as ruler and a vast bureaucracy through which the pope amassed wealth and power and agents (archbishops and bishops) themselves siphoned off riches and became rich and powerful. Like a state, it sold protection and justice; but in addition it sold salvation and so had a unique hold over the population in a world where hell and damnation were believed to be the foredestined lot of most of the populace. This ideological conviction together with the ascetic side of the Church actively imposed a distinctive stamp on medieval life.

Northwest Europe, where feudalism gradually emerged, was a climatic contrast to the Mediterranean rim, which had been the seat of Greco-Roman civilization. The former had abundant rainfall, was thickly forested, and had heavy soils in contrast to the Mediterranean area. While viticulture moved northward up the Rhone Valley, Gaul and England were more suitable to raising livestock and cereal production than was the Mediterranean rim. Small changes in climatic conditions produced large and sometimes disastrous changes in agricultural output.

Characterizing the structure of this millennium, we can say that it was an era in which a melding of Germanic and Roman institutions was in a state of flux as a result of repeated warfare,

---

[1] For a discussion of the organization of the Benedictine Monastery at Cluny see Duby (1974:213–21).
[2] See Previtt-Orton (1966), vol. I, chapter 12.

invasions, and chaos. The Carolingian Empire emerged and under Charlemagne appeared to be a resurrection of the Roman Empire in the West; its disintegration came quickly, aided by the invasions of Vikings, Magyars, and Moslems. There was a more gradual emergence of a feudal structure of decentralized political organization, hierarchical fiscal obligations, and manorial economic structure marked by relative self-sufficiency. Economic activity revived, local and long-distance trade grew, towns developed, output from urban artisans increased, and the money economy expanded. Finally, the feudal/manorial structure disintegrated in a century characterized by famine, plague, and warfare and was gradually replaced by larger political units and a set of property rights over land, labor, and capital which varied depending upon the bargaining strength of monarchs and constituent groups.

II

The focus of this chapter is upon the emergence and decline of feudalism; population change and warfare provide the keys to explaining the associated structural transformations. Warfare was the decisive factor in the size and structure of the political unit; population change, through its effect upon the relative price of land and labor, played an equally decisive role in changing economic organization and property rights. Let me first specify the general features of the feudal/manorial system and then explore the role of population and warfare in the rise and decline of this set of institutional arrangements.

The economy of tenth-century western Europe had the following initial conditions. Law and order generally existed only within the boundaries of settled areas, a condition that severely limited trade and commerce; goods were generally much less mobile than labor because they were subject to higher transaction costs. Land was abundant but valuable only when combined with labor and protection. Labor exhibited constant costs when combined with land to produce goods because of the relative abundance of land. Because of the indivisibility of a castle there were, up to a point, economies of scale in protection. As the number of inhabitants protected by a lord grew, however, the distance of farmed lands from the castle increased and eventually led to rising costs of protection. In short, protection exhibited the U-shaped cost curve so familiar to economists. The "efficient" size of the manor was determined at the point where the marginal cost of providing protection equaled the value of the lord's share of the marginal product of labor (that is, the tax).

A local castle and knights were the keys to protection. The local lord was linked to overlords all the way up to the greatest lord—the king in a hierarchy of feudal obligations. Between the local lord and the king there might be several intermediate levels; but at each level the lower lord provided knight service for his immediate superior. Property rights under feudalism were in effect a conditional grant of tenure in return for military service. In the course of feudalism's emergence out of the centuries of chaos following the demise of Rome, the lord and his knights had become both a warrior class and a highly specialized ruling class whose survival and raison d'être depended on military prowess.[3] The ideological gloss overlying this class was chivalry, a term that brings to mind King Arthur, the Round Table, knight service, and courtly love, but in practice was more a rationale for a class that lived by violence.

The underpinnings of this structure, which provided the productive output of goods and services in return for whatever measure of protection and justice existed, were slaves, serfs, and free laborers. While some slavery persisted into the Middle Ages, the characteristic organization of the manor was built upon villeins and freemen; its structure is admirably summarized in the *Shorter Cambridge Medieval History* (pp. 424–25) as follows:

> The most characteristic version of the manorial village, although narrowest in its distribution, was the English "manor," which became the most closely organized and most durable of the type. It consisted of two once distinct elements, the economic and the administrative, and thus strove towards two intimately connected aims, the subsistence of the villagers and the lord's profit and authority. The village community lay at the basis of the whole. In a brief description only an average account, subject to countless irregularities, can be given. The normal villager (*villanus villein*) would hold a *yardland* or *virgate* of thirty acres (or its half, a bovate), distributed in scattered acre-strips in the three or two open fields of the manor, which might coincide with the village or be only a part of it. He followed the manor routine (its

---

[3] The French title of Duby's book referred to earlier in this chapter was "Guerriers et Paysans," and the original title captures the spirit of Duby's study of the seventh to the twelfth century better than the bland English title.

"custom") in the cultivation, the ploughing, sowing, and reaping, of his strips; independent husbandry was barely possible in the open fields. In each year one field in rotation out of the two or three (as the case might be) was left fallow and unenclosed for beasts to graze in; the cultivated field or fields were fenced round. His own livestock up to a stated number were free to pasture in the "waste"; he had his share of the haymeadow. Intermingled with the tenants' strips in the open fields lay the strips kept by the lord of the manor in his own hands, his *demesne.* There was a strong tendency, however, to isolate the demesne in a home-farm. In this connection arose the greater part of the labor service which the villager owed for his tenement. Each villein household owed *week-work* (one laborer) of usually three days a week on the demesne farm, which included its share of the ploughs, oxen, and implements for all kinds of work and cartage. The *cottars,* whose holdings were much smaller, owed of course less labor. At the peak periods of mowing and reaping, *boon-work* of all kinds was required in addition, and in this the freemen, socagers and others, who occupied their tenements for a rent or other terms implying free contract, took their part. A freeman, however, might hold land on villein tenure, and *vice versa.* The *assarts,* or reclamations from the waste, were commonly less burdened with the heavy dues of villeinage. Dues of all kinds, indeed pressed on both villein and freeman of the manor, render of hens, eggs, special payments, etc. The villein, besides being tied to the soil, was subject to the servile fine of *merchet (formariage)* on his daughter's marriage and the exaction of his best beast as heriot (*mainmorte*) on his death; he paid the money levy of tallage at the lord's will; his corn was ground in the lord's mill; in France the lord's oven and his winepress were seigneurial monopolies. The villein might be selected as reeve or other petty official of rural manorial economy. His condition, however, was mitigated by the growth of the custom of the manor, which at any rate fixed the exactions he labored under and secured him in his hereditary holding. Like the freeman he attended the manorial court, which declared the custom of the manor and its working. The lord of many manors would send round steward or bailiff to receive his profits and collect produce for his support in those in which he periodically resided. Besides the subsistence of the villagers, in short, their labor was to provide that of the warrior governing class and the allied ecclesiastical dignitaries, to both of whom they owed as a rule what little peace, justice, and enlightenment they had.

Like the superstructure of the feudal hierarchy, the property rights of villeins and freeholders were a conditional grant of tenure in exchange for the variety of labor services, goods in kind, and money payments described above. Three aspects of this manorial structure have been the subject of a great deal of controversy. They are the persistence of labor services as a major part of the serf and free laborers's obligation to the lord; the basic characteristics of serfdom as an institution; and the scattering of strips of the individual laborer in the open fields as described in the above quotation.

In an earlier study (1971, 1973) Robert Thomas and I provided an explanation for labor services and the characteristics of serfdom. We maintained that labor services were a result of the extremely high transaction costs of forming organized markets precluding specialization and exchange. In this situation the items desired for consumption could be realized at a lower cost by allocating labor services to produce the desired mix of goods and services. In short, it was less expensive for the lord to employ the labor dues owed to him to grow the goods he desired than to negotiate with his serfs every time he wished to consume different goods during the next season. The absence of a market made labor dues the most efficient form of economic organization, despite the incentives to shirk which were entailed in such arrangements. Shirking costs were reduced by the customs of the manor (laws) specifying the amount of labor time for various tasks, establishing a manager to oversee the serfs's efforts, and providing for the fining of detected shirkers.

With respect to the issue of serfdom as an institution we argued that it was essentially a contractual one as described above and that the most striking feature of manorialism was the nature of the enforcement of the serf-lord contract. There was no impartial third party to enforce the bargain. The manorial court, in which the lord of the manor or his representative presided as the judge, enforced the customs of the manor—the unwritten law. Yet the lord of the manor was an interested party in dealing with his serfs. Such an arrangement, it would appear, provided ample opportunities for the lord to exploit his serfs. The lord did, however, face a constraint that effectively limited his power. Labor was scarce, and lords were frequently in competition for serfs and, accordingly, unlikely to return a runaway serf. Therefore, the lord had an incentive to abide by the contractual arrangements imbedded in the custom of the manor and to interpret them with "restraint." If he failed to do so, his serfs might break the contract by fleeing the manor.

The argument we advanced both about labor services and about the contractual relationships of serfdom have produced a substantial amount of controversy from which we have benefited; in light of those criticisms and subsequent literature on the subject, I would modify both arguments.[4]

[4] See Fenoaltea (1975a).

The major criticism of our labor-services argument was that markets were far more widespread in the tenth to twelfth centuries than we implied, and, accordingly, the transaction cost of acquiring the bundle of consumption goods through markets was not a higher cost alternative than allocating labor services. Postan (1972: chapter 11) makes a convincing case for more trade in medieval England than our model would imply. Duby paints a picture of disintegration of labor services after 1100 in the northern half of the Continent in which the growth of a money economy played a critical role. Lords found it more profitable to sell freedom, to receive income from their monopoly of bread ovens and mills, and to substitute rent payments for labor services. In short, "it was wiser to abandon a 'work' which because of 'the carelessness, uselessness, listlessness, and shiftlessness' of those owing labor services was yielding very little and costing a great deal. . . . It would therefore be preferable to exchange this 'work' for the cash that was falling into the peasants' hands much more readily than in times past" (Duby:226).[5] The inference of Duby's analysis is that the growth of trade and monetary exchange in both factor and product markets occurred earlier than our analysis suggested, although his argument is not inconsistent with the view that the earlier existence of labor services could have come from high transaction costs before the growth of a money economy.[6]

The argument that Thomas and I advanced about the essential nature of serfdom is open to more vulnerable criticism, both because we put the relationship into the framework of a contract and because we did not lay sufficient stress on the one-sided nature of the arrangement. As we described the structure, it looked too much like an equal trade of protection and justice for payments in services and in kind. But Fenoaltea (1975a) was correct in pointing out that protection and justice were not really public goods, since peasants could be excluded at low cost. A more accurate perspective, and one consistent with the theory of the state advanced in Part I, was that the warrior class was analogous to the Mafia in extracting income from the peasantry.

---

[5] Chapter 8 discusses the general trend toward money payments.

[6] Fenoaltea (1975b) offers a different transaction cost argument for labor services based on the superior technology the lord used on his own demesne or alternatively a form of economic organization that was economically inefficient but maintained the lord's superior social status.

Arcadius Kahan (1973) in a thoughtful discussion of serfdom stresses that carrying over the modern-day notion of contract to the serf-lord relationship is imposing a modern-day concept which is misleading. The serf was bound to the lord and his actions and movements were severely constrained by his status; no voluntary agreement was involved. Nevertheless, it is crucial to reemphasize a key point of our analysis; namely, that it was the changing opportunity cost of lords and serfs at the margin which changed manorialism and eventually led to its demise.

The persistence of scattered strips has provoked a number of transaction cost arguments to explain the evident inefficiency of an individual peasant working a large number of separated strips of land scattered throughout the three fields of the typical manor. Two types of explanations have developed. In one it was the result of decisions by the peasant village and, variously, a response to the high risk of concentrated land holding—that is, an insurance scheme—(McClosky 1976), a consequence of a dual production function which required that the large fields be maintained as a unit in order to realize the scale economies in animal pasture—and therefore was insisted upon by the village ruling unit—(Dahlman 1980), or the consequence of an egalitarian attitude of a majority of the village members (Georgescu-Roegen 1969).

A different explanation stresses the exploitative relationship of rulers to ruled and argues that the persistence of scattered strips stemmed from the efforts of lords to monitor the output of villein and free laborers in order to be able to reduce shirking (Hall, unpublished) and to adjust the size of the landholding of peasants to the bare minimum and thereby increase the demesne (and income) of the lord (Kula 1976).

The diversity of conditions and the wide variety of arrangements that existed have not made it possible to discriminate effectively amongst these alternative explanations for the persistence of strips. There is evidence both supporting and contradicting each. However, given the model of the state advanced in Part I, it would have been a rational response of the lord to have monitored output in order to increase his income at the expense of the peasant—if the opportunity cost of the lord made this a feasible alternative.[7]

---

[7] The late serfdom in eastern Europe appears to fit this pattern and is the heart of Witold Kula's important study.

III

Of the two major forces for change in the millennium, population and military technology and organization, our knowledge of the first is fragmentary at best. Scholars generally believe that population was declining in the late Roman Empire. This decline probably accelerated in the sixth century with the outbreak of bubonic plague, which appears to have remained endemic well into the seventh century. If population began to expand thereafter, as Duby (1974:71) believes, it must have been very slow given the chaotic conditions that persisted.

But feudalism provided a measure of order and security in this chaotic world and led to a concomitant expansion of both population and economic activity. Northwest Europe was still largely forested and had abundant room for population growth. As an expanding population led eventually to crowding and to diminishing returns in local areas, the logical outcome was colonization: the creation of new manors carved out of the wilderness. A frontier movement developed. New manors spread across northwest Europe and increased the potential gains from trade by reducing the unsettled areas between manors that had harbored brigands, by encouraging the growth of towns where specialized skills could develop to produce manufactured goods, and by settling areas with significantly different factor endowments. The wine of Burgundy, Bordeaux, and the Moselle, the wool of England, the metal products of Germany, the wool cloth from Flanders, the fish and timber from the Baltic all betoken different factor endowments in both resources and human capital investment. In short, the frontier settlement movement resulted in reduced transaction costs of trade, and gains from trade increased.

Towns established their own body of law and gradually their own commercial courts. While early enforcement of town law may have been by ostracism, there subsequently developed the police power of a local political unit. As merchant codes became established, they were recognized over a wider area—the Chart D'Oleron (near La Rochelle, France), for example, during the twelfth century was widely recognized in Flanders, Holland, and England.

Within the towns, guilds developed to serve the needs of local manufacturers as well as merchants. The property rights surrounding the production of non-agricultural goods were inextricably tied to the guilds, which in their early form were voluntary associations but which soon became a legally recognized part of the state. Guilds provided an early set of rules with private policing for the protection of the property of their members, but by the end of the twelfth century they had become a part of the political administration in the Italian cities.

General diminishing returns to a growing population in Western Europe appear to have set in in the twelfth century. In turn, relative factor scarcities changed: labor became less valuable; land, more. The rising value of land led to efforts to provide for exclusive ownership and transferability. Within the manor the common fields would tend to be overexploited if every resident had equal access. The response to this exploitation was to embody in the customs of the manor regulations which restricted access. Stinting arrangements that limited the number of animals a family could pasture on the common became customary. Thirteenth-century England witnessed the development of an extensive body of land law, the beginnings of enclosure, and, finally, formalization of the ability to alienate land. Similar developments took place in Burgundy, Champagne, and France. The rising value of land increased the incentives to alter property rights so the now increasingly scarce resource could be used more efficiently.[8]

The twelfth and thirteenth centuries were a period of a flowering of international commerce. There is not sufficient space in this chapter to trace the institutional arrangements that were innovated in the development of organized product and factor markets to replace local self-sufficiency and barter. The Champagne Fairs, the burgeoning Mediterranean trade of Venice, Genoa, and other Italian cities, the urbanization of metal and cloth trades of Flanders were only a few of the major manifestations of commercial expansion of the era. From the viewpoint of this chapter the most interesting aspect was the shift in the protection of property rights from private policing by voluntary groups to the state. Everywhere kings and princes were guaranteeing (for a fee) safe conduct to traveling merchants, protecting alien merchants and providing them with exclusive trading

---

[8] A more thorough discussion of the alteration in property rights in land and labor is described in North and Thomas (1973).

privileges, enforcing the judgments of commercial courts, and granting or delegating property rights to the burgeoning towns.

There can be little doubt that there was substantial productivity increase in the non-agricultural sector as a result of reducing transaction costs; nevertheless, this sector still accounted for only a tiny fraction of total economic activity. Population growth was causing the prices of agricultural goods to rise relative to other goods, and real wages were falling. A growing population coupled with diminishing returns was reducing the standard of living of most people. Agricultural production was affected: relatively fewer animals and relatively more cereal grains were raised. This change was reflected in the diets of the peasant as carbohydrates replaced protein. The population of western Europe was approaching a subsistence level, and the margin of existence became precarious. The famines that enveloped much of western Europe in the early 14th century demonstrate this, and they were a harbinger of worse things to come. The plague in 1347 became endemic, returning again and again so that probably population fell for a century. Trade and commerce, as a consequence, declined in volume. Western Europe was experiencing a Malthusian crisis.

In the non-agricultural sector the most striking result of this crisis was the emerging strength of guilds organized to protect local artisans in response to rapidly declining markets. The strength of the guilds in preserving local monopolies against encroachments from outside competition was frequently reinforced by the coercive power of kings and great lords. On a large scale the Hanseatic League represented such a defensive alliance of cities to protect their shrinking markets from the competition of rival cities.

In the agricultural sector there was a return to an era of abundant land and scarce labor. Everywhere poorer land went out of production; there was a shift from crops to livestock production; and real wages rose, and rents fell. The relative bargaining strength shifted from the lords to the peasants. The opportunity cost of peasants improved as escape to towns (which resulted in freedom after a year and a day) offered an alternative to the oppression of a local lord. Despite repeated efforts to regulate maximum wages, competition among landlords led to increasingly liberal terms for tenants as well as to rising wages; as a consequence, the master-servant aspect of serfdom gave way to recognition of copyhold rights and an end to servile obligations (although it was not until 1666 in England that they were legally swept away). Freemen had already escaped the jurisdiction of the manorial court in England in the thirteenth century and come under the aegis of the king's court. Gradually villeins also came under the king's justice, and the manorial court slowly lost jurisdiction. The great contraction that took place during the fourteenth and fifteenth centuries did cause some reversion back to the Dark Ages in terms of chaotic conditions and ubiquitous warfare, which made property rights increasingly insecure. But trade, while diminished, did not disappear; markets survived and with them a money economy.

The changes described in the previous pages of this section took place throughout western Europe. There were regional variations in population pressure and in the incidence of famine and of the plague, but to one degree or another all of western Europe felt the changing relative factor scarcities. However, the response in terms of evolving institutional arrangements and property rights differed throughout western Europe. In order to understand the diverging pattern of adjustment to these changes we must turn to the other factor contributing to change in the medieval world, the technology and organization of warfare.

IV

The previous chapter ended on the theme that the economies of scale associated with military organization, which permitted large states and order over a substantial territory, had either disappeared or been substantially weakened in the late Roman Empire. During the ensuing millennium a warrior class that lived by pillage, raids, and ransom dominated the scene. This class was only briefly constrained by the Carolingian Empire, and even the relative increase in protection and order that emerged with feudalism did not fundamentally change this way of life. Warfare was typically small scale but ubiquitous. By the end of the era, however, the character of warfare was basically altered and this warrior class had become obsolete.

The chaos of western Europe was briefly interrupted when Charles Martel turned back the Arabs at Poitiers in 753. By 800 Charlemagne had annexed or conquered a vast area, from the borders of Islamic Spain to Saxony, Bavaria, and Lombard Italy; on Christmas Day of that year he was crowned emperor by the pope in St. Peter's Cathedral. The subsequent Carolingian Renaissance was a striking contrast to the earlier "dark ages," but its partition and breakdown in the ninth century were convincing evidence that the viable size of the political-economic unit was small. No centralized administration and fiscal structure emerged, and it was in effect Charlemagne's genius that briefly held his empire together. Internal warfare was abetted by partible inheritance; dissolution hastened by the assaults from three directions of Vikings, Moslems, and Magyars.[9] Vikings appeared off the coast of England in 786, Ireland in 795, and Gaul in 799. London was sacked in 841, and Vikings moved up the rivers in their long boats to attack such widely separated cities as Rouen in the north and Toulouse in the south. Moslem corsairs attacked Christian ships in the Mediterranean and raided from southern Italy to Provence. Hungarian horsemen following the ancient Roman roads raided Bremen in 915 and reached as far west as Orleans in 937.

A distant king was of little protection against these marauding bands. The viable response was the fixed fortification and the heavily armored knight. The latter's comparative advantage over infantry was immensely increased by the diffusion of the stirrup which provided the leverage for the armored knight on horseback to use the combination of human and animal muscle to destroy opposition (White 1962). The hierarchical decentralized structure of feudalism outlined above was the result. There was the revival of local order and economic expansion described earlier in the chapter, with the addition of the Vikings who had settled into northern Europe and became a part of the structure.

The military result was a stalemate which reinforced the persistence of small political-economic units. The castle was impregnable to all but the most persistent and well-financed military excursions that could afford the prolonged siege to starve out the inhabitants; the character of warfare was typically small scale between heavily armored knights.

But if the technology of warfare solidified the feudal structure, the resultant revival of economic activity gradually undermined it. The growth of a money economy led to scutage—a money

---

[9] From a description of the breakdown of the Carolingian Empire. See Previtt-Orton (1966), vol. I, chapter 14.

payment in lieu of knight service. Kings could now hire mercenaries in lieu of relying on forty days a year of knight service. The size of a king's army now depended on his purse. In the long run the de facto power of vassals, who had always posed the threat of becoming militarily more powerful than the king, was decreased. But in the short run—through the fifteenth century—greater warfare and chaos attended the growing market for mercenaries, who once organized into existing bands became the scourge of western Europe as they discovered the profitability of extortion, ransom, and plunder. Between periods when they were hired by one or another side in a war they lived off such profitable opportunities.

Between the thirteenth and the end of the fifteenth centuries there occurred a major series of technological changes in military warfare.[10] The pike, the longbow, the cannon, and eventually the musket in warfare on land and improvements in naval architecture combined with the cannon at sea. At Courtrai in 1302 Flemish pikemen demonstrated that heavily armored cavalry were vulnerable to the pike-phalanx; at Crecy the combination of English longbowmen with dismounted knights routed the French as it did again at Poitiers and again at Agincourt. In the fifteenth century (at Formigny in 1450 and Castillion in 1453) the French turned the tables with field artillery that devastated the English ranks before their archers could get in range. Moreover the development of the siege cannon destroyed the centuries-old impregnability of the castle; the French in 1449–1450 recaptured most of the fortified sites of the English in Normandy.

We have seen that mercenary specialists ranging from Swiss pikemen to English archers were effective and profitable in the late Middle Ages. They were dangerous not only to the enemy but to their employer when during those periods they were unemployed and unpaid they ravaged the countryside. It was in direct response to such ravaging by hired mercenaries that Charles VII of France created the first standing army in western Europe in 1445.[11] The Compagnies d'Ordonnance were eventually made

---

[10] For a discussion of land warfare in the fifteenth century see *Cambridge Medieval History* (1969), vol. VIII, chapter 21. For a discussion of naval warfare see Cipolla (1966).

[11] The Turkish Janisseries had already demonstrated the superiority of a standing army in Eastern Europe.

up of twelve thousand troops paid at the rate of ten livre tournois per month for a man at arms and four or five livre tournois for each of his "retinue."

Whether the development of an exchange economy was a sufficient condition for expanding the optimum scale of warfare or technological innovations augmented the scale may still be argued. What cannot be argued is that it expanded. As a consequence, the conditions for political survival were drastically altered. Survival now required not only a larger army, but a trained, disciplined fighting force supported by costly equipment in the form of cannons and muskets. The age of the armored knight with lance passed; the age of chivalry was ended. Warfare on land and at sea (where the size and armaments of naval ships increased dramatically) had dramatically altered the size of the financial resources necessary for survival.[12]

At this point we can usefully pause in our historical narrative to offer an analogy from economic theory. Let us examine the case of a competitive industry with a large number of small firms. Introduce a change which leads to significant economies of scale relative to the size of the market so that the efficient-size firm must become larger. The path from the old competitive equilibrium to a new (and perhaps unstable) oligopoly solution will be as follows. The original small firms must increase in size or combine, or they will be forced into bankruptcy. The competition for survival will be fierce. The inevitable result is a smaller number of large firms of optimum size. Even then the equilibrium is likely to be unstable. In an oligopoly there will be endless efforts toward collusion and price fixing, but there are always advantages for an individual firm to cheat on the arrangement. The result is periods of collusion interrupted by eras of cutthroat competition.

If we compare the above description with the political world of the late Middle Ages, we find remarkable similarities. Between 1200 and 1500 the many political units of western Europe went through numerous conflicts, alliances, and combinations as the local manor gave way to the emerging nation-state. These centuries witnessed intrigue and warfare on an ever-expanding scale. While the size of states sometimes increased, the critical

[12] See Bean (1973) and comments by Ringrose and Roehl (1973).

factor was the ability to increase tax revenues rather than simply to increase the size of the political unit. The contending nation-states faced enormously growing expenses. A year of warfare represented at least a fourfold increase in the costs of government—and most years were characterized by war, not peace. Kings who in the past had lived on their own could no longer do so. Monarchs were continuously beset by fiscal crises and growing indebtedness and often were forced to desperate expedients. The spectre of state bankruptcy was a recurring threat, and bankruptcy was often a reality.

As late as 1157 the Count of Flanders received a significant share of his revenues in kind. Income in kind shows up in French crown receipts well into the thirteenth century. During the feudal period it had been customary for the king's court to move from one part of the country to another to consume the goods and services in kind. With the growth of a money economy, the revenues became increasingly monetized. They were, however, declining during the fourteenth and fifteenth centuries as a result of the fall in land rents due to a declining population—at precisely the time when more revenue was required for survival.

In the face of declining revenues and growing financial needs, the princes of Europe faced an ever-worsening dilemma. Custom and tradition set limits to the exactions they could obtain from lesser lords. As the Magna Carta amply attests, a king who stepped over the boundary of accepted custom faced the possibility of revolt. Many of the king's vassals were almost as powerful as he (in fact, the Dukes of Burgundy were at this time much more powerful than the kings of France), and certainly in concert they were more powerful. There was frequently more than one contender for the throne. Even in the absence of an active contender, powerful vassals posed an imminent threat either to overthrow the king or to collaborate with an outside invasion, as the Burgundians did with England against the French crown. Increased taxation could place a European Crown in jeopardy.

There was the possibility of borrowing money—and indeed this was a major source of meeting short-term fiscal crises brought on by war. Since a prince could not be sued for debt, the lender exacted a high interest rate, usually disguised to avoid usury laws. As compensation for the high risk, the loan often was backed by collateral (frequently it was crown lands, the crown jewels, farming of the customs, or certain monopoly concessions). Default was common. Edward III ruined the Peruzzi and Bardi, and at a later date Charles V and Phillip II ruined the Genoese and the Fuggers.

A king could rely on loans to tide the government through a war; but, facing the awesome task of repayment, he required fiscal revenues. The necessity to establish a regular source of revenue to repay war loans influenced and then determined the relationship between the state and the private sector.[13]

The degrees of freedom of the ruler varied widely. He could confiscate wealth. He might be able to exact a forced loan when he could convince his subjects that they were threatened by attack or invasion. He could grant privileges—property rights and the protection of property rights—in return for revenue. Clearly there were economies to be gained by the state taking over from manorial lords the protection of property rights. As trade and commerce grew beyond the boundaries of the manor and the town, the farmers, merchants, and shippers found that the private costs of protection could be reduced by a larger coercive authority. The basis for a mutually advantageous exchange existed between the private sector and the state. Since individuals in the private sector always had the free rider incentive to evade a tax, the state had of necessity to discover a source of income that was measurable and easy to collect. In contrast to present-day tax structures, there was no institutional structure available to undertake such activities. The emerging nation-state thus sought revenues from economic activities that were relatively easy to tax. A number of possibilities were open to a ruler.

Where foreign trade was a significant part of the economy, the costs of measuring the extent of trade and of collection of the tax were typically low—particularly so in the case of waterborne trade, since the number of ports was limited. But where trade was primarily local within a town or small geographical area or

---

[13] It also played a critical role in the relative decline of the Church, which possessed the major accumulation of wealth in the Middle Ages. As noted earlier in this chapter, the Church had been a competitor state throughout this period and played a central part in the endless intrigue; but as emerging secular political units searched for revenue, taxation and confiscation of the income and wealth of the Church was an increasingly tempting option. The threat of ex-communication by the pope appeared to be a lesser evil than destruction at the hands of a rival.

primarily internal to the economy, the costs of measurement and collection were typically much higher. Foreign trade was thus a more attractive source of potential revenue than domestic trade.

Another alternative, frequently employed at this time, was to grant certain property rights to groups who could pay for them, or to pass laws prohibiting practices that threatened government revenues. Here we can no more than list some of the multitudinous (and ingenuous) ways by which princes traded property rights for revenue. The right to alienate land was granted to free peasants in England in 1290 (by the Statute of Quia Emptores) and to nobles in 1327, because the king would otherwise lose revenue by the practice of subinfeudation. Later, the Statute of Wills (1540) was enacted to permit inheritance because the crown was losing revenue through the extensive device of "uses." Similar laws were enacted in France, Champagne, and Anjou. Such laws not only prevented loss of revenue but allowed the state to tax land transfers. Towns were granted trading and monopoly privileges in return for annual payments, and alien merchants were granted legal rights and exemption from guild restrictions, again in return for revenue. Guilds were granted exclusive monopoly privileges in return for payments to the crown, and customs duties were established on exports and imports in return for monopoly privileges.

In most cases the crown was initially forced to grant to "representative" bodies (Parliament, Estates General) control over tax rates in return for the revenue they voted. In some instances these representative bodies retained this privilege; in others, they lost it. This last point requires special emphasis and further elaboration since it is the key to future differential patterns of development which we observe within Europe. What did the ruler have to give up in order to get the essential tax revenues for survival? That is, what determined his bargaining strength *vis-à-vis* his constituents? The argument advanced above suggests that three basic considerations influenced the bargaining process: (1) the extent of the potential gains to constituents created by the state taking over protection of property rights from local lords or voluntary associations; (2) the ability of rivals of the state to provide the same service; and (3) the structure of the economy which determined the benefits and costs to the government of various types of taxation.

In the next chapter we shall examine how these three factors effected the type of government that emerged in France, Spain, the Netherlands, and England and how the type of government influenced the economic growth of these nations.

Chapter 11

Structure and Change in Early Modern Europe

I

The two centuries from 1450 to 1650 were marked in Europe first by extended exploration, exploitation, trade, and settlement to the New World and the Indies, and second by a structural transformation, of crisis proportions, of political-economic units. The consequence of the expansion was ultimately to integrate the rest of the world with the western European nations; but its shorter-run consequences were a widening of the market and increased opportunities for profit and, in turn, political pressure for structural changes to realize those opportunities. The resultant structural transformation produced the essential conditions that underlie the economic growth of the past three centuries.[1]

II

Henri Pirenne, writing in the early twentieth century, argued that European development during the Dark Ages had been fundamentally influenced by Islamic forces that had hedged-in

[1] An equally important force for secular change was the beginning of modern science in these centuries, but since the economic consequences of the development of scientific disciplines come much later it will be treated in subsequent chapters.

Europe, stifled trade, and ultimately reoriented Europe away from the Mediterranean toward the Atlantic (1939). Historians have advanced a similar argument to explain a later pattern of exploration and settlement; here it was the conquest of Constantinople by the Turks in 1453 that closed off the spice trade with the Orient, leading the Portuguese (and others) to search for an alternative route to the Indies.

Neither hypothesis has survived critical scrutiny untarnished. Trade continued throughout the Mediterranean basin during the Dark Ages, albeit at a greatly reduced level; and the spice trade continued through the Levant after the Turks captured the gateway to the oriental trade. Both hypotheses, however, contain an important element in an explanation: the alteration of relative prices. In the case of the Pirenne thesis, the Mediterranean trade became more insecure *relative* to other potential trades; in the case of the spice trade, the Turkish conquest raised the potential rate of return of discovering alternative routes to the Indies.

The motives that led Prince Henry of Portugal to undertake the exploration of the African coast were to "serve God and grow rich." It would be a mistake to underestimate the zealous ideological cast to this materialistic endeavor, since the service of God throughout this era constrained the range of choices of the participants (at least in the short run). But the search for gold, spices, silver, slaves, and more prosaic trade goods was the fundamental driving force that led the Portuguese, Spanish, Dutch, English, and French to round the Cape of Good Hope (called the Cape of Storms for good reason); to rediscover America; to capture and pillage the Mayan and Incan civilizations; to search for the Northwest Passage; to fight interminable wars with each other, as well as with Moslems and native populations. By the middle of the seventeenth century the general contours of the world had been discovered (or rediscovered) and patterns of colonial settlement having lasting consequences for subsequent development had been established. A papal bull put forth an imaginary dividing line which gave Brazil to Portugal and the rest of Central and South America to Spain. The Dutch, while pre-eminent in trade, had only temporary success in ousting the Portuguese from the Brazilian sugar coast and in maintaining a foothold (New Amsterdam) in North America. However, their efficiency in shipping and trade played a major role in shaping the external policies of France and, particularly, England. The English, relatively latecomers in the search for profitable trade ventures, gradually developed a system of colonial settlement and preference trade between its West Indian and North American colonies. This system was designed defensively to exclude the Dutch (and others) and positively to integrate the colonies and the mother country. The division of costs and benefits of the Navigation Acts, as between the colonies and the mother country, is the subject of a substantial literature.[2] In the Far East the superiority of Western sailing ships and cannons established Portuguese, Dutch, and English trade. As Cipolla makes clear, their trade was not confined simply to east-west trade, but in addition they were "middlemen in a vast network of commercial activity among Asian nations . . ." (1965:136).

In terms of the framework advanced in Part I, there were two fundamental consequences of this European expansion and integration of the rest of the world into the Atlantic nations: the institutions and property rights carried over from the mother country shaped the subsequent development of the colonial areas, and the pattern of trade and flow of productive factors (labor and capital) helped shape the pattern of development of the Atlantic nations themselves.

The contrast between the economic organization of the Spanish, Portuguese, and French settlements on the one hand and the English on the other stemmed from a combination of the property rights carried over from the mother country and the factor endowments of the colonial area. The Spanish encomienda system in Mexico substituted the overlordship of Spanish encomenderos for Aztec rulers. In return for "protection and justice" the new rulers received tribute and forced labor. The Portuguese sugar colonies were built by slaves imported from Africa. The French attempted to settle French Canada in a pattern mirroring feudal land organization of the mother country—with the predictable result that it provided little attraction to settlers.

English settlement, coming a century after Spanish and Portuguese settlement, mirrored the changing structure of property rights emerging in that country. While the Virginia Company and some of the other colonial ventures started out by working land in common, the disastrous consequences quickly led to

[2] For a survey of the literature see Walton (1971).

modification and the de facto development of private property rights in land. The scarcity of labor produced diverse results in the different colonies, depending on the resource endowments. The indenture system initially provided an attractive opportunity for the poor to pay for their passage in return for a fixed period of obligatory labor. In the South, where relatively large-scale tobacco, rice, and indigo plantations developed, indentured servants were replaced by slaves. In contrast, the New England and middle colonies were characterized by individual land holdings and the early development of an economy based on agriculture, fishing, and shipping.

The development of America is the subject of a subsequent chapter. The focus of this chapter is upon the emerging national economies of western Europe; the above-described expansion influenced each of them. For the Portuguese and the Spanish it initially meant riches and economic opportunity, but ultimately these gains were to prove illusory as the Spanish sank into stagnation. For the Dutch it meant an economy built on their comparative advantage in shipping and trade; for the English the colonies became a part of an empire. We must examine the structural crisis of the seventeenth century to see the differential pattern of European development.

III

There is widespread agreement that there was a crisis in the seventeenth century but no agreement on its sources or character. It was an era marked by devastating wars, such as the Thirty Years' War in Germany; falling wages; widespread social upheaval; and religious strife. By the time it was over the structure of some of the political-economic units had been radically transformed. For the Marxist the seventeenth century is part of a larger puzzle in the dialectical process of development, since feudalism appears to have died by 1500, but capitalism, traditionally associated with the Industrial Revolution, does not emerge for almost three centuries. Because the exogenous variable in the Marxian system is technological change, which leads to the emergence of new classes, the Marxists have a three-century void. Their explanation is that it took the emerging bourgeois class almost three centuries to come to political power and create the essential property rights which led to the Industrial

Revolution. The English and French revolutions were the critical breakthroughs that opened the gates of modern capitalism.[3]

For Hugh Trevor-Roper the crisis was one of an overburdening parasitic bureaucracy with a consequent tax burden that produced strain, casualty, and bankruptcy when Europe ceased expanding in the seventeenth century.[4] There can be no doubt there was a fiscal crisis, but as J. H. Elliot points out in his comments on Trevor-Roper, it was engendered by war rather than the extravagance of Renaissance courts.[5] Thus the Marxian argument appears to fit the evidence better, as it was a structural crisis over control of the state which ultimately led to the emergence of a set of property rights encouraging modern economic growth. The Marxian emphasis on technology has led Marxians astray, however, since the technology of the Industrial Revolution followed rather than preceded the structural changes. While gunpowder, the compass, better ship design, printing, and paper all played a part in the expansion of western Europe, the results were widely divergent. The technological change associated with the Industrial Revolution required the *prior* development of a set of property rights, which raised the private rate of return on invention and innovation. The explanation advanced below begins with population change and is built on the interplay between changing economic opportunities and the fiscal requirements of the state.

IV

The late medieval world was characterized by cycles. The population growth of the preceding two centuries was followed, between 1300 or 1350 and 1475, by famine, pestilence, and economic contraction; a second cycle of expansion, 1475–1600, was followed by a contraction during the seventeenth century. The crisis of the seventeenth century spread with differential results throughout Europe. England and the Netherlands were barely, if at all, affected, while France and especially Spain suffered extensively. England and the Netherlands had escaped the Malthusian crisis as output grew faster than population; France, while

[3] See Hobsbawm, "The Crisis of the Seventeenth Century" in Aston, ed. (1967).

[4] "The General Crisis of the Seventeenth Century" in Aston, ed. (1967).

[5] See the comments by J. H. Elliot following the Trevor-Roper essay.

not stagnating, was clearly falling relatively behind England; and Spain, previously the most powerful nation in Europe, fell into a state of absolute decline.[6]

The reason for the differential growth rates among the merging nation-states of Europe during the seventeenth century is to be found in the nature of the property rights that had developed in each. The type of property rights established was the outgrowth of the particular way each nation-state developed. The interplay between the government and its subjects with respect *to the expansion of the state's* right to tax was particularly important. We have seen that each emerging nation-state was desperate to obtain more revenue. It is the manner in which this was accomplished that was crucial to the state's economy, for in each case a modification of property rights was involved.

In the case of the two successful countries, the property rights established provided incentives to use factors of production more efficiently and directed resources into inventive and innovating activity. In the case of the less successful countries, the absolute level of taxation and the specific forms by which fiscal revenues were obtained resulted in personal incentives to do just the opposite. This section briefly surveys how such a divergence came about.

Let us begin with France. The emergence of a nation-state in France began as a response to the devastation caused by the Hundred Years' War. English armies occupied parts of France, marauding bands of unpaid soldiers preyed upon the countryside, and the great nobles engaged in seemingly endless squabbles. France was a country in name only when Charles VII took the throne in 1422. He faced the awesome task of reestablishing law and order and of recovering more than half his claimed kingdom from the English and Burgundians.

Such a task required a large and growing crown revenue. A representative body called the Estates General had been established to vote the crown special levies to meet emergencies. Charles VII repeatedly had to ask the Estates General for new revenues during the early years of his reign. The amounts that he could ask for and expect to receive were limited by the levels of taxation in competing English-occupied France and Burgundy. Charles VII used his fiscal revenues effectively, making an ad-

---

[6] This section is drawn from North and Thomas (1973) Part III. For a more detailed discussion of the economies of western Europe see De Vries (1976).

vantageous peace with the Burgunidans, pushing the English back, and clearing the countryside of outlaws. As a consequence of his increased power, he began to treat as his prerogative the regular leveling of taxes which had first been voted as special ones by the Estates General. The fervent desire of the Estates General to bring an end to chaos within France allowed the crown to seize the right to tax without the consent of the governed, a right that would outlast the emergency that created it.

The ability to enforce property rights effectively, the removal or neutralizing of local rivals, and the acquisition of the unconstrained power to tax gave the French crown the exclusive right to grant or alter property rights. The rivalry between the emerging nation-states caused a continuing need for ever-more fiscal revenues. The crown sought revenue wherever it could be found. The trading of property rights for tax revenue was a fruitful short-run solution that had deleterious long-run consequences.

The kingdom of France as it emerged after the Hundred Years' War was not a national economy even if it was becoming a nation-state. The economy was composed of many regional and local economies. The crown was forced to tax each region specifically—a task which required a large bureaucracy and the assistance of existing voluntary organizations. With the decline of economic activity in the fourteenth and fifteenth centuries, guilds had become a growing power in the towns of France. They attempted to protect the shrinking local markets from outside competition by employing monopoly restrictions. The crown found in these guilds an already developed infrastructure for raising fiscal revenue. The crown strengthened the guilds by guaranteeing a local monopoly in return for a fee. The crown in effect traded monopoly rights in local areas for an assured source of revenue. This fiscal system was expanded and elaborated under Colbert in the seventeenth century. Potential rivals within France (the nobility and the clergy) were neutralized by being excluded from taxation. A large administrative bureaucracy was created to control the fiscal system. Once such a bureaucracy was in place, it was relatively easy to use it to regulate the economy, as the system implemented by Colbert demonstrates.[7]

---

[7] This system is discussed in the classic sources of Hecksher (1955), Nef (1957), as well as in North and Thomas (1973), chapter 10. For a recent analysis see Eklund and Tollison (1980a).

The logic and consequences of this fiscal system can be readily interpreted in terms of the analytical framework of this study. With a reduction in the power of external and internal rivals the crown increased its ability to exact income from its constituents but was constrained by the costs of measuring wealth and income which were predominantly derived from local and regional production and trade. The system of trading property rights for revenue provided a solution but required an elaborate agency structure to monitor the system. The resultant bureaucracy not only siphoned off part of the resultant income but became an entrenched force in the French political structure. While revenue to the crown and bureaucracy increased, the consequence for productivity was to discourage economic growth. The French economy remained regional in nature and as a result the gains from a growing market were sacrificed. The benefits of competition were lost to numerous local monopolies that not only exploited their legal position but also discouraged innovation. The benefits of improving the efficiency of markets were in France sacrificed to the fiscal needs of the state. As a consequence, France did not escape the Malthusian crisis of the seventeenth century.

Neither did Spain. Earlier in Spanish history when land was still abundant, the wool industry had developed. Sheepherders moved their flocks between the highlands in summer and the lowlands in winter. In 1273 the local sheepherders guilds, called *mestas,* were consolidated by Alfonso X into a single guild called the Honorable Assembly of the Mesta of the Shepherds of Castile.

> The motive was merely one of the king's financial embarrassments; he realized that it was much easier to assess taxes on livestock than on men and formed the mestas into an organization that would provide considerable sums to the monarchy. In exchange for these taxes the herders wrested a series of privileges from Alfonso X, the most important of which was the extension of supervision over all migratory flocks, including stray animals, in the whole kingdom of Castile. This supervisory function was gradually extended, in time, even to "permanent" sheep pastured in local mestas and to the "riberiegas," animals which were pastured along the river banks within the district of a particular town. (Vives (1969:25)

In return for being the principal source of revenue of the crown to finance the war with the Moors, the mesta was given expanded privileges to move sheep back and forth across Spain; in consequence, the development of efficient property rights in land was thwarted for centuries.

The Council of the Mesta by the sixteenth century had become a privileged institution, with protected routes across the kingdom, with its own itinerant legal staff and armed guards accompanying the annual flocks, with authority to override conflicting interests, to prevent the enclosure of fields in their path, empowered to engage in collective bargaining with the most powerful landowners, exempt from the payment of the *alcabala* and from municipal sales taxes. It had judicial powers and economic prerogatives which placed it outside the reach of other institutions. (Schwartzman 1951:237)

It was under Ferdinand and Isabella that a nation-state emerged, after centuries of strife with the Moors and an almost ceaseless internal warfare among feudal lords. Weary of internal chaos, the representative body of Spain, the Castile Cortes, surrendered control over taxation to the crown. Between 1470 and 1540 tax revenues grew twenty-twofold and, as in France, the granting of monopoly rights by the state was a major source of income with similar—if more damaging—consequences.

With Charles V's ascension to the throne in 1516, the great era of Spanish hegemony over Europe began. It was initially a period of great prosperity with enormous increases in fiscal revenues from Aragon, Naples, and Milan, but particularly from the prosperous Low Countries, which in some years exceeded by tenfold revenues from all other sources, including treasure from the Indies. However, increased revenues were matched by increased expenditures as Charles V maintained the largest (and best-trained) army in Europe, as well as a large navy. Charles V and his successor Philip II were required to spend more each year to maintain this empire. When revenues from the Netherlands stopped with the revolt of the Low Countries and the treasure from the New World declined, the need became especially critical. Guilds in the towns were granted exclusive local monopolies for new revenues. Property was confiscated, and noble status, which was exempt from taxation, was sold. Even such desperate expedients could not keep the crown from bankruptcy. Bankruptcies occurred in 1557, 1575, 1596, 1607, 1627, and 1647.

As a consequence of monopoly, high rates of taxation, and confiscation, trade and commerce declined. The only areas safe from the crown were in the church, government services, or the nobility. The widely reported observation that the hidalgos had an aversion for trade and commerce and a preference for careers in the church, army, or government suggests that they were rational men. The structure of property rights that evolved in response to the fiscal policies of the government simply discouraged individuals from undertaking many productive activities and instead encouraged socially less-productive activities that were sheltered from the reach of the state.

The experiences of France and Spain were similar in many ways. In both cases the initial desire on the part of the people for protection and the enforcement of basic property rights was so great that the state was able to acquire control over the power to tax. The need for ever-larger fiscal revenues caused both states essentially to trade property rights for fees. The property rights that were granted did not foster efficiency—rather the opposite. Spain even more than France suffered the consequences during the seventeenth century.

While France and Spain were suffering setbacks throughout the seventeenth century, the population and income per capita of the United Provinces experienced a sustained increase. As a consequence, the Dutch achieved a political importance all out of proportion to their small size. The success of the Dutch is all the more interesting because it was a country with relatively few resources. The Dutch overcame their lack of resources by developing an efficient economic organization relative to their larger rivals and by taking advantage of the expanding world trade associated with the discoveries and trade in the Indies and Americas.

The United Provinces had been the possession of the Duke of Burgundy until by inheritance they passed to the king of Spain. Their rulers, whether Burgundian or Hapsburg, actively discouraged the existence of monopoly privileges in the established cloth towns, such as Bruges and Ghent. While opposed by these towns, the rulers were supported by new centers of industry and commerce that were springing up, the result of a reviving international trade. The efficiency of these new areas was due in large part to the absence of guild and trade restrictions. As a consequence, the Low Countries in general and Antwerp in particular rose to unparalleled importance in industry and commerce.

The fact that the rulers of this area discouraged restrictive practices and actively encouraged competition and the growth of trade and commerce may appear peculiar in the light of opposite developments in France and Spain. The answer to this puzzle lies in the nature of the major economic activities of the area. The Low Countries were the natural center of European trade. Their initial comparative advantage in the manufacture of cloth had led to the development of an international market place where a wide range of goods was traded.

In 1463 Philip the Good had created a representative body, called the States General, which enacted laws and held the authority to vote taxes for the ruler. The make-up of this assembly favored legislation that fostered the growth of trade and commerce and the granting and protection of private property rights that made such growth possible. Furthermore, the Dutch were willing to pay for those rights by a series of small taxes on trade in general. The level of tax on any one item was always relatively low. The Hapsburgs went along with the desires of the assembly so long as sufficient revenues were approved. The prosperity of the Low Countries made this possible. The Low Countries became the jewel of the Hapsburg Empire, delivering to the Spanish king the majority of his revenues. Eventually, however, the ever-more exacting demands of Philip II led to the successful revolt of the seven northern provinces. During the rebellion Antwerp was sacked by the Spanish, and commercial leadership shifted to Amsterdam. The republic that emerged retained the structure of law and property rights that had led to the commercial eminence of the Dutch in the first place.

The expansion of trade and commerce was the prime mover of the Dutch economy. The expansion of trade led to improvements in the efficiency with which Dutch markets operated. Markets, which develop to reduce transaction costs, are subject to economies of scale. As the volume of trade grows, the cost of making an individual trade falls. First in Antwerp and then in Amsterdam, trades began to be made in continuous auction markets. Price lists reporting the current market transactions were circulated for all to read. Standard contracts and law courts dealing exclusively with trade were established.

A thriving capital market developed alongside commerce and produced innovations of its own. Gradually the existing letter obligatory was transformed into a bill of exchange allowing merchants an expanded means of payment.

The property rights that favored the growth of commerce also favored increased efficiency in agriculture. Dutch agriculture became more capital intensive, waste lands were drained and cleared, and fertilizer was used extensively. The rise of international markets led to regional specialization within the Low Countries. Vineyards disappeared and dairying expanded. New crops were introduced to service the urban commercial sector.

The Dutch during the early modern era became the economic leaders of Europe. Their centrally located geographical position was combined with a government that encouraged an efficient economic organization by granting and protecting private property rights and discouraging restrictive practices. The development of the pre-eminent European market at Antwerp and then at Amsterdam made commerce the easiest sector for the state to tax. The numerous goods traded on the commercial exchanges came from all parts of Europe, and they came to the Low Countries because the markets there were competitive and efficient. The merchants of the Low Countries in recognition of this situation paid their rulers through the States General to establish and enforce private property rights and end restrictive practices. The Netherlands as a result became the first country to achieve sustained economic growth. Moreover, the United Provinces continued to prosper even after the center of the European economic stage shifted to England when this larger country, consciously or unconsciously, imitated the success of the Dutch.

The success of the English economy in escaping the crisis of the seventeenth century is directly traceable to the system of private property rights that had evolved. The English government faced the same fiscal demands as did the other emerging nation-states of Europe (although the threat of invasion was less pressing). The size of France, the fiscal endowments of Spain, and the efficiency of economic organization of the Netherlands made these countries European powers. England was forced to contend with these emerging nation-states. She sought a middle ground, constructing a New World empire in defiance of Spain and attempting to quarantine the Dutch on the one hand while instituting similar property rights and institutional arrangements on the other. By the year 1700 England had succeeded in replacing the Dutch as the most rapidly growing nation in the world.

Yet two centuries earlier there was little indication that England would take the path that led to economic growth. As in France the emergence of a nation-state in England was a long and costly process. During the fourteenth and fifteenth centuries

England suffered through the Hundred Years War and the War of the Roses with the attendant disorders, rebellions, and maladministration of justice that went along with the reduction of the powers of the barons.

The Tudors, as a consequence, raised the English monarchy to its height. Henry VII, while still expected to live on his own, did manage to expand his revenues in ways now very familiar to us—by selling grants and privileges. His successor, Henry VIII, managed the same way and added the confiscation of monastic lands. The process of consolidating the power of the king and at the same time increasing crown revenues left the Tudors decidedly unpopular with many, perhaps most, of the nobility and clergy. The Tudors relied for their support on the rising merchant class and on the House of Commons where, along with the landed gentry, this class was well-represented. The Tudors were as opportunistic in their dealings with property rights as any continental king. They sought revenues wherever they could be found without regard to economic efficiency. They cultivated, rather than suppressed, Parliament because it was expedient to do so.

The Stuarts inherited what the Tudors had sown. The Stuarts viewed the government as their exclusive prerogative, while Parliament saw the crown as circumscribed by the common law. Caught up in the ever-more expensive rivalry between nations, the Stuarts sought new sources of funds; Parliament proved intractable, and the scene was set for a conflict that the crown would lose.

The right of Parliament to grant taxes was by this time of long standing, having emerged late in the fifteenth century out of the struggle for control of the wool trade. Wool, long the staple export in English international trade, was an obvious source of crown revenue. A tripartite struggle over the extent of the tax developed between the crown, the merchants exporting the wool, and Parliament, where the wool growers were well-represented. The outcome of this struggle was a compromise with something for everyone. The crown received the revenues from the tax, but Parliament won the right to set the level of the tax, and the merchants achieved a monopoly of the trade. The wool monopoly eventually disappeared, and the wool tax became a minor source of government revenues; but Parliament's exclusive right to tax endured.

Hence in England, the representative assembly retained its crucial powers to tax even though the issue was not finally settled until 1689. When challenged by the Stuarts, Parliament's authority survived. Thus, the crown's initial control over property rights for two centuries passed to a representative assembly composed of merchants and landed gentry—a group whose interests were to halt restrictive practices and ensure private property rights and competition by constraining the powers of the king.

Let us examine some of the reasons why a representative assembly thrived in England while it declined and disappeared in France and Spain. England's geographical position as an island insulated the country from its rivals. Foreign invasion was never as serious a threat as it was on the Continent, and so the central provision of protection was not as significant to the English as it was to the French. Internally there were often several contenders for the throne, the presence of whom limited the powers of the English king or queen. The nature of the economy led to a dependence upon an export staple, wool, which provided an easily measured and collected source of fiscal revenues. The collection of this tax did not require a large bureaucracy dependent upon the crown but could be farmed out to a voluntary organization of merchants. In short, little reason existed to concentrate authority in the crown over property rights and taxation, and still less reason existed to support a large central government.

The rise of Parliament caused the nature of English property rights to diverge from the Continental pattern. The power to grant property rights increasingly fell to a group whose own interests were best served by private property and elimination of crown monopolies. Had such a shift not occurred, the economic history of England would have been much different. As we have seen, the economic policies of the Tudors were the same as those of the continental kings. Had they been able freely to trade monopolies and other restrictive rights for revenue, the outcome for economic efficiency also would have been similar. But in England the crown ran into effective opposition. The regulations enacted by the Tudors in an attempt to develop a comprehensive system of industrial regulation proved ineffective.[8] These regu-

---

[8] For a further discussion see Eklund and Tollison (1980b).

lations, similar to the ones successfully enacted in France, were simply evaded. Finally, the crown's prerogative to create monopolies was itself ended by an act of Parliament.

It was in the context of the development of an efficient set of property rights that the growth in population during the sixteenth century occurred. In France and Spain a growing population encountered a restrictive set of property rights that made an efficient adjustment to the changing factor proportions impossible; in England, as in the Netherlands, the opposite occurred. In England a growing population meant the revival of trade and commerce. Institutional arrangements evolved to further the gains from trade. The reduced cost of using the market to organize economic activity was the main source of productivity gains during this era. As the market expanded, commercial, industrial, and agricultural innovations familiar to the Dutch were adopted by the English. It was the reduction in transaction costs due to the establishment of private property rights and competition in trade and commerce that allowed England to escape the Malthusian check that both France and Spain suffered during the seventeenth century.

Chapter 12

The Industrial Revolution Reconsidered

I

The Industrial Revolution has been widely considered by modern economic historians as a watershed dividing human history. The eras that preceded it are regarded as a prelude to the rapid social and economic change unleashed in Great Britain beginning with the last half of the eighteenth century. It is easy to understand this preoccupation with the Industrial Revolution. The process of sustained economic growth that historians believe began between 1750 and 1830 radically altered the manner and standard of living of Western men and women. If an ancient Greek had been miraculously transported through time to the England of 1750, he or she would have found much that was familiar. The Greek alighting two centuries later, however, would discover what would appear to be an "unreal" world in which little would be recognizable or even understandable, so much had the state of mankind been altered in that relatively brief historical time span.

What were the changes? They can be stated as follows:

1. Population growth occurred at an unprecedented rate. Demographers estimate that world population was approximately eight hundred million in 1750. It was in excess of four billion by 1980. (Coale 1974:43)

2. The Western world achieved a standard of living which had no counterpart in the past. The average citizen enjoyed luxuries which were not available to even the richest man of earlier societies. Moreover, the average length of life almost doubled in the developed countries.

3. In the Western world agriculture ceased to be the dominant economic activity; industry and service sectors of the economy replaced it in significance. This change was made possible by the tremendous increase in agricultural productivity. In the United States the 5 percent of the population engaged in agriculture could feed the other 95 percent and still have enough left over to make the United States a world leader in the export of agricultural goods. In colonial times these percentages were reversed.

4. In consequence, the Western world became an urban society with all that term implies concerning increasing specialization, division of labor, interdependence, and inevitable externalities.

5. Continuous technological change became the norm. New sources of energy were harnassed to do men's work, and new materials and substances constantly created to satisfy human wants.

While these developments are not in question, how these changes occurred, when they began, and what we mean by the term Industrial Revolution have been the subject of a substantial debate. It is the argument of this chapter that the Industrial Revolution was an acceleration in the rate of innovation, the origins of which go back well before the traditional chronology (1750–1830). It was better specified property rights (not the same thing as laissez faire) which improved factor and product markets as described in the previous chapter. The resultant increasing market size induced greater specialization and division of labor, which increased transaction costs. Organizational changes were devised to reduce these transaction costs and had the consequence of radically lowering the cost of innovating at the same time that the increasing market size and better specified property rights over inventions were raising the rate of return on innovating. It was this set of developments which paved the way for the real revolution in technology—the Second Economic Revolution—which was the wedding of science and technology. It was this later development, in the second half of the nineteenth century, which produced the elastic supply curve of new knowledge and the unprecedented developments briefly summarized above.

In order to set this story in perspective we must first review the traditional story of the Industrial Revolution and explore the nature of technological change; then we shall be in a position to examine the interrelated process of organizational change and technological development which made up the Industrial Revolution as it is defined in this chapter.

II

Historians agree that these changes in organization and technology began in Britain during the middle decades of the eighteenth century. Over the next hundred years, the population of Britain tripled; some towns grew into big cities; the average income of an Englishman more than doubled; agriculture fell from roughly one-half of the nation's output to under one-fifth; and manufacturing and services expanded to assume the farmer's former role. In the process the manufacture of textiles and iron was undertaken in steam-powered factories of greatly improved efficiency.

This combination of events has appeared more startling to the historian than it did to contemporaries. Adam Smith, writing the most important book on economics in the middle of these occurrences, did not mention them. Further, he predicted that his nation of merchants, farmers, and handcraftsmen would continue to increase its wealth at a moderate pace by further specialization and trade; in fact, national income rose at an unprecedented rate in the next eight decades.

Smith was in good company. David Ricardo suggested that rising rents would absorb any increase in productivity. In the decades immediately after Ricardo wrote, rents as a share of a rising national income fell by half. Thomas Malthus predicted that the enormous increase in population would keep wages from rising for long times above subsistence; and Karl Marx, writing at the end of the era, predicted that the lot of the worker would not improve. Instead, the share of labor income in national income rose markedly, and real wages increased dramatically. The classical economists simply failed to understand the events that were occurring around them.

It is not that all contemporaries were unaware of change occurring. Some were aware, as evidenced in Frederick Engel's *Conditions of the Working Class in England,* published in 1844. But the term "Industrial Revolution" was not popularized until Arnold Toynbee employed it in a series of lectures delivered in 1880–1881, five decades after the date customarily accepted as the end of the transformation to which it refers.

Why did most classical economists miss the Industrial Revolution while living through it? Perhaps because the significance of this century of change lies more in the analyses of historians than in actuality. Population, for instance, was growing prior to the century of Industrial Revolution; large cities existed before the industrial towns grew up; and the income of Englishmen increased prior to the birth of Adam Smith as well as during his life and the lives of other classical economists. During this period there were more and more agricultural workers in total; agriculture would not have appeared a declining industry to a contemporary observer. Large factories had existed prior to the Industrial Revolution, and steam engines had been employed in coal mines for decades before James Watt's steam engine. The fabled Watt engine was simply an improvement over the previously existed Newcomen engines. So perhaps it is not surprising that the classical economists missed the Industrial Revolution: for what was new was the magnitude of the changes, not their revolutionary character. While the average Briton marveled at the wonders of the Crystal Palace Exhibition of 1851, he would have found the transformation of the next 125 years to be simply unbelievable. And while the classic era of the Industrial Revolution was certainly an acceleration in economic change, the revolutionary transformation I described at the beginning of this chapter is predominantly a happening of the past 150 years. It was after the middle of the nineteenth century that everyday life was transformed in such a fashion that our mythical time-travelling Greek would no longer recognize earth as a familiar place.

The enormous growth in population, for instance, which began prior to the Industrial Revolution, had been transformed into a world population explosion by the middle of the twentieth century. The cause of this modern explosion has been declining mortality from infectious disease as a result of improvement in nutrition and in the environment. Similarly, an urban world is a development that has occurred during the last hundred years and is associated not so much with the industrial city as with a dramatic decline in the costs of transportation, the increase in agricultural productivity, and the agglomerative benefits of central places for economic activity. Nor does the industrial sector dominate the employment of the developed nation's labor force; services, not manufacturing, employ the vast majority of modern workers. Further, the rate of economic growth during the Industrial Revolution was not particularly impressive when compared with later eras, especially the rates achieved by more recently developing nations.

In short, our stereotyped views of the past two centuries are in need of revision. The period that we have come to call the Industrial Revolution was not the radical break with the past that we sometimes believe it to have been. Instead, as I shall show below, it was the evolutionary culmination of a series of prior events. The real revolution occurred much later, in the last half of the nineteenth century. The technological events of the Industrial Revolution period were largely independent of developments in basic science.[1] The technological events of the recent past, on the other hand, all have required major breakthroughs in science. Learning by doing can explain the technology developed during the Industrial Revolution, but only scientific experimentation can account for the development of nuclear power or the petrochemical industry. The great technological strides of the last hundred years depended upon the scientific revolution; and the combination of science and technology produced the Second Economic Revolution.

III

To understand what occurred during the Industrial Revolution it is necessary to explore the process of technological change. Most of the existing literature, concentrating on the great inventions such as Watt's steam engine, Arkwright's water frame, or Crompton's mule, ignores the day-to-day progress in technological change which produces the sustained productivity increase in economic activity; nor is it integrated into a transaction cost

---

[1] For a discussion of the role of science in the Industrial Revolution see Musson, ed. (1972).

framework that would permit us to understand the complex reciprocal relationship between economic organization and technical change.

From initial conceptualization to establishment of technical feasibility—that is, from invention to commercial feasibility, innovation to subsequent diffusion—is often a long and intricate process.[2] Consider, for example, the development of the steamship. Watt's steam engine was an eighteenth-century invention. Its application to water transportation occurs at the beginning of the nineteenth century. Yet we do not observe that the steamship replaced the sailing ship until the end of the nineteenth century. As late as 1880 most of the world's bulk cargo was still being carried by sailing ships. Thus, one of the most dramatic inventions took almost a hundred years to replace its predecessor.

The transformation took place only gradually because successive modifications and improvements in the reciprocating engines were required to reduce fuel consumption (and thereby increase carrying capacity) and, equally, continued improvements in the sailing ship which increased speed and reduced the size of crews allowed the sailing ship to keep pace with the steamship for most of the nineteenth century.

The process of technology improvement depends upon not only the day-to-day improvements in a new technique but also the developing human skills using the new technique. The process of learning by doing must also accompany technical change. In addition, technical changes in one area may outrun technical knowledge in other fields. We are familiar with the fact that Watt's steam engine could not be efficiently produced until Wilkinson's boring machine enabled Watts to bore precision cylinders. Even more famous is the fate of the celebrated notebooks of Leonardo da Vinci: a vast array of original ideas could not be implemented with the companion technologies of the time. Indeed, the relationship between the development of new techniques and the development of new knowledge is a major issue.

Innovations draw upon the stock of existing fundamental knowledge which men possess. That knowledge is today embodied in such formal scientific disciplines as physics, chemistry,

[2] See Rosenberg (1972) for an excellent elaboration of the incremental character of technological change.

and biology. These disciplines are of recent origin, beginning in the late Renaissance and early modern eras. It is not that man's fundamental knowledge of his environment had not expanded since neolithic times: I have discussed a number of these advances in earlier chapters. But these developments did not depend upon structured formal disciplines. We must make this distinction, because the incentives to expand pure knowledge are not necessarily the same as those that lead to practical innovation.

Historically, there has always been a gap between pure scientific knowledge and the techniques that man has utilized; indeed, until very modern times the systematic development of new knowledge was not necessary for man to make enormous progress. It is only in the last one hundred years that advances in basic knowledge are necessary to continued technological change.

What determines the rate of development of new technology and of pure scientific knowledge? In the case of technological change, the social rate of return from developing new techniques had probably always been high; but we would expect that until the means to raise the private rate of return on developing new techniques was devised, there would be slow progress in producing new techniques. And, in fact, we have observed in the previous historical chapters of this book that throughout man's past he has continually developed new techniques, but the pace has been slow and intermittent. The primary reason has been that the incentives for developing new techniques have occurred only sporadically. Typically, innovations could be copied at no cost by others and without any reward to the inventor or innovator. The failure to develop systematic property rights in innovation up until fairly modern times was a major source of the slow pace of technological change.

It is only with the Statute of Monopolies in 1624 that Britain developed a patent law. It is true that prior to that time prizes had sometimes been awarded for the development of new techniques and at times governments had subsidized men searching for new techniques. Prince Henry the Navigator, for example, called together a group of mathematicians to search for a new method of determining latitude. Governments also have often subsidized the development of military technology and provided a ready market for new weapons. But a systematic set of incentives to encourage technological change and raise the private rate of return on innovation closer to the social rate of return was established only with the patent system. It would of course be misleading to put too much stress on a single law. Eli Whitney spent a good part of his life attempting to protect his patent for the cotton gin. More important than patent law per se is the development and enforcement of a body of impersonal law protecting and enforcing contracts in which property rights are specified.

Let me restate the argument in a more rigorous fashion. Rules designed to constrain behavior with respect to an economic return to ideas face basic difficulties associated with the measurement of the idea itself. Trade mark, copyright, trade secret, and patent laws are all designed to provide some degree of exclusive rights to the inventor and innovator and have generated a controversy, spanning more than a century, over the value of patents.[3] But much of the controversy misses the point. The inability precisely to define and delineate an idea means that surrogate rules will be required; and such rules, embodying imperfect measurement and some degree of monopoly restriction, will result in real revenue losses. But as compared to no protection at all, the value of some property rights over invention is not an issue. Idle curiosity or learning by doing will produce some technological change of the type we have observed throughout human history. But the sustained devotion of effort to improve technology—as we observe in the modern world —is stimulated only by raising the private rate of return. In the absence of property rights over innovation, the pace of technological change was most fundamentally influenced by the size of markets. Other things equal, the private return upon innovation rose with larger markets. An increase in the rate of technological change in the past was associated with eras of economic expansion.

In summary, economic historians of the Industrial Revolution have concentrated upon technological change as the main dynamic factor of the period. Generally, however, they have failed to ask what caused the rate of technological change to increase during this period: often it would appear that in arguing the causes of technological progress they assume that technological progress was costless or was spontaneously generated. But in sum, an increase in the rate of technological progress will result

[3] For a review of the controversy see Machlup (1958).

from either an increase in the size of the market or an increase in the inventor's ability to capture a larger share of the benefits created by his invention.

IV

The most convincing explanation for the Industrial Revolution as an acceleration in the rate of innovation is one drawn from straightforward neoclassical theory in which a combination of better specified and enforced property rights and increasingly efficient and expanding markets directed resources into new channels. Its origins go back in time well before the traditional chronology. Let us return to the shipping illustration used at the beginning of this chapter. The competition of steam and sail in the nineteenth century really is the middle of the story. Productivity increase as a result of declining transaction costs had been going on since at least 1600, when the Dutch flute (a specialized merchant cargo ship) was used in the Baltic trade and subsequently adopted on other routes. The declining transaction costs —a result of reduced piracy, increases in size of ships, growing trade, and reduced turnaround time—led to substantial productivity growth beginning 150 years (at least) before the Industrial Revolution; and they, more than technological change, were responsible for productivity increases.[4]

What happened in ocean shipping was paralleled by equal transformation in other product and factor markets. There certainly is nothing new in this argument. It was a central part of Toynbee's celebrated lectures published in 1884. He wrote, "The essence of the industrial revolution is the substitution of competition for the medieval regulations which had previously controlled the production and distribution of wealth."[5] The same theme is picked up by Phyllis Deane and R. M. Hartwell.[6] What has been missing in the argument, however, is that while laissez faire is identified as the key to the development, the term "laissez faire" not only has misleading ideological overtones but at least in part misses the point. It is true that the decline in mercantilist restrictions including repeal or reform of the Statute

---

[4] See North (1968).
[5] Arnold Toynbee as quoted in Hartwell (1971:249).
[6] See Deane (1965:203) and Hartwell (1971, chapter 11).

of Artificers, poor laws, acts of settlement, usury laws, navigation acts, and so forth is part of the story. Particularly significant to the developing of more efficient markets, however, is the better specification and enforcement of property rights over goods and services; and in many cases much more was involved than simply removing restrictions on the mobility of capital and labor—important as those changes were. Private and parliamentary enclosures in agriculture, the Statute of Monopolies establishing a patent law, and the immense development of a body of common law to better specify and enforce contracts also are part of the story.[7] Laissez faire implies an absence of restraints; efficient markets imply well-specified and enforced property rights, which means the creation of a set of restraints encouraging productivity growth. The removal of restrictions widening the gap between private and social returns frequently required positive action by government—a government which we have seen was, as a result of the English revolution, oriented toward such developments. Indeed, a part of the process was the wholesale evasion of restrictions which remained on the books—and became a dead letter through lack of enforcement; such a development could only occur with the tacit approval of Parliament.

V

The Industrial Revolution, as I perceive it, was initiated by increasing size of markets, which resulted in pressures to replace medieval and crown restrictions circumscribing entrepreneurs with better specified common laws (chapter 11). The growing size of the market also induced changes in organization, away from vertical integration as exemplified in home and handicraft production to specialization. With specialization came the increasing transaction costs of measuring the inputs and outputs, as described in chapter 4. The resultant increased supervision and central monitoring of inputs to improve quality radically lowered the cost of devising new techniques.

It is in the evolution of economic organization of manufacturing that we can best observe the interplay between transaction costs and technical change which characterized the Industrial Revolution. From handicraft to putting-out system to the factory

[7] See Hartwell's discussion (1971, chapter 11).

system spans more than three centuries; the key to explaining the transformation is growth in the size of the market and problems of quality control (that is, measurement of the characteristics of the good). In the course of the transformation in economic organization wage labor developed, the metering of inputs and outputs sharply changed, and the incentives for technical change increased.

The putting-out system which developed in Tudor and Stuart England was a response to the expanding market demand of those centuries.[8] It was characterized by raw materials being put out to geographically spread locations and wages (predominantly piece-rate) being paid for each step in the manufacturing process from raw material to finished good. In contrast to handicraft manufacturing, putting out was marked by growing separation of tasks—a classic example of Smithian growth in the size of the market inducing specialization. While its initial main focus was in textiles, it gradually spread to newer branches of textiles, leather goods, small metal wares. Clapham maintained that this system still predominated manufacturing in Britain as late as the 1820s. While escape from the urban guilds and a cheap labor supply as a byproduct of part-time agriculture explain the dispersion of manufacturing, they do not explain the form that it took. Why not simply a series of market transactions rather than a central merchant-manufacturer employing wage labor? The most convincing answer is that the costs to the merchant of ensuring quality control were less by the latter form of organization than by the former. A major argument of chapter 4 is that where quality was costly to measure, hierarchical organization would replace market transactions; the putting-out system was in effect a "primitive firm" in which the merchant-manufacturer attempted to enforce constant quality standards at each step in the manufacturing process.[9] By retaining ownership of the materials throughout the manufacturing process, the merchant-manufacturer was able to exercise this quality control at a cost lower than the cost of simply selling and buying at successive stages of the production process. The gradual move toward central workshops was a further step in efforts at greater quality control and presaged the development of the factory system that was in effect the direct supervision of quality throughout the production process.

[8] It also has been located in such widely diverse times and places as thirteenth-century Flanders and twentieth-century China, Asia, and Africa.
[9] For an elaboration of the argument here see Millward (forthcoming).

The gradual move to central work places cannot be explained by a central power source. Space in factories could be and was rented out to individual entrepreneurs before as well as after the development of central power sources. Rather, the impetus for the factory system was monitoring of the production process by a supervisor. With the development of direct supervision and monitoring, the costs of devising technical improvements are reduced because the role of the monitor is to "rationalize" each step in the production and this process consists of devising means to measure the output of each input unit and of creating more productive combinations. Team production played no significant role in the putting-out system; but once the workers were gathered in a central place, the productivity gains from team production were evident. With the better measurement of individual contributions came reductions in the cost of devising machines to replace men's and women's hands.

The Industrial Revolution came about as a result of organizational changes to improve the monitoring of workers. This factory discipline was itself a step in quality control but had the additional consequence of suggesting to entrepreneurs new productive combinations and specifically machines to replace human hands in the production process.

The emphasis in much of the literature on the Industrial Revolution goes the wrong way—that is, from technological change to the factory system; rather than from central workplace, to supervision, to greater specialization, to better measurement of input contributions, to technical change. Transaction costs and technology are of course inextricably intertwined: it was increased specialization which induced organizational innovations, which induced the technical change, which in turn required further organizational innovation to realize the potential of the new technology.

In terms of the theoretical framework of this study, one additional point must be raised. In chapter 4 I argued that the measurement costs of constraining behavior in the absence of effective ideological constraints would be so high as to make the new organizational forms non-viable. Both the political and the economic changes described above created impersonal factor and product markets and broke down old ideological loyalties. Factory discipline (that is, rules and penalties to enforce behavior) had to be supplemented by investment in legitimating the new organizational forms. The Industrial Revolution was characterized by sustained efforts to develop new social and ethical norms. Peter Mathias described this effort as follows: "A set of social norms, embodied in emergent social institutions, did develop in response to these new needs, however imperfectly they were practised. The virtues of hard work—the gospel of work preached by Samuel Smiles—saving, thrift, sobriety became the new social imperatives dinned into the heads of the working classes by their social betters by every known means of communication. They were enshrined in nonconformist and evangelical doctrine. In Sunday schools, pulpits, the mechanics' institutes after 1824 and all forms of literature in the hands of middle-class publicists were preached the golden rules as they attempted to diffuse the bourgeois virtues down the social scale" (1969:208). I shall have more to say about this issue in examining the implications of the Second Economic Revolution.

Chapter 13

The Second Economic Revolution and Its Consequences

I

The term "economic revolution" is intended to convey two distinct changes in an economic system: a fundamental change in the productive potential of the society as a consequence of a basic change in the stock of knowledge, and a consequent, equally basic, change in organization to realize that productive potential. Both economic revolutions deserve that title because they altered the slope of the long-run supply curve of output so as to permit continuing population growth without the dismal consequences of the classical economic model. The First Economic Revolution created agriculture and "civilization"; the Second created an elastic supply curve of new knowledge which built economic growth into the system. Both entailed substantial institutional reorganization. The organizational crisis of the modern world can only be understood as a part of the Second Economic Revolution.

The Second Economic Revolution made the underlying assumption of neoclassical economics realizable. That optimistic assumption was that new knowledge could be produced at constant cost and that substitution at all margins made possible persistent and sustained growth. The realization was possible only with the wedding of science and technology. The Industrial Revolution was a part of the evolutionary process that led to the marriage, and indeed we may get bogged down in semantics and technical trivialities if we wish to date precisely the exchange of the marriage vows. The important point is that the Second—as indeed the First—Economic Revolution was the inflection change in the supply curve of new knowledge, rather than the clustering of a set of innovations or any of the other characteristics used to describe the Industrial Revolution. There is also nothing automatic about a society's ability to realize this productive potential since its realization involves a basic restructuring of property rights. The internal and international turmoil of the past century provides us with abundant evidence of the chaos that has resulted from the tension between the technology of the Second Economic Revolution and political-economic organization.

In this chapter I propose to examine how the Second Economic Revolution came about and what its implications have been for economic organization and then to explore the social, political, and ideological reactions which characterize our modern world.

II

The steps in the development of the Second Economic Revolution were, first, the development of the scientific disciplines. Currently there is no convincing explanation for the early development of scientific knowledge. It surely was related to a decline in the monopoly the church had possessed over ideas about the relationship of man to his environment. The Protestant Reformation was a symptom of such a change in perspective. Galileo, Copernicus, Kepler, and, particularly, Newton were leading a revolution in man's view of the world around him. Who sponsored such people? What kinds of incentives existed for the development of new knowledge? During the Renaissance it was fashionable to support scientists; but the systematic demand for scientific knowledge is a modern phenomenon and is surely related to a growing perception of its usefulness in solving practical problems. A distinctive feature of its institutionalization in universities and research organizations is the recognition of social demands on a broad front. Advances in scientific knowledge must proceed along a wide variety of lines so that our ability to employ developments in one area is not impeded by bottlenecks in another.

A second step, emphasized by A. E. Musson, E. Robinson,

and others, concerns the intellectual interchange between scientists and inventors during the Industrial Revolution.[1] This interchange contributed to the growing consciousness of the high social (and potential private) rate of return from increase in basic knowledge; a consequence was growing public and private expenditure on basic research. An awareness of the growing relevance of science to invention led to increasing investment in human capital. Germany's pre-eminent late–nineteenth-century role in the chemical industry was in good part due to the early training of large numbers of chemists. Schmoockler (1957) shows a dramatic rise between 1900 and 1950 in the ratio between patents taken out by state residents and scientists and engineers in the state. The most crucial feature of this evolution was that public and private organizations came to appreciate that the underlying key to success was basic and exploratory research. The result of this development is what has come to be called the invention industry.[2]

Still a third important step is the evolution of property rights which raised the private rate of return closer to the social rate. In earlier chapters I have emphasized the importance not only of the development in patent laws but also of the growth of complementary law (such as that over trade secrets) aimed at raising this private rate of return. The development of intellectual property rights posed complex issues in the measurement of the dimensions of ideas as well as complex problems over the trade-off between raising the private rate of return on innovation and monopoly-restraining of trade as a result of the grant of exclusive rights over time. While the private rate of return has been raised by better specified property rights over invention and innovation, a good part of the basic research has been financed by government and takes place in universities—reflecting the growing public awareness of the high social rate of return to scientific advances.

III

The technological breakthroughs that have characterized the Second Economic Revolution are the development of automated machinery to replace man's hands and mind in production; the

---

[1] See Musson, ed. (1972).
[2] See Nelson, Peck, and Kolachek (1967), chapter 3.

creation of new sources of energy; and the fundamental trans-formation of matter.

The first of these developments is a continuation from the In-dustrial Revolution and is in part a simple result of increasing specialization and division of labor, which make the objective of devising a machine to replace a simple task easier for the in-ventors. Eli Whitney's celebrated demonstration of interchange-able parts in the manufacture of muskets and Henry Ford's equally celebrated assembly line for the manufacture of the Model T were classic examples. The high-speed computer is the most revolutionary modern example. Its most striking char-acteristic is continuous high-speed throughput, to use Alfred Chandler's (1977) favorite term. It is a response to large-scale markets that induce high-volume output.

The second also has its beginnings in the Industrial Revolution, with Watt's improved steam engine; but in the ensuing two centuries this improvement has been overshadowed by the de-velopment of the internal combustion engine, sources of elec-tricity, and nuclear power. The result has been a per capita use of energy far exceeding that of the past, when animal and human muscle were the chief source of energy.

The third, the transformation of matter, is also not new. The Bronze Age and the Iron Age were chronological periods named by historians and anthropologists after the technological break-throughs that transformed copper and tin and iron ore into use-able materials. The development of bleaching was an important chemical breakthrough of the Industrial Revolution. But the mod-ern developments in the sciences of chemistry, physics, and genetics are a quantum jump in man's ability to transform matter into useable materials and energy. For example, coal and petro-leum have been transformed into thousands of goods far removed in appearance and composition from the original material. The important underlying basis is the growing scientific knowledge about the fundamental sources of matter which permits their recombination into other materials, energy, and new genetic com-binations. Pasteur, Einstein, Von Newmann, and Crick and Wat-son have become familiar names in the extraordinary scientific revolution of the past century. It is this development that has changed the shape of the supply curve of basic knowledge and made possible sustained economic growth in the face of the un-precedented explosion of population in the past century.

IV

The technology of the Second Economic Revolution was characterized by significant indivisibilities in the production process with large fixed-capital investment. The realization of the potential scale economies required large-volume continuous production and distribution. Ever since J. M. Clark's *The Economics of Overhead Costs* (1923) and Allyn Young's classic article "Increasing Returns and Economic Progress" (1928) economists have discussed the economic implications of scale economies.[3] Economic historians have provided detailed descriptions of mechanization in individual industries, and recently Chandler provided the following summary:

> The rise of modern mass production required fundamental changes in the technology and organization of the processes of production. The basic organizational innovations were responses to the need to coordinate and control the high-volume throughput. Increases in productivity and decreases in unit costs (often identified with economies of scale) resulted far more from the increases in the volume and velocity of throughput than from a growth in the size of the factory or plant. Such economies came more from the ability to integrate and coordinate the flow of materials through the plant than from greater specialization and subdivision of the work within the plant. (1977:281)

Chandler goes on to discuss the integration of mass production with mass distribution as follows:

> As the new mass production industries became capital-intensive and management-intensive, the resulting increase in fixed costs and the desire to keep their machinery or workers and managerial staff fully employed increased pressures on the owners and managers to control their supplies of raw and semifinished materials and to take over their own marketing and distribution. The changing ratio of capital to labor and of managers to labor thus helped to create pressures to integrate within a single industrial enterprise the process of mass distribution with those of mass production. By 1900 in many mass production industries the factory, works, or plant had become part of a much larger enterprise. In labor-intensive, low-level technology industries most enterprises still operated little more than a factory or two. But in those industries using more complex, high-volume, capital-intensive technology, enterprises had become multifunctional as well as multiunit. They had moved into marketing of the finished

[3] For a thoughtful discussion in the context of economic history see David (1975), Introduction.

goods and the purchasing and often the production of raw and semifinished materials. These enterprises did more than coordinate the flow of goods through the processes of production. They administered the flow from the suppliers of raw materials through all the processes of production and distribution to the retailer or ultimate consumer. (1977:282–83)

The managerial revolution in American business, to use the subtitle of Chandler's book, was an effort to realize the productive potential of the new technology. Chandler has persuasively described one part of that effort, but part of the story is missing; a major part of that managerial revolution was the attempt to devise a set of rules and compliance procedures to reduce the transaction costs attendant on the new technology.

This potential required both occupational and territorial specialization and division of labor on an unprecedented scale. The greater the specialization and division of labor, the greater the number of exchanges in the production process. Individual home production is complete vertical integration, and, as noted in chapter 4, there are no measurement costs; but the price is the productivity gains from specialization. The Second Economic Revolution resulted in just the obverse. Specialization and division of labor resulted in an exponential multiplication of exchange, with immense gains in productivity; the price, however, which is the transaction costs arising from these exchanges, is also great. Obviously the productivity gains from specialization have exceeded the increasing transaction costs in the process; hence the quantum leap in living standards that makes the modern Western world unique in history. But the transaction costs associated with this development use up immense amounts of resources.

While historical statistics are not organized to specifically mirror specialization and division of labor, the changing proportion of blue collar (production) workers to white collar workers gives some indication. Between 1900 and 1970 the United States labor force grew from 29 million to 80 million. Manual workers increased from 10 million to 29 million, while white collar workers increased from 5 million to 38 million (Historical Statistics Series D 182, 183, 189). But that is not all. If the coordination and integration of the production process involves an ever-growing proportion of the labor force within manufacturing firms, the Second Economic Revolution equally fostered a growing number of firms specializing in transactions from producer to consumer. Between 1860 and 1960 employment in trade grew twice as fast as the labor force. A specialized monitoring profession, accounting and auditing, grew from 2300 in 1900 to 712,000 in 1970 (Historical Statistics Series D235). During the same period employment in government grew from 1 million to 12.5 million (Historical Statistics Series D131).

Chandler glosses over the transaction cost problems associated with the new technology. How does one devise and measure exchange relationships in "high-speed throughput"? While Chandler implies that vertical integration was the answer, it should be clear both that measurement is still necessary at each step in the production process, and that one has the additional dilemma of monitoring the inputs. The problems of quality control at each step in the lengthening production chain and the growing problems of labor discipline and bureaucracy were the accompaniment to this radical change in production. Much of the technology was designed to reduce the attendant transaction costs by substituting capital for labor, by reducing the degrees of freedom of the worker in the production process, or by automatically measuring the quality of the intermediate goods.[4]

The underlying problems were, first, the problem of measuring inputs and outputs so that one could ascertain the contribution of individual factors and measure the output both at successive stages of production and finally. For inputs there was no agreed-upon measure of the contribution of an individual input; equally there was room for conflict over the consequent payment to factors. For output not only were there residual unpriced outputs (waste, pollutants) but also there were complicated costs of specifying the desired properties of the goods or services produced at each state in the production process.

The second problem was that the large fixed-capital investment, which had long life and low alternative value (scrap value), required exchange relationships and contractual agreements extending over long periods of time. During these periods there were uncertainty about prices and costs and abundant possibilities for opportunistic behavior on the part of one or the other party to the exchange.

In consequence there were, first, increasing resource costs of measuring the quality of output. While the production potential

---

[4] Chandler does discuss the growth of scientific management, pp. 272–81. The high-speed computer is the most striking technological change that reduced transaction costs.

resulted in a quantum leap in the per capita consumption of goods and services it produced a comparable growth in measuring the quality of the goods and services produced. Sorting, grading, labeling, trade marks, warranties, and licensing are all costly devices to measure the characteristics of goods and services.[5] Yet despite the resources devoted to measuring the "quality" of goods and services the dissipation of income is evident all around us in the difficulties in measuring automobile repairs, in evaluating the safety characteristics of products or the quality of medical services, or in measuring educational output. We have consumer testing services such as *Consumer Reports* and trade associations and Better Business Bureaus to police quality. A major political consequence has been the demand for government intervention to provide quality standards.

Second, while team production permitted economies of scale it did so at the cost of increased shirking. The "discipline" of the factory system is nothing more than a response to the control problem of shirking in team production. From the perspective of the employer the discipline consisted of rules, regulations, incentives, and punishments. Innovations such as Taylorism were methods of measuring individual performance. From the point of view of the worker they were inhuman devices to foster speed-ups and exploitation. Since there was no agreed-upon measure of output that constituted contract performance, both were right.

Additionally, the potential gains from opportunistic behavior were equally enhanced and led to strategic behavior both within the firm (in labor-employer relations, for example) and in contractual behavior between firms. Everywhere in product and factor markets the gains from withholding services or altering the terms of agreement at strategic points offered large potential gains. Vertical integration, horizontal integration, bonding of the participants were efforts to limit such activity; and an increasing appeal to government to act as a third party to contracts underlay a great deal of the growth of regulation.[6]

Further, the development of large-scale organization produced the familiar problems of bureaucracy. If the multiplication of rules and regulations inside large organizations is a device to

---

[5] See Barzel (1980) and McManus (1975) for a further discussion of the measurement costs of the quality of output.

[6] For an elaboration of this argument see Goldberg (1976).

reduce shirking and opportunism, the deadweight losses associated with bureaucracy are so familiar that they require no further elaboration here.

Finally there were the external effects: the unpriced benefits and costs that were a consequence of employing this technology are an equally familiar story. The growth of the business firm was a method of internalizing unpriced benefits.[7] The unpriced costs are reflected in the modern environmental crisis in which the problems of measuring and reducing them have both altered voluntary organization and induced the growth of government intervention in the twentieth century. William Baumol's *Welfare Economics and a Theory of the State* (1952) was an early attempt to relate the growth of government intervention to external costs.

The burgeoning modern literature on industrial organization offers ample evidence of organizational innovation to reduce transaction costs. But the growth of specialization and division of labor was both occupational and territorial. As the new technology lowered transportation and information costs, it led to regional, national, and world-wide specialization which produced markets sensitive to world-wide supply and demand conditions, transmitted changes in economic conditions throughout the world, and encouraged opportunism on an international scale. The result was to raise the rate of return on using government to protect groups from market instability and international opportunism. Political instability as well as economic interdependence was the price of specialization.

V

The Second Economic Revolution ushered in an era of unequaled prosperity in the Western world. It also induced a massive reaction against market economies and market forms of resources allocation. The labor movements that came into existence were predominantly socialist and communist in England and Europe and played a major role in the emergence of socialist and communist political systems and political parties in these countries; peasant and farm movements if not actively hostile to market economies have at the least spearheaded successful movements

[7] See Davis and North (1971).

to protect themselves from market competition; Third-World countries have shown little enthusiasm for market forms of resource allocation; and even in countries that have remained predominantly market economies the growth of government has reflected a radical alteration in the control of those political systems and consequent change in the structure of economic organization. What has made the market system tend to self-destruct?

It is clear that control of the state was, for a brief period of time, in the hands of groups whose self-interest promoted the growth of market forms of resource allocation. That is the story of the two preceding chapters. It is equally clear that control of the state passed into the hands of groups that favored the elimination, or at the very least modification, of market forms of resource allocation. Two hypotheses are advanced below to account for this transformation; both have their origins in the specialization and division of labor which as we have seen was an integral consequence of the Second Economic Revolution. One is that market competition induced massive alienation because the particular characteristics of the exchange relationship that emerged energized groups to overcome the free rider problem and gain control (or at least participate in control) of the state; the other, that market competition induced interest groups to shield themselves from its consequences by using the state to alter property rights and hence reduce competitive pressures. The first hypothesis stems primarily from the occupational, the second from the geographic, division of labor—both part of the Second Economic Revolution. Let us examine each in turn.

It was Karl Polanyi who, in *The Great Transformation* (1957), first made a forceful case that a market society would tend to self-destruct. Polanyi argued that the market-based society which dominated the Western world in the nineteenth century was inherently unstable because the commoditization of land, labor, and money (via the International Gold Standard) destroyed the social fabric of society. It is worth quoting his colorful language to get the flavor of his criticism of the market economy.

To allow the market mechanism to be sole director of the fate of human beings and their natural environment, indeed, even of the amount and use of purchasing power, would result in the demolition of society. For the alleged commodity "labor power" cannot be shoved about, used indiscriminately, or even left unused, without affecting also the human individual who happened to be the bearer of this peculiar commodity. In disposing of a man's labor power the system would, incidentally, dispose of the physical, psychological, and moral entity "man" attached to that tag. Robbed of the protective covering of cultural institutions, human beings would perish from the effects of social exposure; they would die as the victims of acute social dislocation through vice, perversion, crime and starvation. Nature would be reduced to its elements, neighborhoods and landscapes defiled, rivers polluted, military safety jeopardized, the power to produce food and raw materials destroyed. Finally, the market administration of purchasing power would periodically liquidate business enterprise, for shortages and surfeits of money would prove as disastrous to business as floods and droughts in primitive society. Undoubtedly, labor, land, and money markets *are* essential to a market economy. But no society could stand the effects of such a system of crude fictions even for the shortest stretch of time unless its human and natural substance as well as its business organization was protected against the ravages of this satanic mill. (1957:73)

Polanyi's criticism was in the tradition of Durkheim and Weber; but it was Polanyi who most vividly described the disintegrating effects of the "unregulated market" in terms of the social instability it created. His analysis, in contrast to his colorful description, is vague, imprecise, and at times simply nonexistent. He emphasizes that it was the state that created the impersonal markets; but nowhere does he provide a theory of the state which accounts either for its creation of the body of property rights or for the way that groups influenced the state to bring about the demise of the "self-regulating market"; he graphically describes the destruction of the social fabric of society without providing a theory of ideology; and he continually identifies non-market forms of resource allocation with social, that is, non-economic, objectives when in fact they frequently stemmed from efforts to reduce transaction costs as described in the previous section of this chapter. But Polanyi's basic intuition was correct and he provides the clues with which to develop a theoretical reconstruction.

We can begin by agreeing with Polanyi that it was change in control of the state that led to the breakdown of the restrictions on factor and product markets as described in the previous chapter. The creation of large-scale impersonal factor and product markets was an essential prerequisite to realizing the productive potential of the Second Economic Revolution. But the price paid was massive ideological alienation. It is only necessary to go back to the dilemma posed at the beginning of chapter 5, on ideology, to get to the heart of the issue. The stability of any society requires an ideological superstructure to legitimize the rules of the game.

The personalized exchange described in chapter 4 with reference to transaction costs minimized the gains from shirking and opportunism because of both repeated dealings and personal contact. Moreover the exchange process was overlaid with a social ethic of the justice of the rules and property rights. Reciprocity certainly reinforced these codes of behavior, but it would be a mistake to conceive of the "consensus" ideology that overlaid personalized exchange as pure reciprocity. It was in effect a way of life and under those conditions formal rules of exchange and monitoring would be minimal.

In contrast the exchange process of impersonal markets first of all fostered diverse perceptions of reality which in turn led to differing and conflicting ideologies. The experiences of the laborer were those in common with other laborers increasingly cut off from the personal ties that had produced a common set of values. Informal agreements had to be replaced with formal contracts; the consequent structure of impersonal market organization encouraged the very behavioral characteristic that posed the Hobbesian dilemma. That is, a formal set of rules evolved to constrain behavior in market exchange but also created conditions in which there was a large pay-off to disobeying those rules. Those whose behavior was constrained by the consensus ideology of personalized exchange soon came to perceive that they were being taken advantage of in this new environment where there was a large pay-off to maximizing behavior by the parties to exchange. Impersonal market competition introduced a basically antagonistic relationship to exchange. Traditional status relationships, a "fair rate of return," honesty, and integrity were replaced by ubiquitous conflict over the terms of exchange. In particular the inability to measure the output of labor in team production induced conflict over what constituted shirking versus the speedup.

It is not surprising that in such an environment Marx could construct a theory of history around class conflict, with technology as the exogenous variable; or that Joseph Schumpeter could maintain that the very success of capitalism produced ideological alienation that would lead to its downfall. But what is missing in Schumpeter's and in Polanyi's analyses, and only incompletely and inadequately dealt with by Marx and his followers, is a theory of the way the free rider problem would be overcome to lead to a capture of the state (or at the very least partial control of the state) by groups intending to use the political process to safeguard their terms of exchange.

The growth of class consciousness in nineteenth-century Britain and Europe has been a favorite topic of social historians, and the ideological perspectives of many of the writers who have been Marxists has provided for real insight into the process of worker alienation. Marx's emphasis on consciousness being basically conditioned by one's relationship to the mode of production remains an important contribution. The creation of an impersonal labor market cut the old ideological ties of the worker and led him to identify with other workers in a common antagonistic interest against employers. To quote Charles Tilly, Marx's account "Class Struggles in France has stood the passage of time rather well" (1969:13). The succession of movement from Luddism to Chartism to the Labour Party reflected the evolution of the British worker's ideological perspective. On the continent the later development of class consciousness mirrored the lag in growth of impersonal labor markets; but despite disparate origins similar patterns of protest evolved.[8] However, on the continent Marx had a far greater influence on the ideological perspective of the worker than he did in England.

The consequences of occupational specialization and division of labor were to break down the communication and personal ties that had formed the fabric of a consensus ideology, and to produce diverse ideologies built upon the new and conflicting perceptions of reality that emerged from the environment of occupational specialization. Alienation activated groups to participate in control of the state to alter their terms of exchange.

In contrast, the second hypothesis suggests that the self-destruct tendency of the market system comes from the inherent instability of the competition that emerged from the reduction in transportation costs leading to regional, national, and international specialization and division of labor. This competition in turn led to sharp fluctuations in the terms of exchange (and in the case of labor markets, to unemployment) and induced interest groups to devote resources to attempting to influence or control

---

[8] See Rimlinger (1960). See also Tilly (1975).

the policies of the state in the interest of reducing competitive pressures. In the case of farm groups, large group action was induced by the deep conviction that the farmer was a victim of the adverse terms of trade of an industrial system. In the case of manufacturers the new competition broke down the local monopolies that had existed and induced participation in influencing the state. In the Marxian literature this is frequently viewed as the class struggle of a rising bourgeoisie to overthrow the political dominance of the landlord class, as in the repeal of the Corn Laws; this emphasis obscures, however, the ubiquitous struggle of propertied groups to curtail market competition. The triumph of free trade in Europe was spectacular but brief. It was quickly replaced not only by the revival of barriers against external competition, but equally by efforts to reduce market competition internally.

VI

The structural transformation of Western economies in the past century as a consequence of the Second Economic Revolution has been the subject of a vast literature by social scientists. There have been important contributions to our understanding, but no description has been complete; and because of ideological differences and the compartmentalization of academic disciplines, an integrated overview of the structural transformation is still lacking.

Neoclassical economics has recognized and elaborated the productivity implications of this revolution in a context of zero transaction costs and more recently explored the implications of positive transaction costs for economic organization. But it has failed to come to grips with the ideological consequences and therefore to provide more than a superficial theory of the political process. The new economic historians, basing their analysis on neoclassical theory, have had very little to say about structural change in history; even the literature on positive transaction costs is just now filtering into economic history research.

The strength of the Marxian analysis has been precisely that it focused on structural change and the tension between the production potential of a society and the structure of property rights; but the emphasis on class divisions has obscured the intra-class conflict inherent in economic organization. The most serious shortcoming of the Marxian analysis, however, has been that it has conceived of the problems of alienation as stemming from capitalism, rather than perceiving that the problems are inherent organization consequences of the Second Economic Revolution. Shirking, opportunism, and externalities are as prevalent in the Soviet Union and other socialist countries as they are in capitalist countries. Indeed the widespread view of Marxists in the Western world that the Soviet Union is not socialist is at base a misreading of the nature of the modern organization crisis.

The sociological tradition from Durkheim to Talcott Parsons has recognized the disintegrating effects of modern social organization. Parsons's *The Structure of Social Action* (1937) was a pioneering effort to come to grips with many of the issues, but Parsons failed to solve the free rider dilemma and to produce a coherent body of theory. Nor have political scientists evolved a theory of the state, although they have examined the rise of pluralism, that is, the multiple interest-group control of the political process.

And finally we come back to Karl Polanyi. The sources of the self-regulating market that was the basis of modern distress were the impersonal labor market, the impersonal land market, and the gold standard. All three have either disappeared or been so altered structurally that they bear no resemblance to Polanyi's description of their nineteenth-century character. But the consequences bear little resemblance to Polanyi's cautiously optimistic view of such change. The pluralist control of the state which emerged from the struggle of workers, farmers, and business groups has produced the disintegration of the earlier structure of property rights and replaced it with a struggle in the political arena to redistribute income and wealth at the expense of the efficiency potential of the Second Economic Revolution. Moreover, this resultant struggle has not led to a new ideological social fabric that resolves the organizational tensions.

The erosion of the gold standard since 1914 and especially since the 1930s has eliminated the nominal anchor of the money supply and therefore the forces that limited changes in the price level. In consequence manipulation of the money supply by contending interest groups is a major destabilizing force in the modern world.[9]

9 See Barro (1979).

Polanyi concludes, "Socialism is, essentially, the tendency inherent in an industrial civilization to transcend the self-regulating market by consciously subordinating it to a democratic society" (1957:234). Despite his perceptive examination of the issues, Polanyi, too, failed to understand the Second Economic Revolution.

Chapter 14

Structure and Change in the American Economy 1789–1914

I

All the economies of the Western world underwent profound structural change as a consequence of the Second Economic Revolution. While the initial political-economic structures were diverse, the ensuing changes all led to the rise in the role of government. The case of the United States is unique only in its origins.

The growth of government was not only an increase in government income as a percentage of gross national product; it was also a widening of the groups that participated in the governmental process (pluralism), a change in the set of constraints that specified the economic structure, and a change in the locus of those constraints.

Under the assumptions of the analytical framework developed in Part I and expanded thus far in the historical chapters of Part II of this book it can hardly be surprising that government grew; it is far more surprising that there was a brief period when the state's role was relatively so confined. The American colonies were in the extraordinary position of taking over from England not only the body of property rights (and common law) that had been evolving there, but also the deep distrust of a powerful state that emerged from the English Revolution; the American

Revolution and the behavior of the individual states themselves during the period of confederation furthered this distrust. The story of this chapter is how the framers of the Constitution attempted to control the state and how ultimately those controls broke down. It is tempting to carry the story up through the Great Depression, since that event is typically associated with this structural change; such a view, however, is simply incorrect. The groundwork for the change, in the United States and elsewhere in the Western world, had already been laid by World War I; the Great Depression was merely an episode that was the immediate vehicle for the acceleration of this transformation. The economist's and the economic historian's failure to analyze structural change has led them to misread the economic history of the twentieth century.[1]

II *

I begin by examining the constitutional structure of the Founding Fathers. James Madison argued that there are always numerous conflicting propertied interests and that their internecine struggles—if not controlled—could bring the political-economic system to its knees. Conflicting groups (propertied or propertyless), given access to political restructuring of property rights, would use this avenue to redistribute wealth and income at the expense of others and at the expense of the viability of the system.

Madison's Federalist Paper Number 10 laid out in detail the fundamental dilemma of all political systems. It is worth reading again.

> The most common and durable source of factions has been the various and unequal distribution of property. Those who hold and those who are without property have ever formed distinct interests in society. Those who are creditors, and those who are debtors, fall under a like discrimination. A landed interest, a manufacturing interest, a mercantile interest, a monied interest, with many lesser interests, grow up of necessity in civilized nations, and divide them into different classes, actuated by different sentiments and views. The regulations of these various and inter-

---

[1] Hughes (1977) and Anderson and Hill (1980) are exceptions to this general indictment.

* This section is drawn from North (1978).

fering interests forms the principal task of modern legislation, and involves the spirit of party and faction in the necessary and ordinary operations of the government. . . .

The inference to which we are brought is that the causes of faction cannot be removed and that relief is only to be sought in the means of controlling its effects.

If a faction consists of less than a majority, relief is supplied by the republican principle, which enables the majority to defeat its sinister views by regular vote. It may clog the administration, it may convulse the society; but it will be unable to execute and mask its violence under the forms of the Constitution. When a majority is included in a faction, the form of popular government, on the other hand, enables it to sacrifice to its ruling passion or interest both the public good and the rights of other citizens. To secure the public good and private rights against the danger of such a faction, and at the same time to preserve the spirit and the form of popular government, is then the great object to which our inquiries are directed." (1937:87–88)

The political structure which Madison helped erect at the Constitutional Convention was explicitly oriented to preventing domination by factions. He wished to make it unprofitable for groups in society to devote their efforts toward redistributing wealth and income through the political process. A system of checks and balances was designed to make it extremely costly for any faction, whether a majority or a minority, to use the political system in this fashion. The tripartite system of government—the executive, the legislative, and the judicial; the further division between the two houses of legislature; and the operation of the Federal, state, and local governments all were designed to make efforts at restructuring property rights to redistribute wealth and income very difficult.[2]

John Marshall, Chief Justice of the U.S. Supreme Court from 1801 to 1835, was concerned with the insecurity that had afflicted the rights of private property before the Constitution was ratified, when a "course of legislation had prevailed in many, if not all, of the states which weakened the confidence of man in man and embarrassed all transactions between individuals by dispensing with faithful performance of engagements."[3] The strengthening of the institutions of private property consisted to a very important degree in legally limiting the power of gov-

---

[2] In fact the abolition of slavery, the one major change in property rights in the nineteenth century, and consequent redistribution of wealth, took a civil war to accomplish.

[3] *Trustees of Dartmouth College* vs. *Woodward* (1819), reprinted in Commager (1948:220–23).

ernment. The objective was to embody a set of comprehensive rules in an impersonal legal structure—rules that would not be subject to political whim and change by legislative bodies. Thus, the contract clause of the Constitution as interpreted by the Marshall Court was designed to rectify the insecurities of private property that stemmed particularly from the behavior of the individual states comprising the confederacy.

It perhaps requires emphasizing that the Constitution broadly reflected the interests of the framers. While their interests were diverse and resulted in many compromises, the basic constitutional structure was consistent with the argument advanced in chapter 3. It has become fashionable to discredit Charles Beard's *An Economic Interpretation of the Constitution* (1913), but it would be equally foolhardy to return to the naïve view that the constitution reflected disembodied wisdom. The ideological perspective that it reflected was broader than any particular set of interests but was, within the vision of the framers, generally consistent with their interests. While the aim of the framers was to discourage all factions, the costs of using the government were lower to some factions than to others, as evidenced by the tariff legislation in the first half of the nineteenth century.

The "release of energy" which Willard Hurst cites in his *Law and the Conditions of Freedom in the Nineteenth Century* (1956) had as its source the growth of private law which in the first sixty years of the nineteenth century transformed the interpretation of property rights from an explicitly anti-developmental bias to one where "the relative efficiencies of conflicting property uses should be the paramount test of what constitutes legally justifiable injury" (Horwitz 1977:38). In brief, the legal structure of American society that had emerged by mid-nineteenth century was one that explicitly reflected the same efficiency criteria as that of neoclassical theory.

However, it should be recognized that just as national income accounting is a limited and myopic measurement of social costs and benefits, so also is the efficiency criteria in both law and economics of the nineteenth century. As the previous quote from Horwitz makes clear, there were costs as a consequence of measuring injury that way; they simply were not taken into account. It would be more accurate to say that the benefits that were internalized and the costs that were externalized were consistent with a high rate of growth as measured by national income accounts.

It is not surprising that neoclassical economic theory emerged in this era. Within an historical context of growing, unfettered markets, neoclassical economists made exchange within a system of private property rights the cornerstone of their theory. Their main concern was economic efficiency implied by characteristics attached (by welfare theory) to the equilibrium price and quantity in the market place.

What were the consequences of this political-legal structure on the performance of the American economy? Economic historians have investigated these at length and I want here simply to emphasize two points about performance as measured by national income accounts. One, our imprecise statistics suggest that per capita real income grew at a rate of 1.3 percent per annum in the first part of the century and at 1.6 percent in the latter part. This second figure translates into a doubling of real per capita income every forty-three years. Two, the distribution of both wealth and income appears to have become more unequal over the century.[4]

The transformation toward greater government intervention had its origins in the last quarter of the nineteenth century, but it is important to take note of its long antecedents. There had been state and local regulation of business in colonial times (and before that all the way back in the economic history of Britain). The shift in the last quarter of the nineteenth century was from state to federal regulation and from encouragement and promotion to control.

The landmarks along the way of this transformation are familiar. There was *Munn* vs. *Illinois* in 1877, which affirmed that private businesses "affected with the public interest" were subject to regulation and control by the state of Illinois. A decade later the commerce clause of the Constitution was held to prevent state regulation which obstructed interstate commerce, and the Federal Interstate Commerce Commission was created to regulate railroads. The Sherman Antitrust Act came three years later; the Pure Food and Drug Act, in 1906; the Federal Trade Commission, in 1914.

The succession of farm protest movements (the Greenbacks, the Grangers, the populists) led to state regulation which was the predecessor of federal regulation and to the demand for

---

[4] However, the statistical bases of this conjecture are weak and the one major structural change in the American economy of the nineteenth century—the freeing of slaves—would work in the opposite direction.

radical alteration of the structure of agriculture. While in the short run the farmers achieved few of their objectives, they did initiate a major break with the Madisonian tradition. They were protesting the distributional justice of an unregulated market and demanding fundamental political and economic structural change to alter the distribution of income.

The "closing of the frontier" in 1890, while certainly not the end of the availability of land under the various land acts, nevertheless led to a growing awareness that the supply of land and resources was no longer unlimited and to a fundamental questioning of the degree to which unrestricted marketing of this land from public to private hands was consistent with the welfare of society.

The transformation from an agrarian society to the leading industrial nation in the world was mirrored by a shift from a rural to an urban society, the growth of large-scale economic organization, and the inflow of immigrants to provide a labor force. The symptoms of malaise accompanying this change are well-known. The Knights of Labor, the Haymarket riot, the Pullman strike, and the vote for Eugene V. Debs in the election of 1912 all were reflections of this transformation.

Less spectacular but equally portentous were the efforts of an evolving urban society to deal with growing "public bads." In 1890, 26 percent of cities over 10,000 population had no sewers at all, and of those that did only 45 percent of the dwellings were connected to a sewage system. By 1907 nearly every city had a sewage system. In 1900 less than 3 percent of cities had treated water supplies; by 1920 nearly 37 percent were so supplied.

It is important to stress these nineteenth- and early–twentieth-century forerunners because we are all too accustomed to thinking of the transformation as a later–twentieth-century phenomenon. But as Hughes points out in *The Governmental Habit,* "Munn put the Supreme Court's stamp on the idea that in American capitalism private property was subject to government regulation even if that property had not benefited from a special license or franchise, or was subject to eminent domain" (1977: 112). Similarly, the platform of the farmer movements was ultimately incorporated into the major parties's platforms and adopted, piece by piece; and the conservation movement led to the withdrawal of large blocks of remaining public lands from sale into private hands. There were also the beginnings of labor legislation limiting the contractual freedom of employers and employees—most evidently in regard to women and children.

By 1914 the size of government had not grown significantly as a percentage of the GNP, but the foundation for fundamental structural change which would lead to the disintegration of the Madisonian system had been laid. I propose in the next section briefly to describe the incremental changes that were altering the relative prices of using the market versus using the political process and then to examine the way by which the organizational pressures of the Second Economic Revolution were inducing groups to modify the market system.

III

It was change in the political structure as well as in the judicial attitude that reshaped the cost/benefit structure of decision making. Specifically, there were alterations in the cost of increasing federal government revenue; in rule-making decisions, from the legislative branch to departments of the executive branch or from the legislative branch to independent commissions appointed by the executive branch; in the control of the money supply, to control by the executive branch. Let us look at these in turn.

The Constitutional amendment legalizing the income tax in 1913 was the initial opening wedge to increasing the size of government income and providing the basis for transfer payments. Once this amendment was in place the subsequent costs of changing the rate simply required Congressional enactment.

Departments within the executive branch of government were created which became lobbying bodies for special interest groups and increasingly assumed decision- and rule-making powers as the executive branch was delegated rule-making powers by Congress. The evolution of rule-making powers by the Department of Agriculture (which achieved cabinet status in 1889) is illustrative of the trend. For the meat packing industry the export market was a major source of income; but from 1879 on, one European country after another restricted American imports because of diseases. The restrictions hurt both farmers and meat packers and the Grange as well as meat packers lobbied for meat inspection by the federal government. In 1884 Congress established the Bureau of Animal Husbandry within the Department of Agriculture and in 1891 Congress passed the first meat inspection law; all meat for export had to be inspected by a Department of Agriculture inspector, and violation could be punished by fines and imprisonment. A result was to provide and enforce uniform measurement of the quality of goods: indeed, on the same day in 1906 that Theodore Roosevelt signed the Meat Inspection Act he also signed the Pure Food and Drug Act, which had similar objectives of enforcing quality standards in other food and drugs.

The enforcement of quality standards was the ostensible reason for the delegation of such rule-making power to the Department of Agriculture, and the costs of passage of the 1906 law were greatly reduced by the public outcry that came following Upton Sinclair's *The Jungle.* But if quality standards were all that was at issue they certainly could have been realized by voluntary group action of the big meat packing firms. These firms' vigorous support of government regulation suggests two other objectives: ridding themselves of the costs of inspection and reducing competition from the numerous small meat packing firms.[5] While quality standards served as the ostensible reason, control of competition was at the very outset a key to the shift of rule-making decisions from Congress to the Department of Agriculture. The constituency of the Department of Agriculture continued to press for further shifts of rule-making power from Congress to the Department under various disguises, but the major thrust was to reduce or eliminate the competitive pressures of the market and to increase demand. Price supports, school lunch programs, Food for Peace, and milk marketing acts were just around the corner.

The Department of Commerce and Labor was established in 1903 and a decade later split into separated departments of commerce and labor. Their history with respect to the evolution of rule-making powers to alter property rights was similar to that of the Department of Agriculture.

The shift in rule-making power from the legislative to the executive branch was implemented by a set of court decisions between 1892 and 1911 which acknowledged the power of the legislative branch to grant discretionary power to the executive

[5] See Kolko (1963:98–108).

branch. These decisions recognized the power of executive agencies to make rules within the broad policy objectives set out by Congress. In *United States* vs. *Grimaud* (1911) the court decreed that administrative rulings had the force of law.[6]

The development of "commission government" has in recent years been assigned a major role in the structural change of the American economy. The substitution of a small number of commissions in place of the cumbersome Madisonian machinery of government immensely reduced the costs of utilizing the political process to alter property rights. The Interstate Commerce Commission created in 1887 is correctly awarded a major role in American economic history, and the history of the development and extension of its rule-making powers has been amply documented in recent studies.[7] The shift in rule-making powers from legislature to commission paralleled the delegation of rule-making from the legislative to departments of the executive branch. In 1906 the Hepburn Act gave the ICC the power to set maximum rates. In 1910 the Mann-Elkins Act extended ICC control to telephone, telegraph, and cable services. It not only played a major role in the decline of competition in the transport industries, but also served as a model for the creation of subsequent commissions. The Federal Trade Commission created in 1914 was a logical extension of commission government to deal on a broader basis with unfair competition and price discrimination. The "alphabet soup" of the New Deal was only two decades away.

The creation of the Federal Reserve System in 1914 is regarded in standard economic histories as a consequence of the studies of the National Monetary Commission; as a response to the inelastic supply of money which became apparent in the 1907 panic; and as a compromise with the thought of a too powerful single central bank. But a more significant aspect of its creation was a structural change which closely tied monetary policy to the political system. In the short run this change led to the preeminence of Benjamin Strong and the Federal Reserve Bank of New York and, eventually, to a strong Board of Governors and political control of the money supply.

[6] See Anderson and Hill (1980), chapter 6, for a further discussion of this shift and implications for both executive departments and regulatory agencies.
[7] McAvoy (1965) and Hughes (1977:115–20).

While a major share of the credit for the structural change lies at the door of interest-group pressure using the political process, the role of the judiciary was also important. The Munn case had long judicial precedent in state courts, as Harry Scheiber has shown (1972). After the Munn decision, the Court appeared to follow no hard and fast line, supporting state regulatory powers over federal in some cases but not in others. At times the Court appeared almost to repudiate the Munn doctrine. Yet one indisputable fact emerged. By 1914 much of the structural change was in place and could not have been so without the help, or at least the acquiescence, of the Court.[8]

IV

It is easy to see the interest group pressures that played a hand in the structural transformation; but the story is incomplete without examining the forces of the Second Economic Revolution that energized the interest groups and the role of ideological change that altered the range of choices open to the participants.

The farm movement was a reaction to the growing world-wide competition of agricultural producers which subjected the farmer to sharp price fluctuations; it was also a reaction to effective price discrimination by railroads, grain elevators, and processors. The Granger movement concentrated on local and state political intervention to alter the terms of exchange with railroads and grain elevators; but the desire to reduce competition and alter the terms of exchange between agricultural and non-agricultural goods (as well as judicial interpretation of the limits of state intervention) shifted farmers' focus to the national level.

The history of business enterprise during this era has been characterized on the one hand as a story of Robber Barons and on the other hand as the development of "The Visible Hand." Both approaches do in fact mirror elements of the organizational consequences of the Second Economic Revolution. In the previous chapter I briefly described the managerial revolution so eloquently detailed by Chandler. But equally a part of the story are the events detailed in the muck-raking literature: the manipulation of railroad finance by Drew, Fisk, Gould, and others; the

[8] For a discussion of the evolving attitude of the courts see Hughes (1977, chapter 4) and Keller (1977, chapters 9, 10, 11).

control of the New York State legislature by the life insurance companies; Rockefeller's rebating agreement with the Pennsylvania Railroad; Morgan's ubiquitous efforts to consolidate industries; and a thousand and one other occurrences of this gaudy era of business activity. They all reflect the immense gains from opportunism and from limiting competition that accompanied the Second Economic Revolution. They also reflect the instability of voluntaristic solutions because the gains from cheating on "gentlemen's agreements" were simply too tempting to produce lasting stability. Between 1874 and 1898 the major trunk lines connecting the agrarian west with the eastern seaboard went through four major and numerous minor reorganizations as rate agreements constantly broke down.[9] Only the trust was an effective response to opportunism, and the Sherman Antitrust Act of 1890 was at least partly designed to close that door. The use of the machinery of government was a natural step. Life insurance companies had utilized the machinery of state government to reduce competition and prevent discontented policy holders from demanding an accounting of poor dividend showings by major companies (North 1953); other business and financial interest groups found that they could more effectively curb competition through departments and commissions at the federal level.[10]

While in Europe the labor movement early turned to the political process, it did not play a major role in the structural transformation of the American economy. The American Federation of Labor of Samuel Gompers was dominated by craft unions with substantial strategic power to limit entry and engage in opportunistic activity to improve their terms of exchange. The large immigrant component and the resultant ethnic and linguistic diversity of the labor force in the industries of the Second Economic Revolution were used strategically by employers to raise organization costs. This diversity equally raised the costs of widespread united political activity by workers. Much of the social legislation that was initiated (and frequently declared unconstitutional by the courts) or enacted cannot be traced to the

---

[9] Keller (1977:424). Ulen (1980) stresses that voluntaristic collusion worked effectively in periods of expansion but tended to collapse during contractions. He also raises doubts about the supremacy of any particular pressure group in dominating the ICC in the years up to 1920.

[10] See Kolko (1963).

door of the AFL. Indeed, right up through the Social Security
Act of 1935 that body was largely hostile to such endeavors. It
requires the introduction of ideological considerations to account
for the early development of social legislation largely instigated
by middle-class reformers.

I am not aware of evidence that could be used to weigh
definitively the importance of ideological conviction versus interest group pressures in the passage of legislation during this
era. The constitutional amendment for the income tax was a part
of the populist platform and, like the entire farm movement, is
not explicable without ideological considerations, since it involved large group action which successfully overcame the free
rider problem. Gabriel Kolko in *The Triumph of Conservatism*
(1963) makes a convincing case that the Progressive movement
was used by interest groups to achieve their objectives. As noted
already, Upton Sinclair's *The Jungle* was important in aiding the
passage of the 1906 Meat Inspection Bill. Miller (1971) shows
that the most important force behind the Granger laws was commercial interests in localities adversely affected by the competition from railroad development.

What is clear is that the ideological convictions of the farmers
and the Progressive movement led to actions which were used
by interest groups in altering the system. The clearest reflection
of ideological transformation was the evolving attitude of the
judiciary. The gradual transformation of the attitude of the Supreme Court was a long process, from Chief Justice Waite's position in the Munn Case to the conflict between Justice Field
and Justice Holmes, to the case of *Nebbia* vs. *New York* (1934),
where the Court declared "there is no closed case or category of
business affected with the public interest. . . ." [11] The ideological
transformation was still in process by 1914, but it would be established definitively in the 1930s.

[11] Cited in Hughes (1977:213). Hughes and Anderson and Hill (1980),
chapter 7, provide a description of the ideological transformation.

Theory and History

Part III

Theory and History

Chapter 15

A Theory of Institutional Change and the Economic History of the Western World

I

Institutions provide the framework within which human beings interact. They establish the cooperative and competitive relationships which constitute a society and more specifically an economic order. When economists talk about their discipline as a theory of choice and about the menu of choices being determined by opportunities and preferences, they simply have left out that it is the institutional framework which constrains people's choice sets. Institutions are in effect the filter between individuals and the capital stock (as defined in chapter 1) and between the capital stock and the output of goods and services and the distribution of income.

The word 'structure' in the title of this book refers to the institutional framework. The word 'change' refers to the way institutions are created, modified, or destroyed over time. In this chapter I propose to pull together as completely as possible the theory of institutional change developed in Part I and used as a framework to explore economic history in Part II.

II

Institutions are a set of rules, compliance procedures, and moral and ethical behavioral norms designed to constrain the behavior of individuals in the interests of maximizing the wealth or utility of principals. In the case of political or economic institutions, wealth or utility is maximized by exploiting the gains from trade which are a result of specialization (including specialization in violence). A key distinction in this model is between agents and principals. Put simply, agents work for principals, or, in the more formal terminology of Meckling and Jensen, the principals "engage another person (the agent) to perform some service on their behalf which involves delegating some decision making authority to the agent" (1976:308). The relationship that concerns Meckling and Jensen is a voluntary one; it should be noted that in my framework it may be voluntary or involuntary (such as is slavery). And it is important to stress that even in involuntary relationships there is some latitude in decision-making power by the agent as a result of the inability of the principal to perfectly constrain the agent's behavior. Most individuals are agents in one role as employees and principals in another role as consumers. While social scientists from other disciplines perhaps do not customarily think of consumers as principals in the sense used in the foregoing definition, such usage is consistent with the central thrust of neoclassical economics—that is, consumer sovereignty. Nor is there any implication from the definition that all principals are equally powerful or influential, or that all agents are equally "powerless." What the definition does focus on is the contractual relationship between parties.[1] It does not, for example, imply that lords and serfs were equal; it does imply that the specification of the exchange relationship between them was a contractual one even though the terms of exchange heavily favored the lord. The interesting question is what determined the limits of the lord's favorable terms and how did those terms change over time.

I shall explore below the determinants of the terms of exchange; but first it is essential to specify the individual behavioral characteristics that lead to the constraints that make up institutions. We do so by invoking the individualistic maximizing postulate of economic theory. That postulate assumes that in-

---

[1] An additional important advantage to this contractual approach to a theory of institutions is that contracts are typically specified in writing so that they provide the potential for a set of observations from which to derive testable hypotheses, essential for useful theorizing. The limitation is that the behavioral norms are not typically a part of written contracts.

dividuals in the absence of any constraints maximize at any and all margins; it is, then, constraints that make possible human organization by limiting certain types of behavior.[2] In the absence of constraints we exist in a Hobbesian jungle and civilization is impossible.

The constraints on behavior range from taboos to rules to exhortation. While some of the constraints are common to all societies (there are certain minimal behavioral patterns necessary for any cooperative activity), others are specific to the interests of principals in different contextual settings. By contextual setting I mean not only the existing stock of capital as described in chapter 1 but also the stock of constraints as specified in existing institutions (a subject to be further explored below in examining institutional change). While it is useful to separate constitutional rules, operating rules, and normative behavioral codes, in practice they are frequently overlapping.

Constitutional rules are the fundamental underlying rules designed to specify the basic structure of property rights and control of the state. They are intended to be more costly to modify than are operating rules, which, either as statute laws, common law, or voluntary contracts, specify terms of exchange within the framework of the constitutional rules. Normative behavioral rules are codes of behavior aimed at legitimating the constitutional and operating rules. Thus the customs of the manor in feudal society were a set of constitutional rules but also embodied some operating rules and normative behavioral codes.

The rules are devised relative to the perceived costs of compliance. Therefore the existing technology of measurement, costs of enforcement, and moral and ethical behavioral norms all enter into the calculus of rule making.

The evolving transaction cost literature has produced a whole family of terms designed to illuminate the costs associated with human economic interaction. Information costs, agency costs, the costs of shirking and opportunism are prominent. Another strand

[2] The argument at this point parts company with some of the industrial organization and public choice literature which has *some* individuals "maximizing with guile" in opportunistic behavior or *some* individuals "rent seeking." In my model such individuals are simply differently constrained than other individuals. The distinction is important because the former approach implies that some individuals maximize and others don't but does not provide a consistent logical explanation for differential behavior. What separates the two approaches is that I include ideology as a constraint on behavior.

in the literature emphasizes the costs arising from uncertainty, the amelioration of risk by insurance, and the problems of adverse selection and moral hazard. The costs of compliance are those of detecting violations of the contractual agreement and those of enacting penalties. The cost of detecting violations is that of measurement, and in exchange between principals, measuring the attributes of the goods or services exchanged and the external effects of imperfect measurement are both costly. In principal-agent relationships there are the cost of measuring the agent's performance and the inefficiencies that result from imperfect measurement. The costs of enacting appropriate penalties includes those of assessing damages.

It is the agents of principals who enforce contractual agreements and enact the penalties; and because these agents are not perfectly constrained by the principals, enforcement costs are also related to the political-legal structure and to the perceived legitimacy of the rules. Uncertainty arises from long-term contracts which involve many unknowns with respect to future relative prices over the terms of the contract; investments specific to a particular contractual exchange are often subject to imperfect enforcement and liable to opportunistic behavior.

Opportunism implies a clear violation of a contract, and therefore the costs arise from imperfect enforcement. The costs of shirking, on the other hand, arise because of the difficulties of reaching an agreed-upon measure of the output of labor in that contract. The cost of measuring the quantity and quality of labor output is at the very heart of the agency problem. It underlies the reason why piece-rate wages are not used more extensively; it is central to the conflict over the employment relationship; and it is equally the core of the problem of bureaucracy. There is no agreed-upon measure of performance that both parties to the contract will abide by or be able to costlessly enforce.

Personalized exchange—repetitive dealings and personal contacts—minimizes the need for formal rules and compliance procedures since reciprocity and a consensus ideology (see below) constrain behavior. Where impersonal exchange occurs competition plays the key role in constraining behavior of the parties to exchange. The more competition is diluted in hierarchical organizations the greater is the necessity for formal rules and elaborate monitoring devices to measure performance.

Moral and ethical behavioral norms are an essential part of

the constraints that make up institutions. They are derived from the constructions of reality (ideology) that individuals develop to contend with their environment. Ideology is not the same as morality since it both encompasses a comprehensive way of perceiving the world and acts to economize on the costs information; ideology does, nevertheless, incorporate a judgment about the justice or fairness of institutions and specifically of exchange relationships. Consensus ideologies evolve when the individuals of a universe have similar experiences; divergent ideologies stem from divergent and conflicting perceptions of reality. Consensus ideologies therefore are a substitute for formal rules and compliance procedures. As diverse ideologies evolve it is in the interest of rulers to invest in convincing other principals and agents that the institutions are fair or legitimate and hence to lower the compliance costs. Moreover institutions that are viable within a consensus ideology are no longer viable as diverse ideologies evolve since rules must be formalized and compliance procedures developed with an eye to the costs of detecting and punishing violations.

It is the combination of the constitutional rules with the associated moral and ethical codes of behavior that underlies the stability of institutions and makes them slow to change. The combination produces ingrown patterns of behavior which, like the capital stock, tend to be changed only incrementally.

III

A political-economic system is made up of a complex of institutions bearing specific relationships to one another. The constitutional rules are the most fundamental organizational constraints of such a system. Their objective is to maximize the utility of the rulers by specifying the underlying structure of property rights and of control over coercion. They will be developed with the objectives of (1) specifying a pattern of wealth and income distribution; (2) specifying a system of protection in a universe of competing states; and (3) laying the framework for a system of operating rules to reduce transaction costs in the economic sector.

The characteristics of the existing military technology are important conditioning factors in the first two objectives since they determine the distribution of violence potential within and between states. Within the state the characteristics of military technology together with the costs of compliance (that is, the technology available to measure performance and the costs of legitimating the rules) determine the underlying terms of exchange (property rights structure) between rulers and constituents. Between states military technology together with the costs of agency determines the upper bound of the size of states. However ideology is also important here, both in supplementing the violence potential with a given military technology and in reducing the costs of agency.

The gross terms of exchange between rulers and constituents will be determined by the opportunity costs of the principals involved; the net terms to the rulers are those gross terms minus the agency costs of the bureaucracy.

While the constitutional rules lay out the basic set of property rights, the state both provides the framework to adjudicate and enforce the rules and promulgates codes of behavior designed to lower the compliance costs of the political structure and the transaction costs in the economic sector.

The forms of contractual relations that comprise the economic organization are therefore basically conditioned by the state, first with respect to the diverse opportunity costs of various constituents (which will lead to property rights reflecting the political power of constituent groups) and second with respect to the cost to the ruler of monitoring economic performance. Subject to these qualifications the state will then provide the infrastructure of public goods to promote economic activity. The forms of voluntary organization that will develop within this framework will depend upon relative prices, the stock of technology, and the costs of enforcing alternative forms of economic organization. The first two comprise the traditional production theory of neoclassical economics described in chapter 1, and little need be said here about them except to emphasize the tension between the stock of technology which determines the gains from specialization (via scale economies) and the costs of alternative forms of organization. The greater the gains from specialization, the more steps in the production process and the higher the transaction costs. The degree to which these various steps will be organized by market versus hierarchical organization will depend upon the alternative costs of measurement and enforcement. Since vertical integration into hierarchical organization means the substitution of factor markets for product markets (that is the essential consequence of a firm replacing market transaction), a key determinant will be the cost of organizing factor, and in particular, labor markets. The creation of impersonal factor markets is an essential step in realizing the gains from specialization. The degree to which the state will implement the development of land and labor markets will depend on the two constraints specified above. Such development might, for example, increase potential strife, as in the case of enclosures in Tudor England, and hence threaten a ruler's security.

IV

In the previous section I explored a cross-section slice of institutions that make up a political-economic system at a particular moment in time. Here I take a longitudinal slice and explore changes in the system over time.

At the beginning of this chapter I asserted that institutions are the filter not only between individuals and the capital stock but also between the capital stock and the performance of the economy. They determine the output of the system as well as the distribution of income. As filters, they are inherently conservative since they provide the stability of the society and hence the security of the income of the principals. The introduction of time is a destabilizing influence on institutions because the principals are mortal and the capital stock changes.

Principals make a difference not only because skills and entrepreneurial ability differ but because the legitimacy of an institution is at least in part carried over to the principal. Hence no matter how carefully specified are the rules of succession, the successor is in a different bargaining position with other principals and agents from the previous principal.

The capital stock changes first as a result of changes in population. While we sometimes observe homeostatic population for periods of time, changes in population have been the most obvious source of change in the capital stock. While the secular pattern has been upward there have also been lengthy periods of declining population.

Second, the capital stock changes because knowledge changes. Humans have increased their stock both of pure knowledge and of applied knowledge embodied in technological developments and skills of people. Increased knowledge not only alters relative prices but also, because it has been largely irreversible in history, insures that the changes are not purely cyclical (a subject to be discussed below).

The changes in the capital stock induce changes in institutions in a number of ways. Changing relative prices affects the bargaining position between principals and between principals and agents. Changes in military technology (really a change in relative prices) affect the size of the state and the bargaining position of rulers vis-à-vis constituents and other rulers. Further, ideology is altered by changing individual perceptions of the justice or injustice of exchange relationships; hence, the costs of enforcement of the rules are also altered.

The foregoing very general discussion of sources of institutional change suggests that the more rapid the changes in the capital stock, the more unstable the existing system of institutions. In this framework, revolution is more likely with rapid changes in the capital stock which are improving the well-being of constituents and therefore radically weakening the ruler relative to the constituents.

The cumulation in the stock of knowledge has imposed an evolutionary order upon the secular change of political and economic institutions—the subject matter of the historical chapters of this book. The two great economic revolutions in history initiated radical secular changes in institutional organization. The first took about ten millennia. We live in the midst of the second.

The First Economic Revolution produced the state, the political constraints essential to establish economic order, and the expansion of specialization and division of labor beyond the primitive requirements of tribal hunting and gathering units. While occupational specialization was substantially extended, it was still characterized by personalized exchange and its limits were dictated by the limits to the stock of technology. Major developments in military technology led to the growth in the size of states (and consequent growth of territorial specialization and exchange). The requirements of military technology led to alterations in control of the state as rulers were forced to exchange property rights and political concessions in order to achieve a viable military order in the face of ubiquitous competition among states. With the growth in the size of states came increasing costs of agency and institutional innovation in devising rules and compliance procedures to capture the income from larger political-economic units.

Ideological differences emerged primarily from the diverse geographic experiences of groups contending with their environment and evolved into different languages, religions, customs, and traditions; these in turn formed another basis for conflict in addition to the persistent tension over the distribution of wealth and income within states and between states.

It was growth in the stock of knowledge which made possible the Second Economic Revolution. This growth was preceded by changes in military technology which altered the survival size of states and led to struggles over control of the state and finally the emergence, in northwestern Europe, of a political structure that created a set of property rights which induced economic expansion.

The gains from specialization that resulted from the Second Economic Revolution produced the unparalleled living standards of the twentieth-century Western world. Radical alterations in the size and control structure of voluntary organizations were designed to capture the gains from specialization without a corresponding increase in the attendant transaction costs. The destabilizing consequences within and between states came from the change in the opportunity cost of diverse groups in this new environment of occupational and geographic specialization. The diverse ideologies which have persisted from ethnic (geographic) differences were augmented by ideological diversity that evolved from occupational specialization.

The on-going tension between the gains from specialization and the costs arising from specialization not only is the basic source of structure and change in economic history but is at the heart of the modern problems of political and economic performance. This book is an attempt to tell us how we got from there to here. If the argument has merit it also provides a basis for reevaluating theories dealing with the performance of economies in our time. Economic history conceived as a theory of the evolution of constraints should not only explain past economic performance but also provide the modern social scientist with the evolving contextual framework within which to explain the current performance of political-economic systems. That task remains to be done.

Bibliography

Alchian, A. 1950. "Uncertainty, Evolution and Economic Theory," *Journal of Political Economy*, LIX.

Alchian, A. and Demsetz, H. 1972. "Production, Information Costs and Economic Organization." *American Economic Review* (December).

Anderson, Perry 1974. *Passages from Antiquity to Feudalism.* London: New Left Books.

Anderson, Terry and Hill, Peter J. 1980. *The Birth of a Transfer Society.* Stanford: Hoover Press.

Badian, E. 1972. *Publicans and Sinners.* Cornell University Press. Ithaca.

Barro, Robert 1979. "Money and the Price Level Under the Gold Standard." *The Economic Journal* (March).

Barzel, Y. 1974. "A Theory of Rationing by Waiting." *Journal of Law and Economics* (April).

Barzel, Y. 1980. "Measurement Cost and the Organization of Markets." Unpublished manuscript.

Baumol, William 1952. *Welfare Economics and a Theory of the State.* Cambridge: Harvard University Press.

Bean, Richard 1973. "War and the Birth of the Nation State." *Journal of Economic History* (March).

Beard, Charles 1913. *An Economic Interpretation of the Constitution.* New York: Macmillan and Co.

Becker, Gary 1976. *The Economic Approach to Human Behavior.* Chicago: University of Chicago Press.

Becker, Gary and Stigler, George 1977. "De Gustibus Non Est Disputandum." *American Economic Review* (March).

Berger, Peter L. and Luckman, Thomas 1966. *The Social Construction of Reality.* Garden City: Doubleday and Co.

Bernardi, Aurelio "The Economic Problems of the Roman Empire at the Time of its Decline" in C. Cipolla *The Economic Decline of Empires.*

Binford, Lewis R. 1968. "Post-Pleistocene Adaptations" in Sally R. and Lewis R. Binford (eds.) *New Perspective in Archaeology.* Chicago: Aldine Press.

Bloch, Marc 1947. "Comment et Pourquoi Finit L'Esclavage Antique?" *Annales ESC 2.*

Boserup, Ester 1965. *The Condition of Agricultural Growth: The Economies of Agrarian Change Under Population Pressure.* Chicago: Aldine Press.

Boserup, Ester (forthcoming). *Population and Technological Change: A Study of Long Term Trends.* Chicago: University of Chicago Press.

Braidwood, Robert J. 1960. "The Agricultural Revolution." *Scientific American* Vol. 203.

Braidwood, Robert J. 1963. *Prehistoric Man.* Chicago: University Press.

Breton, Albert 1974. *The Economic Theory of Representative Government.* Chicago: Aldine Publishing Co.

Brunt, P. A. 1966. "The Roman Mob." *Past and Present* (December).

Buchanan, Allen 1979. "Revolutionary Motivation and Rationality." *Philosophy and Public Affairs* Vol. 9 #1 (Fall).

Buchanan, James and Tullock, Gordon 1962. *The Calculus of Consent.* Ann Arbor: University of Michigan Press.

Buchanan, James 1975. "Comment on the Independent Judiciary in an Interest Group Perspective." *The Journal of Law and Economics* (December).

Cambridge Ancient History. 1923–1939, 1970–1977. Volumes II, IV, V, VIII, IX, and X. Cambridge University Press.

Cambridge Medieval History 1969. Vol. VIII. Cambridge: The University Press.

Carniero, Robert 1970. "A Theory of the Origin of the State." *Science,* Vol. 169:733–738 (August).

Cavalli-Sforza, L. L. 1974. "The Genetics of Human Population." *Scientific American* Vol. 231 #3.

Chandler, Alfred 1977. *The Visible Hand.* Cambridge, Mass.: The Belknap Press.

Cheung, Steven N. S. 1970. "The Structure of a Contract and Theory of a Non-Exclusive Resource." *Journal of Law and Economics* XIII.

Cheung, S. N. S. 1974. "A Theory of Price Control." *Journal of Law and Economics* (April).

Childe, V. Gordon 1951. *Man Makes Himself.* London: L. A. Watts Lld.

Cipolla, Carlo 1962. *The Economic History of World Population.* Middlesex: Penguin Books.

Cipolla, Carlo 1966. *Guns, Sails and Empires.* New York: Random House.

Cipolla, Carlo, ed. 1970. *The Economic Decline of Empires.* London: Methuen.

Clark, J. M. 1923. *The Economics of Overhead Costs.* Chicago: University of Chicago Press.

Coale, Ansley 1974. "The Human Population." *Scientific American* Vol. 231 #3.

Coase, Ronald 1937. "The Nature of the Firm." *Economica* (November).

Commager, H. S., ed. 1948. *Documents of American History* 4th Ed. New York: Appleton, Century, Crofts.

Dahlman, Carl 1980. *The Open Field System and Beyond: A Property Rights Study of an Economic Institution.* Cambridge: The University Press.

David, Paul 1975. *Technical Choice, Innovation and Economic Growth.* Cambridge: Cambridge University Press.

Davis, Kingsley 1974. "The Migration of Human Population." *Scientific American* Vol. 231 #3.

Davis, Lance E. and North, Douglass C. 1971. *Institutional Change and American Economic Growth.* New York: Cambridge University Press.

Dean, Phyllis 1965. *The First Industrial Revolution.* Cambridge: Cambridge University Press.

Demsetz, H. 1967. "Toward a Theory of Property Rights." *American Economic Review* LVII.

Demsetz, Harold 1968. "Why Regulate Utilities." *Journal of Law and Economics.*

De Vries, Jan 1976. *The Economy of Europe in an Age of Crisis: 1600–1750.* Cambridge: University Press.

Dickinson, G. Lowes 1958. *The Greek View of Life.* Ann Arbor: University of Michigan Press.

Downs, Anthony 1957. *An Economic Theory of Democracy.* New York: Harper and Row.

Duby, Georges 1974. *The Early Growth of the European Economy.* Ithaca: Cornell University Press.

Dumond, Don E. 1975. "The Limitation of Human Population: A Natural History." *Science* (February).

Ehrenberg, V. 1969. *The Greek State.* London: Methuen.

Eklund, Robert and Tollison, Robert 1980a. "A Rent Seeking Theory of French Mercantilism." Unpublished ms.

Eklund, Robert and Tollison, Robert 1980b. "Economic Regulation in Mercantile England: Hecksler Revisited." *Economic Enquiry.*

Elliot, J. H. 1967. Comment in Trevor Aston, ed. *Crisis in Europe.*

Engels, F., *The Condition of the Working Class in England.*

Fenoaltea, Stefano 1975a. "The Rise and Fall of a Theoretical Model: The Manorial System." *Journal of Economic History.*

Fenoaltea, Stefano 1975b. "Authority, Efficiency, and Agricultural Organizations in Medieval England and Beyond." *Journal of Economic History* (December).

Finley, Moses 1971. *The Ancient Economy.* Berkeley: University of California Press.

Flannery, Kent 1968. "Archaeological Systems Theory and Early Mesoamerica" in B. J. Meggers, ed. *Anthropological Archaeology in the Americas.* Anthropological Society of Washington.

Flannery, Kent 1969. "The Origins and Ecological Effects of Early Domestication in Iran and the Near East" in P. S. Veko and G. W. Dimbley, eds. *The Domestication of Plants and Animals.* Chicago: Aldine Press.

Floyd, John 1969. "Preferences, Institutions and the Theory of Economic Growth." Discussion paper. University of Washington.

Forkes, R. J. 1955. *Studies in Ancient Technology* (Vol. III). Leiden: E. J. Brill.

Forrest, W. G. 1966. *The Emergence of Greek Democracy.* London: Weiderfeld and Nicolson.

Friedman, David 1977. "A Theory of the Size and Shape of Nations." *Journal of Political Economy* (February).

Geertz, Clifford 1973. "Ideology as a Cultural System" in C. Geertz *The Interpretation of Cultures*. New York: Basic Books.

Georgescu-Roegen, N. 1969. "The Institutional Aspects of Peasant Communities: An Analytical View" in C. R. Wharton Jr., ed. *Subsistence Agriculture and Economic Development*. Chicago: Aldine Press.

Gibbon, Edward 1946. *The Decline and Fall of the Roman Empire*, edited by J. B. Bury. New York: The Heritage Press, 3 Vols.

Goldberg, Victor 1976. "Regulation and Administered Contracts." *The Bell Journal* (Autumn).

Gordon, Howard Scott 1954. "The Economic Theory of a Common Pool Resource: The Fishery." *Journal of Political Economy* LXII.

Gunderson, Gerald 1976. "Economic Change and the Demise of the Roman Empire." *Explorations in Economic History*, Vol. 13.

Gunderson, Gerald. "Economic Behavior in the Ancient World." Unpublished ms.

Hall, Chris 1980. "The Predatory State: A Theory of Scattered Strips Agriculture." Unpublished ms. The University of Washington.

Hamilton, Alexander; Jay, John, and Madison, James. 1937. *The Federalist A Commentary on the Constitution of the United States*. New York: The Modern Library.

Harlan, Jack R. and Zahary, Daniel 1966. "Distribution of Wild Wheat and Barley." *Science* CLIII.

Hartwell, R. M. 1971. *The Industrial Revolution and Economic Growth*. London: Methuen.

Hayek, F. A. 1937. "Economics and Knowledge." *Economica* (February).

Hayek, F. A. 1945. "The Use of Knowledge in Society." *American Economic Review* (September).

Hecksher, Eli 1955. *Mercantilism* rev. ed. edited by E. F. Soderlund. Allen and Unwin.

Hicks, John D. 1961. *The Populist Revolt*. Lincoln: University of Nebraska Press.

Hicks, J. R. 1969. *A Theory of Economic History*. Oxford University Press.

Hirschman, A. 1970. *Exit, Voice and Loyalty*. Cambridge: Harvard University Press.

Historical Statistics of the United States 1975. Washington, D.C.: U.S. Government Printing Office.

Hobsbawn, Eric 1967. "The Crisis of the Seventeenth Century" in Trevor Aston, ed. *Crisis in Europe.* New York: Doubleday and Co.

Hodges, Henry 1970. *Technology in the Ancient World.* Middlesex: Penguin Press.

Horwitz, M. J. 1977. *The Transformation of American Law 1780–1860.* Cambridge: Harvard University Press.

Hughes, J. R. T. 1977. *The Governmental Habit.* New York: Basic Books.

Hurst, Willard 1956. *Law and the Condition of Freedom in the Nineteenth Century.* Madison: University of Wisconsin Press.

Isaac, Erich 1970. *Geography of Domestication.* Englewood Cliffs: Prentice Hall.

International Encyclopedia of the Social Sciences 1968. New York: Macmillan.

Jensen, M. and Meckling, W. 1976. "Theory of the Firm: Managerial Behavior, Agency Costs and Ownership Structure." *Journal of Financial Economics* (October).

Jones, A. H. M. 1966. *The Decline of the Ancient World.* London: Longman Green.

Kahan, Arcadius 1973. "Notes on Serfdom in Western and Eastern Europe." *Journal of Economic History* (March).

Kau, James B. and Rubin, Paul 1979. "Self Interest, Ideology, and Log Rolling." *The Journal of Law and Economics* (October).

Keller, Morton 1977. *The Affairs of State.* Cambridge: The Belknap Press.

Klein, B., Crawford, R. C., and Alchian, A. 1978. "Vertical Integration, Appropriable Rents, and the Competitive Contracting Process." *Journal of Law and Economics* (October).

Kolko, Gabriel 1963. *The Triumph of Conservatism.* Glencoe: The Free Press.

Kuhn, T. S. 1962. *The Structure of Scientific Revolutions.* Chicago: University of Chicago Press.

Kula, Witold 1976. *An Economic Theory of the Feudal System.* London: New Left Books.

Ladurie, Emmanuel LeRoi 1979. *The Territory of the Historian.* Chicago: University of Chicago Press.

Landes, William and Posner, Richard 1975. "The Independent

Judiciary in an Interest Group Perspective." *The Journal of Law and Economics* (December).

Latane, Bibb; Silliams, Kipling, and Harkinds, Stephen 1979. "Social Loafing." *Psychology Today* (October).

Lee, Ronald 1978. "Model of Preindustrial Dynamics with Applications to England," Tilly, ed.

Machlup, Fritz 1958. *An Economic Review of the Patent System.* Washington D.C.: U.S. Government Printing Office.

Marglin, Stephen 1974. "What Do Bosses Do?" *Review of Radical Political Economy* (Summer).

Martin, Paul and Wright, N. E., eds. 1967. *Pleistocene Extinctions.* New Haven: Yale University Press.

Mathias, Peter 1969. *The First Industrial Nation.* New York: Charles Scribner and Sons.

McAvoy, P. W. 1965. *The Economic Effects of Regulation, The Trunk Line Railroad Cortels and the Interstate Commerce Commission Before 1900.* Cambridge: M.I.T. Press.

McCloskey, Don 1976. "English Open Fields as a Behavior Towards Risk" in P. Uselding, ed. *Research in Economic History* Vol. I.

McManus, John 1972. "An Economic Analysis of Indian Behavior in the North American Fur Trade." *Journal of Economic History* XXXII.

McManus, John 1975. "The Costs of Alternative Economic Organization." *Canadian Journal of Economics* (August).

McNeill, William 1976. *Plagues and People.* New York: Doubleday.

Meed, Ronald, ed. 1953. *Marx and Engels on Malthus.* London: Laurence and Wishart.

Miller, George H. 1971. *Railroads and the Granger Laws.* Madison: University of Wisconsin Press.

Millward, Robert (forthcoming). "The Emergence of Wage Labour in Early Modern Europe: Exploration of an Analytical Framework." *Explorations in Economic History.*

Musson, A. E., ed. 1972. *Science, Technology and Economic Growth in the 18th Century.* London: Macmillan and Co.

National Bureau of Economic Research 1972. *Economic Growth.* New York: Columbia University Press.

Nef, John U. 1957. *Industry and Government in France and England 1540–1640.* Cornell University Press.

Nelson, R.; Peck, M. and Kolachek, E. 1967. *Technology, Eco-*

nomic Growth and Public Policy. Washington, D.C.: The Brookings Institution.

Niskanen, W. 1971. *Bureaucracy and Representative Government.* Chicago: Aldine Publishing Co.

North, Douglass C. 1953. "Entrepreneurial Policy and Internal Organization in the Large Life Insurance Companies at the Time of the Armstrong Investigation of 1905–6." *Explorations in Entrepreneurial History* (Spring).

North, Douglass C. 1968. "Sources of Productivity Change in Ocean Shipping." *Journal of Political Economy.*

North, Douglass C. 1977. "Non-Market Forms of Economic Organization: The Challenge of Karl Polanyi." *Journal of European Economic History* (Fall).

North, Douglass C. 1978. "Structure and Performance: The Task of Economic History." *Journal of Economic Literature* (September).

North, Douglass C. and Thomas, Robert 1971. "The Rise and Fall of the Manorial System: A Theoretical Model." *Journal of Economic History* (December).

North, Douglass C. and Thomas, Robert 1973. *The Rise of the Western World: A New Economic History.* Cambridge: The University Press.

North, Douglass C. and Thomas, Robert 1977. "The First Economic Revolution." *Economic History Review* (May).

Olson, Mancur 1965. *The Logic of Collective Action.* Cambridge: Harvard University Press.

Parsons, Talcott 1937. *The Structure of Social Action.* New York: McGraw-Hill.

Perrot, Jean 1966. "Le Gisement Natufied de Mallaha (Exam), Israel." *L'Anthropologie* LXX.

Pirenne, H. 1939. *Mohammed and Charlemagne.* London: Allen and Unwin.

Polanyi, Karl 1957. *The Great Transformation.* New York: Rineholt.

Polanyi, Karl 1977. *The Livelihood of Man.* New York: Academic Press.

Postan, M. M. 1972. *The Medieval Economy and Society.* London: Weidenfeld and Nicolson.

Previtt-Orton, C. W. 1966. *The Shorter Cambridge Medieval History* 2 Vol. Cambridge: The University Press.

Renfrew, Colin 1972. *The Emergence of Civilization.* London: Methuen.

Rimlinger, Gaston 1960. "The Legitimization of Protest: A Comparative Study in Labor History." *Comparative Studies in Society and History* (April).

Ringrose, David 1973. Comment on "War and the Birth of the Nation State." *Journal of Economic History* (March).

Roehl, Richard 1973. Comment on "War and the Birth of the Nation State." *Journal of Economic History* (March).

Rosenberg, Nathan 1972. *Technology and American Economic Growth*. New York: Harper & Row.

Rosenberg, Nathan 1974. "Karl Marx and the Economic Role of Science." *Journal of Political Economy* (July/August).

Rosenberg, Nathan 1976. *Perspectives on Technology*. Cambridge: Cambridge University Press.

Rostovtzeff, M. 1926. *The Social and Economic History of the Roman Empire*. Oxford.

Rostovtzeff, M. 1941. *The Social and Economic History of the Hellenistic World* Vol. I. Oxford: Clarendon Press.

Roth, Cecil 1954. *History of the Jews*. New York: Schockin Press.

Samuelson, Paul 1978. "The Canonical Classical Model of Political Economy." *Journal of Economic Literature* (December).

Scheiber, Harry 1972. "The Road to Munn: Eminent Domain and the Concept of Public Purpose in the State Courts," in Flemming and Baily, eds. *Law in American History*.

Schmoockler, Jacob 1957. "Inventors Past and Present." *Review of Economic and Statistics* (August).

Schumpeter, Joseph 1949. "Science and Ideology." *American Economic Review* (March).

Schwarzman, Maurice 1951. "Background Factors in Spanish Economic Decline." *Explorations in Entrepreneurial History* (April).

Smith, Vernon 1975. "The Economics of the Primitive Hunter Culture, Pleistocene Extinctions, and the Rise of Agriculture." *Journal of Political Economy* (August).

Starr, Chester 1977. *The Economic and Social Growth of Early Greece*. Oxford: University Press.

Stigler, George 1961. "The Economics of Information." *Journal of Political Economy* (June).

Struever, Stuart, ed. 1971. *Prehistoric Agriculture*. Garden City: Natural History Press.

Tilly, Charles 1969. *From Mobilization to Revolution*. Reading: Addison and Wesley.

Tilly, Charles, ed. 1978. *Historical Studies of Changing Fertility.* Princeton: Princeton University Press.

Tilly, Charles; Tilly, Louise and Tilly, Richard 1975. *The Rebellious Century.* Cambridge: Harvard University Press.

Trevor-Roper, H. 1967. "The General Crisis of the Seventeenth Century," in Trevor Aston, ed. *Crisis in Europe.*

Ulen, Thomas 1980. "The Market for Regulation: The I.C.C. From 1887–1920." *American Economic Review* (May).

Umbeck, John (forthcoming). *A Theoretical and Empirical Investigation into the Formation of Property Rights.* University of Iowa Press.

Vives, Vincent 1969. *An Economic History of Spain.* Princeton: Princeton University Press.

Walton, Gary 1971. "The New Economic History and the Navigation Acts." *Economic History Review* (October).

Weber, Max 1976. *The Agrarian Sociology of Ancient Civilization.* London: NLB. Translated by R. I. Frank.

White, Lynn 1962. *Medieval Technology and Social Change.* Oxford: The University Press.

Williamson, Oliver 1975. *Markets and Hierarchy.* New York: Free Press.

Wittfogel, Karl 1957. *Oriental Despotism: A Comparative Study of Total Power.* New Haven: Yale University Press.

Young, Allyn 1928. "Increasing Returns and Economic Progress." *Economic Journal* (December).

Index

Agents, 55; definition of, 202; imperfectly constrained by ruler, 26, 27; utility function of, 25
Agency: problems of, 19; theory of, 25, 37
Agriculture: and specialization, 93
Alchian, A., 7n, 21n, 37, 38
Alienation: of land, 12
Ancient World: achievements of, 111–12; bureaucracy, 119; Christianity, 120–21; colonization, 109; decline from within, 115; development of property rights, 110; distribution of wealth and income, 111; economic analysis of, 116–17; economic performance, 109; growth and decline of slavery, 118; ideology and causes of change, 120; income distribution, 92; inequality, 111; irrigation, 93, 96; location of economic activity, 119; organizational forms in, 92; population growth and decline, 114–15; population pressure in, 114–15; reduction in transactions costs in, 110; security of property rights in, 110; suc-

cession, 119–20; technological change in, 111
Anderson, Perry, 63n
Anderson, Terry, 188n, 195n, 198n
Annales School, 15n
Athens: decline, 106; grain trade, 105; property rights, 105. See also Ancient World
Authority: definition of, 34n

Badian, E., 108
Barro, Robert, 185n
Barzel, Yoram, 26n, 36n, 39n, 178n
Baumol, W., 20n, 179
Bean, Richard, 25n, 138n
Beard, Charles, 190
Becker, Gary, 4n, 50, 51
Behavior: altruistic, 11; codes of, 203
Behavioral assumption: common to all models, 63
Behavioral constraints: in institutions, 203; rules, 203; taboos, 203
Behavioral Postulate, 4. See also Maximizing
Berger, Peter L., 48n